FOR A BETTER WORLD

Posters from the United Nations

Edward B. Marks

Foreword by Kofi Annan

Pomegranate

San Francisco

Published by
Pomegranate Communications, Inc.
Box 6099, Rohnert Park, CA 94927
www.pomegranate.com

Pomegranate Europe Ltd.
Fullbridge House, Fullbridge
Maldon, Essex CM9 4LE, England
Catalog Number A547

ISBN 0-7649-1340-9

The descriptions of the United Nations departments and agencies in this volume are largely based on the UN publication *Basic Facts about the United Nations,* © UN Department of Public Information. Biographies of designers of the UNESCO posters reproduced in this volume are largely based on biographical sketches provided as an insert to *UNESCO Through Its Posters,* © 1989 UNESCO. Photographs of black-and-white posters by UN Photo Unit. Color photographs by Sotheby's, Gunter Knop Studios, and the UN Photo Unit. Information regarding title, date, and design and art credits for posters appearing in this book was not always available. This information was determined by the author to the best of his ability.

Library of Congress Cataloging-in-Publication Data

Marks, Edward B.
      For a better world : posters from the United Nations / by Edward B. Marks
          p. cm.
      Includes bibliographical references and index.
      ISBN 0-7649-1340-9 (pbk.)
        1. Posters—20th century—Catalogs. 2. United Nations—Catalogs. I. Title.
    NC1806.8 .M37 2000
    341.23'1'0222—dc21   00-028113
                                                                                        CIP

Cover and interior design by Poulson/Gluck Design

Printed in Hong Kong

09 08 07 06 05 04 03 02 01 00   10 9 8 7 6 5 4 3 2 1

Table of Contents

From its earliest days, the United Nations has highlighted different aspects of its work with engaging and eye-catching posters.

Peacekeeping, human rights, justice, and efforts to combat racism and intolerance; decolonization, sustainable development, and concern for the environment; these are among the many issues and milestones that posters have marked. United Nations posters have also promoted significant world conferences and many commemorative days, years, and decades.

The purpose of this volume is twofold. First, to collect and present some of the best of the hundreds of posters issued by the world organization over the years. Second, to tell the United Nations story in a colorful and graphic way.

Posters usually have a very short life in the public eye, as they are frequently discarded once the event or milestone they have commemorated has passed. But the effort that went into their execution does not diminish in value over time. Quite a number are the work of talented artists and designers, including UN staff members. I am pleased that a representative selection of the best work produced by the United Nations system has been preserved in this volume. Many are from the 1990s, but the reproductions also include prizewinning posters from international competitions held in 1947 and 1948. Whether recent or half a century old, the artwork depicts ideas and values that are timeless. Through them, with an eye on the future, we can gain a fresh perspective on the human condition.

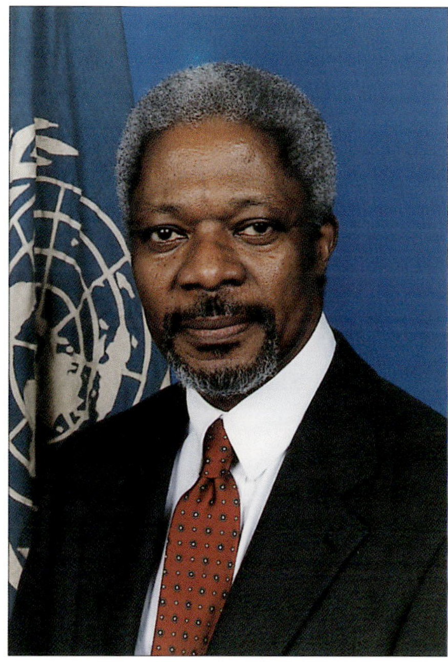

Kofi Annan,
Secretary-General
of the United Nations

Posters are as transitory as the leaves of a tree. Yet they are also the leaves of a diary of popular culture. All posters are created for immediate purposes; they invariably represent a particular moment in time. In addition to their intended message, a poster conveys other information more subtly revealed in the method of reproduction, the typography, and the many forms of visual representation. As a whole, a poster reflects the cultural values of the designer and his or her society. At the same time, they also communicate across borders in universal terms that are understood by people of different languages and cultures.

All posters seem to be related, from works of high art by Toulouse-Lautrec to simple photocopies posted at the supermarket by people seeking their lost pets. Postage stamps are miniature posters. Book magazine covers are essentially posters. The design strategy is the same in each case: attract attention and deliver your message; achieve this end with economy, elegance, and wit.

In an age of multiple media exploding with information, the humble poster is a more popular and powerful form of communication than it has ever been before. This collection of posters is fascinating not only because of the talented design and illustration, but because each was commissioned by the United Nations to address issues and problems of global concern. To behold a single well-wrought poster is a pleasurable thing; to see this array of UN-produced posters is to immerse oneself in the recent history of humanity's most appalling calamities and its most admirable aspirations.

—Paul Davis

I thought about this book for several years before I began work on it. I knew that a treasure trove of United Nations posters existed, but it was difficult to gain access to those produced before the 1990s: the UN has no poster archive. But with time and the cooperation of the people named below, I was reasonably successful in obtaining some gems of the past as well as a bountiful harvest of more recent posters.

Perhaps half of the posters illustrated in this volume originated with the Department of Public Information and other units at United Nations Headquarters in New York. The others were conceived and published by some twenty subsidiary and specialized UN agencies in North and South America, Europe, Asia, and Africa.

First and foremost: Patty Chang helped greatly in every area of this book's preparation. She researched and/or wrote many of the designer biographies, the concise descriptions of the agencies in the UN system, and many of the captions. Her good judgment, reliability, and cooperative spirit were invaluable in sifting through the large number of posters that came in.

Making a final selection of posters was no easy task, but I was fortunate to have the discerning eye of Jan Arnesen, chief of the UN's Exhibition Unit, to help me eliminate many from consideration and select more than two hundred fifty for review by an informal panel. The UN panel members were Arnesen, Judith Brister of the Department of Economic and Social Affairs, and Carolyn Schuler Uluc of the Public Services Section, Department of Public Information. The other panel members were Nicholas Lowry, curator of posters at Swann Galleries, New York, Jan Ralph, a UN retiree and design specialist who formerly directed the UN Photo and Exhibition Units, and myself.

In the course of reviewing the posters, we discussed alternative approaches in making the final selection. We agreed that the posters selected should meet a high aesthetic standard. One member of the panel felt this should be the overriding, perhaps the only, criterion. Others believed that it was important to tell the UN story as fully as possible, even if it meant including posters of acceptable but not outstanding graphic merit. I hope we came out with a selection that reasonably satisfies both objectives.

A few agencies provided satisfactory transparencies of their posters. We were also fortunate to find, in the UN Photo Library, some black-and-white reproductions of very early UN posters. Joyce B. Rosenblum, photolibrarian, and Reynaldo Reyes of the UN Photo Unit were unfailingly helpful. Nevertheless, we had to photograph most of the posters reproduced in the book. Through the good offices of Ambassador Joseph Verner Reed, we were privileged to have Sotheby's photograph about half of the posters as a contribution. We are indebted to Diana Brooks, former president and CEO of Sotheby's, Ben Cohen, its vice president for photography, and Dan Morgan, who actually took the pictures at UN Headquarters. The other posters were expertly shot at Gunter Knop's New York studio, on Agfa film donated to the project by the International Photographic Council.

For their special interest and encouragement I want to thank Kensaku Hogen, UN Under-Secretary-General for Communications and Public Information; Nitin Desai, UN Under-Secretary-General for Economic and Social Affairs; and Gillian M. Sorensen, Assistant Secretary-General for External Relations.

A number of other UN staff members made significant contributions to the realization of the project. They include Mary F. Cherif, Anne Cunningham, Phyllis Dickstein, Hasan Ferdous, Therese Gastaut, Valerie Hampton-Mason, Sonia Lecca, Salim Lone, Vladimir Lubomudrov, Lyutha Al-Mughairy, Manfred Noetzel, and Jay Pozenel.

Members of the UN system who were very helpful in the pursuit and acquisition of posters included Gretchen Bloom, Susan Byng-Clarke, Rocco Callari, Sylvie D. Cohen, Christian Delsol, Mary Duffy, Sylvia Fuhrman, Mona Gillet, Helene Gosselin, James Gunderson, Helga Klein, Roger Kohn, Maureen Lynch, Tracey Martineau, Linda Murray, Celinda Verano, Patricia Waples and Maxim Żhukov.

Both in her capacity as UNICEF's director of design and after she retired, Bonnie Berlinghof was generous with her advice and in giving me free access to UNICEF's substantial poster collection. David White provided transparencies and relevant information for the Rauschenberg posters. After consulting with the League of Nations library in Geneva, George Klein arranged for photos of the two League posters contained in this volume.

Thanks are also due to Vivian Barad, Paul Boyd, Vincent Butler, Iqbal Haji, Ole Hamann, Tom Hinds, John Ingram, Charles J. Lyons, Frieder Mellinghoff, Jennifer Monson, Jack Rennart, Angelo J. Rivera, and many others for their interest and guidance.

It has been a particular pleasure to work with Katie Burke and John Nagiecki at Pomegranate Communications, and I want to acknowledge their interest, encouragement, and cooperation.

It has been said that art is the physical expression of an idea. Posters may not be high art, but they certainly fit this definition. They express ideas, simply and directly.

We all live in a virtual data bombardment. Those who seek to spread information have a profusion of choices. Think of the ceaseless procession of television channels and radio bandwidths—as well as the books, magazines, newspapers, and other print publications. Consider the daily burgeoning number of websites. Most of this torrent of information is targeted at the more affluent West, and much of it is highly sophisticated.

At the other end of the technology spectrum is the poster: a low-tech, relatively straightforward medium whose message is intelligible to people of limited education and experience. Posters can be a bridge between peoples, a common thoroughfare, an instrument of democracy. They are the exclamation points, accenting the high-water marks in the lifestream of an organization or an era.

Of course there are more subtle posters, aimed at a specific, well-informed audience. But the most effective posters—and those of the UN mainly qualify—are lucid and quick to make their point. In contrast to more complicated and sophisticated media they have universal appeal. As an accessible vehicle for communication in the twenty-first century, the poster will endure.

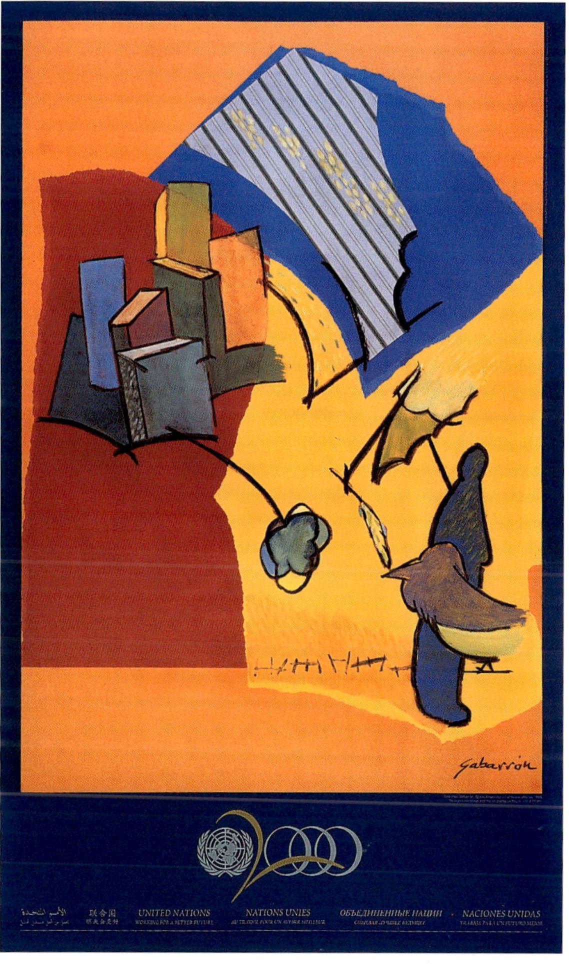

1. *Dawning with the Millennium, 2000, painting by Spanish artist Cristóbal Gabarrón, design by Rocco Callari, Graphic Design Section, UN Department of Public Information. Official poster for UN General Assembly Millennium Summit, September 2000.*

A Brief History of Posters

Posters are a relatively new art form. As far back as the sixteenth century, monarchs and church authorities printed broadsides to announce their decrees. In the centuries that followed, political groups with a public message posted printed sheets on city walls. But it was not until the invention of lithography, in the second half of the nineteenth century, that it became possible to print multiple color copies, and the poster came into its own.

Early posters were used primarily to advertise commercial products and stage or musical attractions. By World War I, the poster had achieved international recognition as an art form. As the twentieth century progressed, other forms of communication, such as radio, the movies, and the ever-increasing use of photography, somewhat reduced the impact of posters, but they remained a powerful medium of expression.

In her foreword to the book *Posters American Style,* the writer Susan Sontag says, "Posters are inexhaustibly rich emblems of the society [and] have become one of the most ubiquitous kinds of cultural objects—prized partly because they are cheap, unpretentious, 'popular' art."

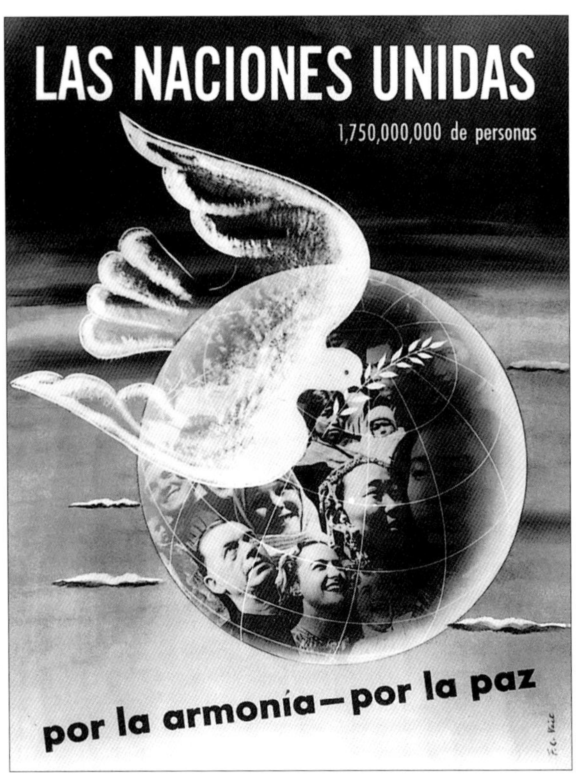

2. Las Naciones Unidas, 1946 (Spanish version).
Possibly first UN poster.

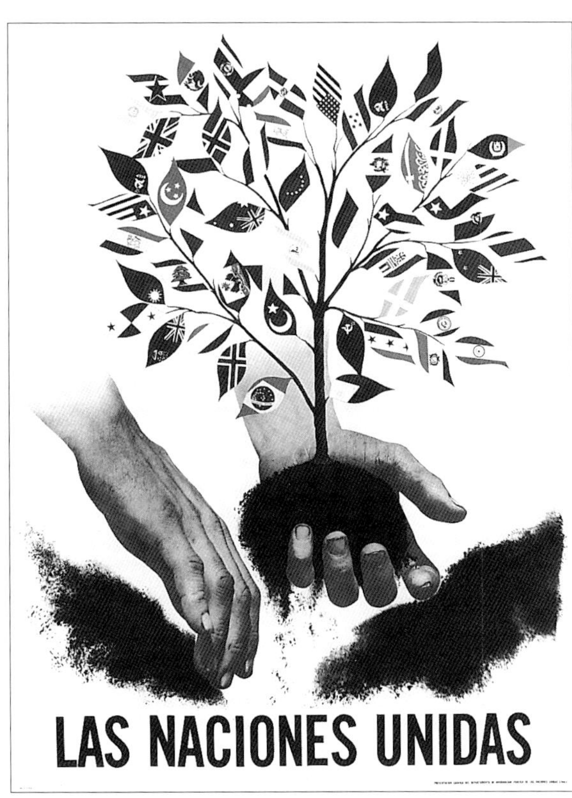

3. Las Naciones Unidas, 1947 (Spanish version), by
Canadian artist Henry Eveleigh. Received first prize
in the inaugural UN poster-of-the-year competition.

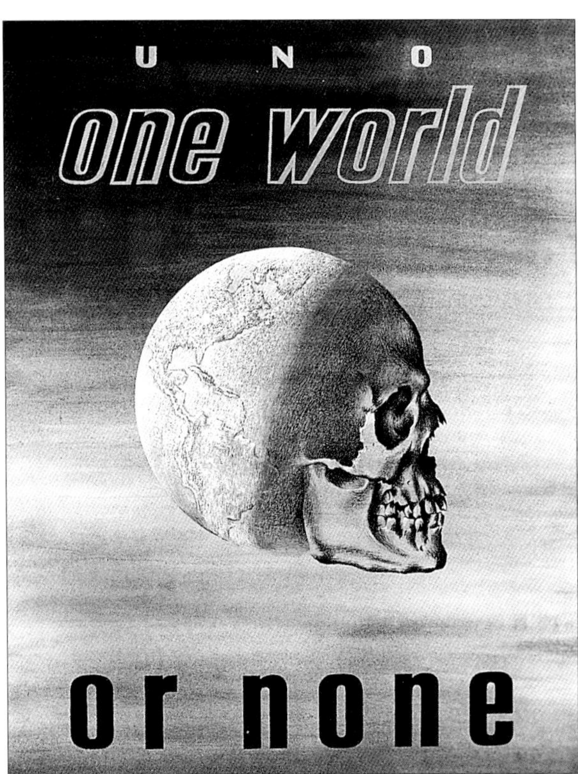

4. One World or None, 1947, by Dutch artist
Jan Bons. Received second prize in the inaugural
UN poster-of-the-year competition.

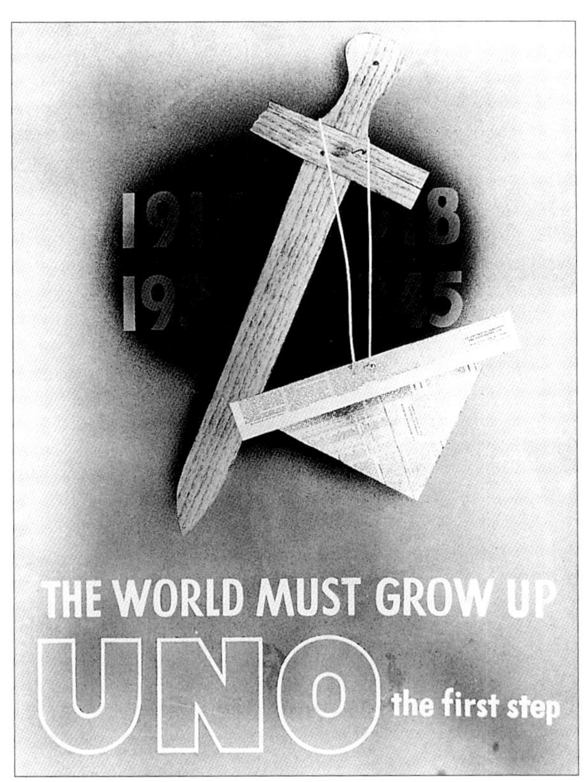

5. The World Must Grow Up, 1947, by South
African artist Rowan Prins. Received third prize in
the inaugural UN poster-of-the-year competition.

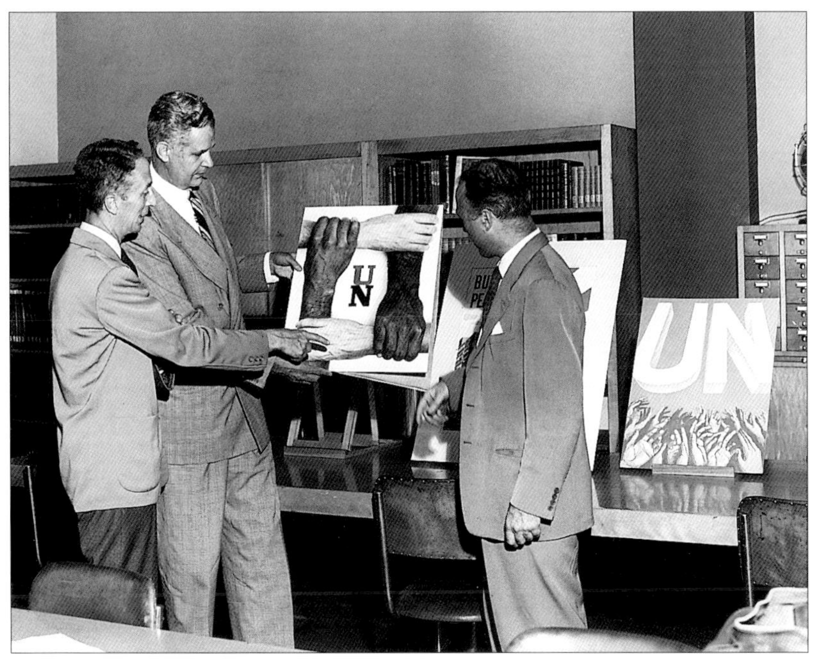

6. *Jury selecting U.S. posters competing for the 1948 UN poster of the year. From left to right: Norman Rockwell, Charles Nagel Jr., director of the Brooklyn Museum, and Toni Palazze, art director at* Collier's *magazine.*

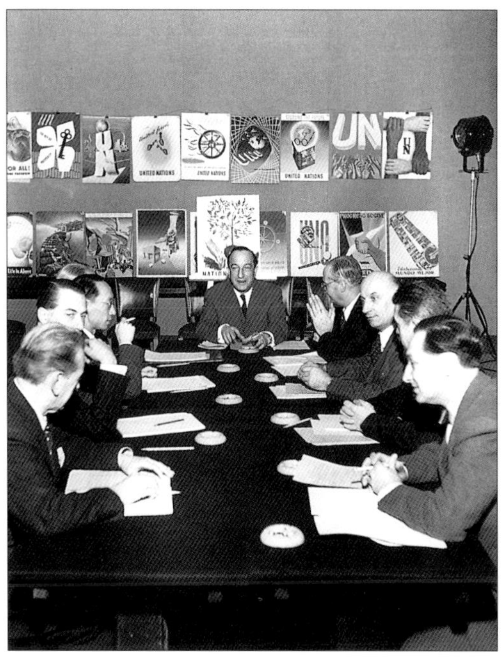

7. *International jury meeting at the Palais de Chaillot in Paris to judge entries for the 1948 poster-of-the-year competition.*

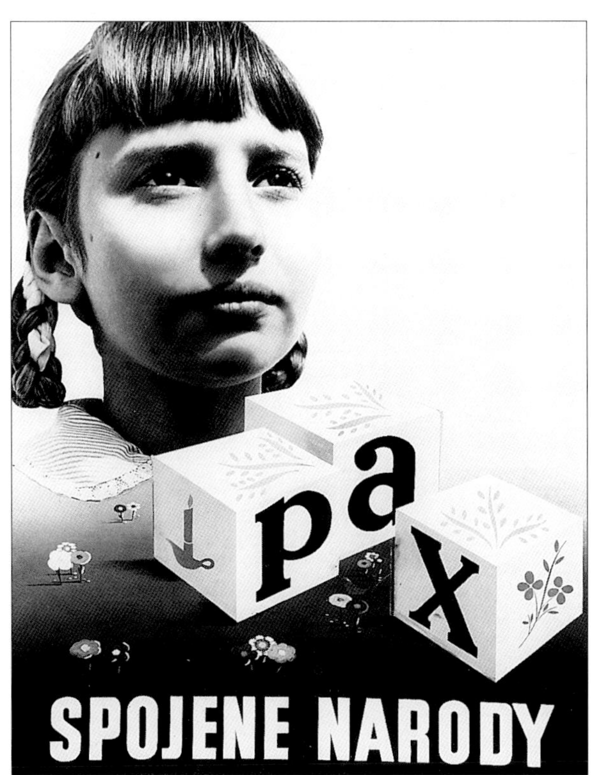

8. Spojene Narody *(United Nations), 1948 (Czech version), by Argentinean artist Armando Paez Torres. Received first prize in the 1948 UN poster-of-the-year competition. Photo by Eskinder Debebe.*

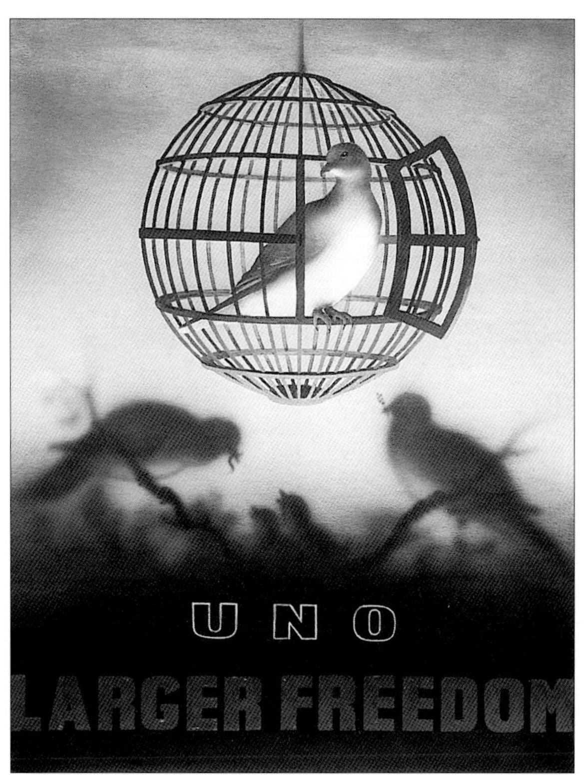

9. Larger Freedom, *1948, by Belgian artist Albert Setola. Received third prize in the 1948 UN poster-of-the-year competition.*

The First UN Posters

The first UN posters were institutional, proclaiming the name and identity of the new global body, known for a time as the United Nations Organization, or UNO. This appellation is found in the early posters, some of which were winners or runners-up in international poster-of-the-year competitions held in 1947 and 1948. Posters were submitted to a panel of judges in each member state. In the United States, a jury comprising the curator of the Brooklyn Museum, the art editor of *Collier's*, and the artist Norman Rockwell reviewed over one hundred submissions. Each national jury forwarded the three best entries for final selection by an international panel of judges. In 1948 this panel met at the Palais de Chaillot in Paris.

No original color posters from these competitions have been located, but the UN photo library retains black-and-white photographs of some of the prize winners. In one of these posters, captioned "UNO—Larger Freedom," a dove is emerging from a cage in the form of a globe. In another, hands are planting in soil a tree whose leaves are the flags of many nations. In a third, the trenchant question "One World or None?" is illustrated by a head in the form of a global map; the face has the features of a death mask (see pages 10 and 11).

Beginning in 1951, a newly designed poster celebrated each United Nations Day, October 24. This series continued into the 1960s. Various motifs are employed: the globe, flags of the nations, clasped hands, searching hands, doves, and other images of peace.

By the 1950s, the Department of Public Information at United Nations Headquarters and the information offices of the specialized agencies were producing posters that spoke not only of the UN and its goals for peace and human rights, but also to a wide spectrum of programs and activities undertaken by the world organization. These include economic and social development; decolonization; disarmament; abolition of poverty, child

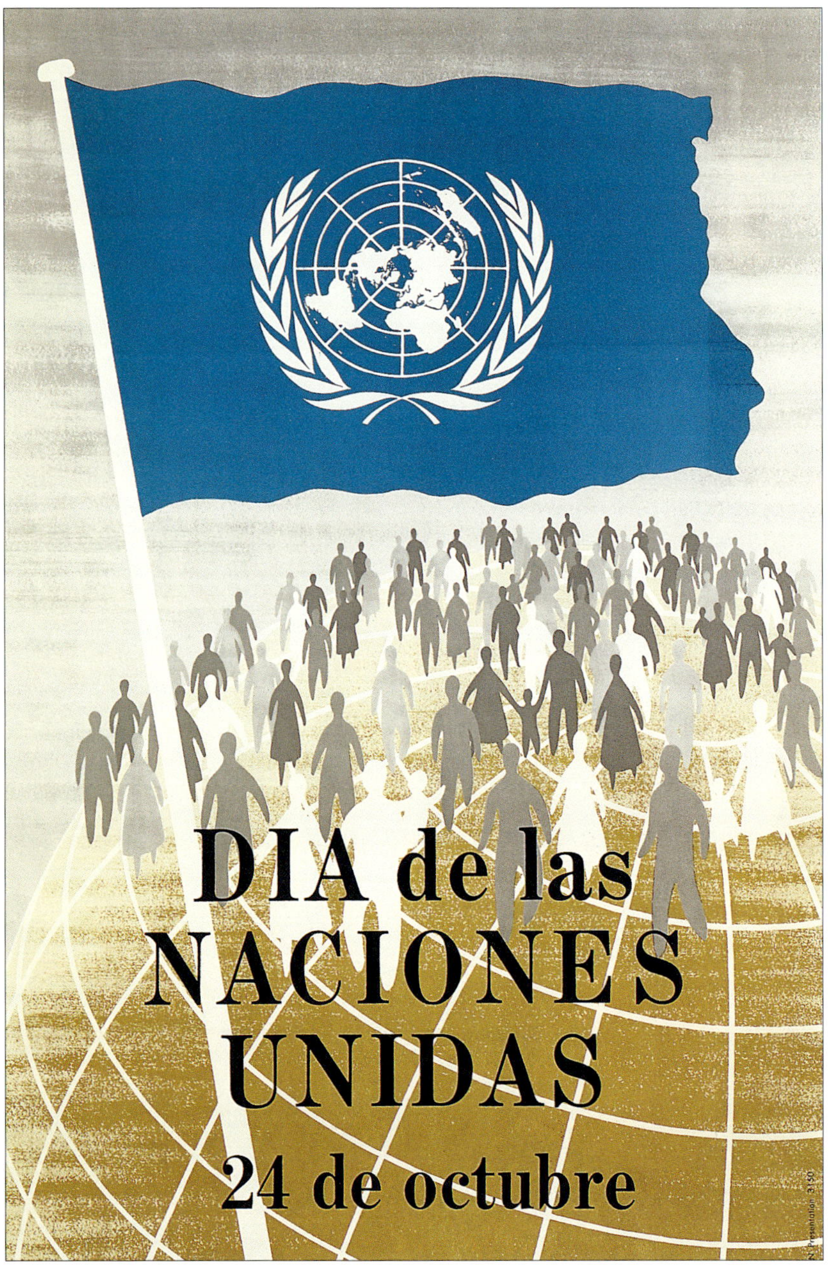

10. Dia de las Naciones Unidas *(United Nations Day), c. 1951 (Spanish version). Probably the first of a series of UN posters issued annually on UN Day, October 24.*

labor, apartheid, discrimination, and racism; actions promoting the well-being of women, children, refugees, the family, older persons, youth, and the disabled; health; population control; civil aviation; food and agriculture; protection of intellectual and cultural property; literacy; education; telecommunications; improvement of the environment; fair labor standards; and many others.

Some UN Poster Targets

Some of the best UN posters and poster calendars celebrate UN days, years, and decades. Others are designed to announce or commemorate international conferences, such as those held on population, the environment, women, and children. A third category signalizes special UN campaigns: against apartheid, for free elections (in Namibia and East Timor, for example), to combat desertification, and to eradicate land mines.

Posters have periodically been issued on a number of special topics not mentioned above, such as small islands, indigenous people, natural disasters, the newly established International Criminal Court of Justice, the United Nations University, protection of national monuments, the biosphere, space, and weather control.

Some posters are institutional. Charts consisting mainly of text with a few photos illustrate the organizational pattern of the United Nations, the UN Charter, the Declaration of Human Rights, and mounting world population. Colorful posters depict the UN's postage stamps and the flags of its member states. Others showing the Secretariat Building, the General Assembly, and the Security Council invite visitors to tour the UN. Some draw attention to UN activity in radio, television, and other media.

Probably the most popular poster theme is peacekeeping. The blue helmets of UN peacekeepers are featured in some, and maps and charts show the areas to which the peacekeepers are assigned. Some of the most striking posters juxtapose the dove and the bomb. Others cite the award to the UN of the Nobel Peace Prize in 1988, and the fiftieth anniversary of the world organization in 1995.

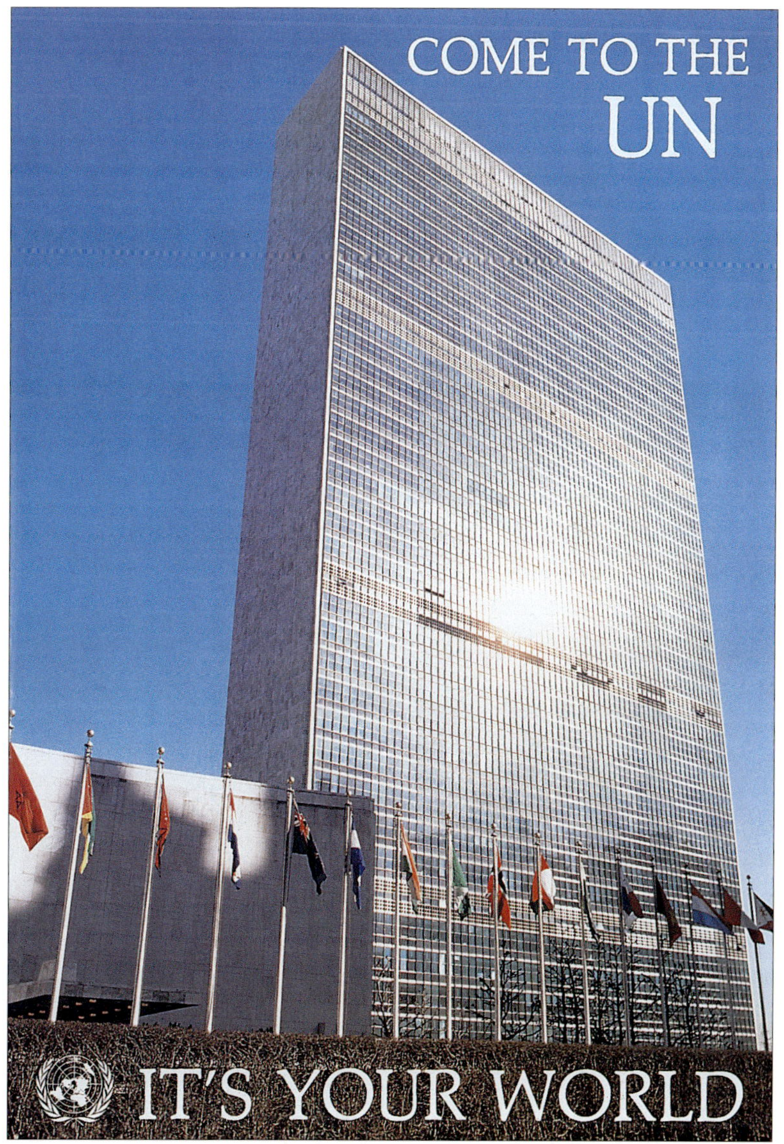

11. Come to the UN—It's Your World, *1988, designed by Gibby's Posters, Bay Terrace, New York. View of the Secretariat Building, one of three buildings that make up the UN complex (one of a series of posters encouraging visits to the UN).*

What is special about the job of designing posters and other informational materials for the United Nations? Maxim Żhukov, former chief of the UN's design section, presents interesting views on this point in his chapter of the book *Cross-Cultural Design: Communicating in the Global Marketplace.*

> *One of the focal problems is translating the UN texts in six official languages. The linguists know that in order to ensure a reliable translation into whatever language, the master copy has to be written simply, with no parochial or slang expressions. Likewise, when looking for an appropriate visual solution we have to rule out those media, tools, and means that might lead to ambiguity or controversy. We must be highly selective in using any visual device. This exactingness affects all constituents and elements of design—for example, the overall layout, the relationship of the 'louder' and 'softer' parts, the imagery, the color palette, the choice of typefaces, and the typographical arrangement.*

A number of UN poster illustrations were the work of well-known artists. Some were adapted from works of art in the UN collection, notably the Chagall stained-glass window and the Norman Rockwell mosaic at the New York headquarters, the Picasso centenary poster based on his painting *The Fall of Icarus* at UNESCO in Paris, and Hans Erni's painting on the same subject at ICAO Montreal (see page 107).

Joan Miró designed a strong poster for UNESCO to celebrate the thirtieth anniversary of the UN Declaration of Human Rights (see page 53). Other notable contributors of art for UN posters include Graciela Rodo Boulanger,

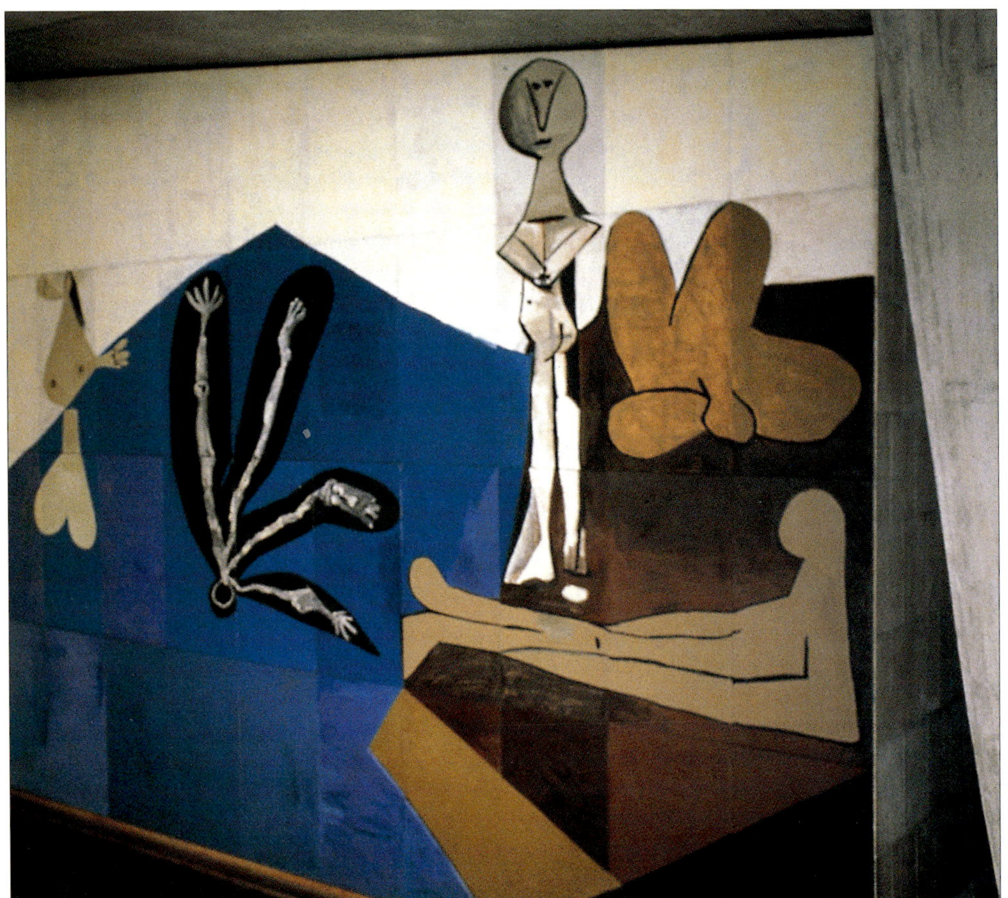

12. La Chute d'Icare (The Fall of Icarus), by Pablo Picasso, 1981. Painting at UNESCO headquarters in Paris (used in poster to commemorate Picasso's centenary, 1881–1981).

Michel Delacroix, Sonia Delaunay, Jean Michel Folon, Osvaldo Guayasamin, Keith Haring, Peter Max, Robert Rauschenberg, Otavio Roth, Maria Elena Vieira da Silva, and Victor Vasarely. Rauschenberg created no less than seven United Nations posters on the environment, apartheid, habitat, and protection of cultural property. Many UN posters are by renowned graphic designers such as Paul Davis, Michel Granger, Ikuo Hirayama, William Mayer, Benn, and Carzou.

With the special purpose of attracting the interest of children, UNICEF has sought and obtained the cooperation of several popular cartoonists. To caution children about the danger of land mines, artists at DC Comics featured Superman in two powerful warning posters. Charles Schulz, widely known for *Peanuts,* enlisted that comic strip's Charlie Brown as an advocate for children's welfare. Dennis the Menace and Kermit the Frog have also been spokesmen for the "Trick or Treat" program—where children go from house to house to collect donations for UNICEF—and other observances of the annual UNICEF day on Halloween (see page 74).

Attractive posters on diverse themes have been produced by past and present staff of the Graphic Design Section and Exhibits Unit of the UN's Department of Public Information, including examples by Jan Arnesen, Rocco Callari, José Castiñeira, Ole Hamann, Jan Ralph, Jim Eschinger, and Maxim Żhukov. In some cases, outside artists were called on to supply the art for an in-house design. Illustrative photographs for many posters were the work of John Isaac, Milton Grant, Evan Schneider, and others of the UN photo unit. Until her retirement in 1999, Bonnie Berlinghof was responsible for the conception and design of a large number of UNICEF's affecting posters.

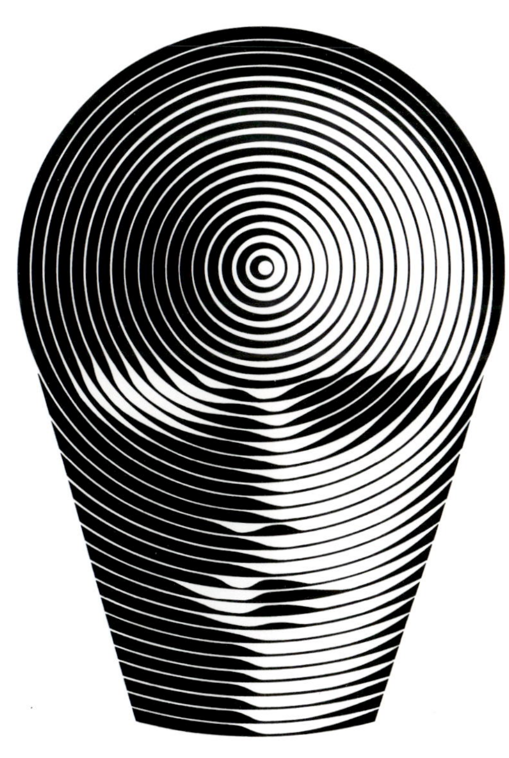

13. UNESCO symbol for International Education Year, by Victor Vasarely.

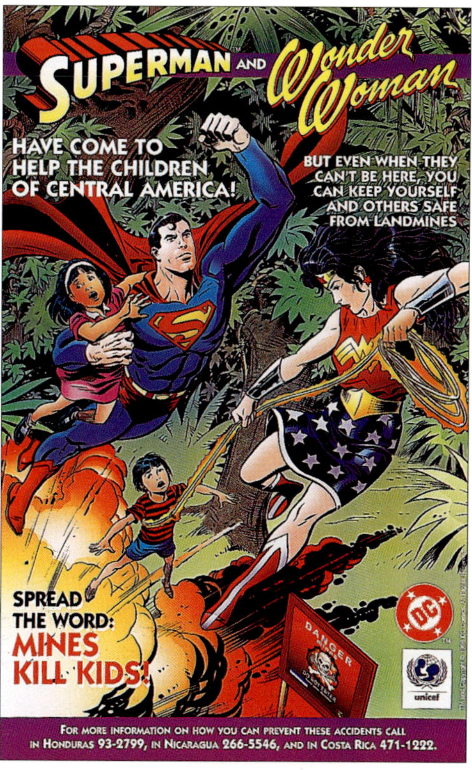

14. Superman and Wonder Woman™, 1998, UNICEF Mine Awareness Campaign poster, art direction by Bonnie Berlinghof. An alert for children to avoid land mines. © DC Comics. All rights reserved.

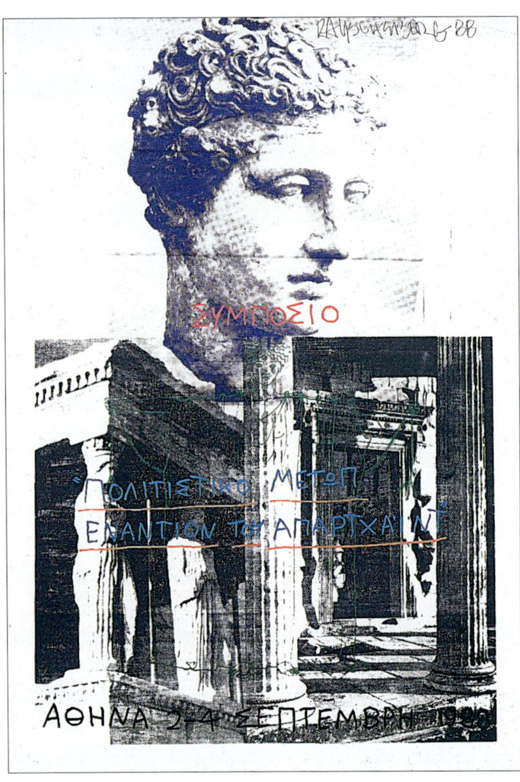

15. *Poster for International Anti-Apartheid Symposium, by Robert Rauschenberg, Athens, Greece, 2–4 September 1988, UN Department of Public Information.*

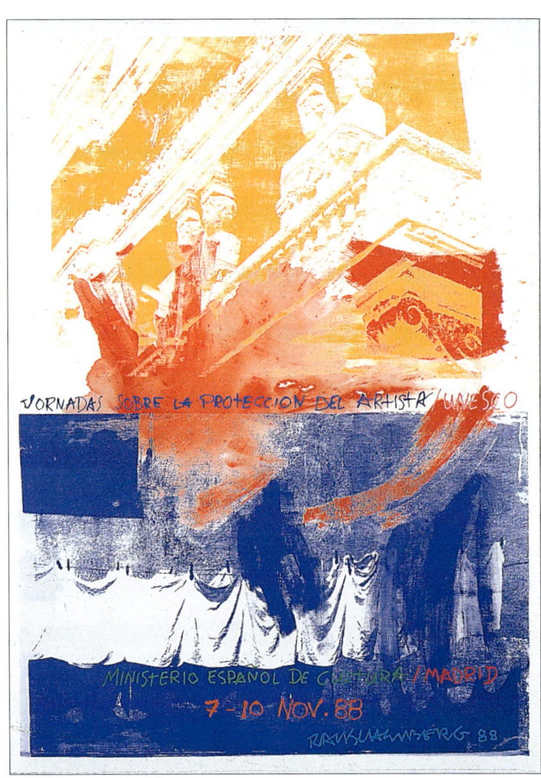

16. *Jornadas sobre la proteccion del artista, by Robert Rauschenberg, for UNESCO conference on protection of artistic property, Madrid, Spain, 7–10 November 1988, in cooperation with Spanish Ministry of Culture.*

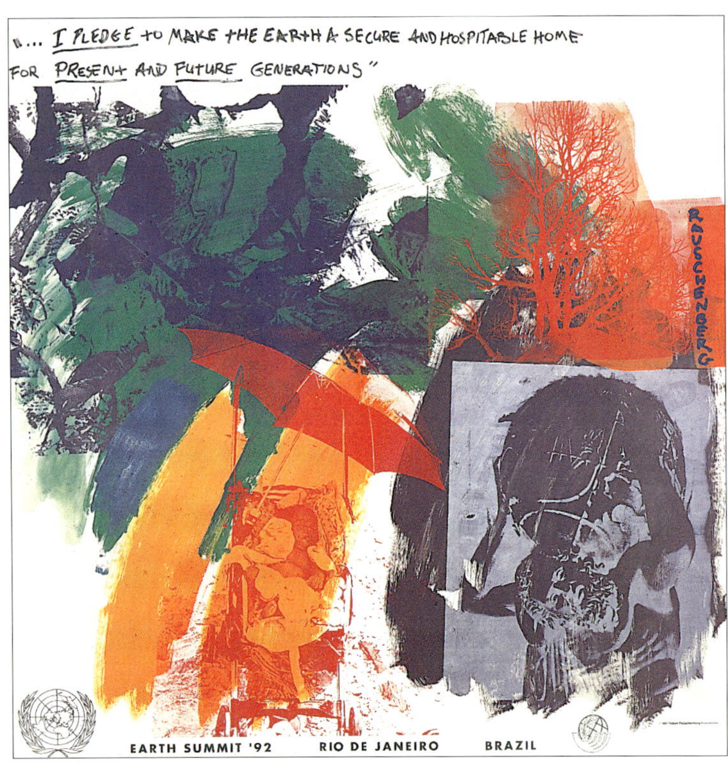

17. *Last Turn—Your Turn, by Robert Rauschenberg, for Earth Summit, Conference on Environment and Development, 1992, Rio de Janeiro, Brazil. Offset lithograph, 25 × 26 in.*

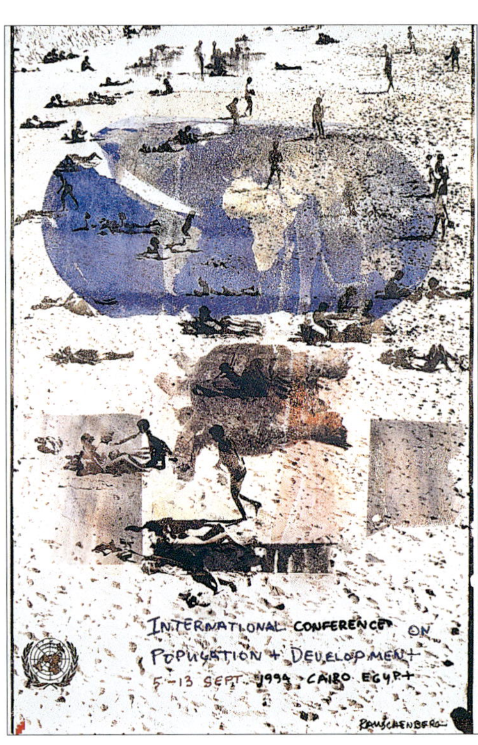

18. *Poster for UN International Conference on Population and Development, 1994, Cairo, Egypt, by Robert Rauschenberg. Offset lithograph, 38 7/8 × 26 7/8 in.*

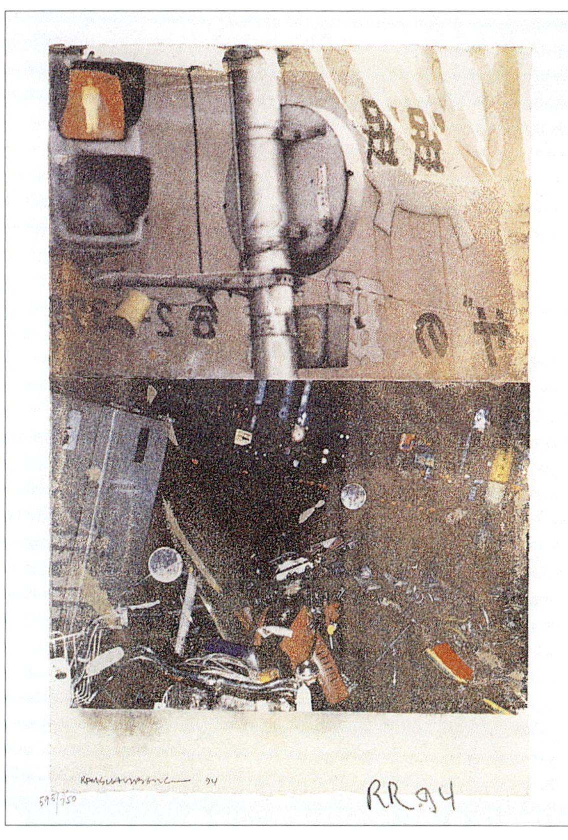

*19. Bulkhead, 1994, by Robert Rauschenberg,
printed to benefit the World Federation of UN
Associations. Offset lithograph, 12 × 8 1/2 in.*

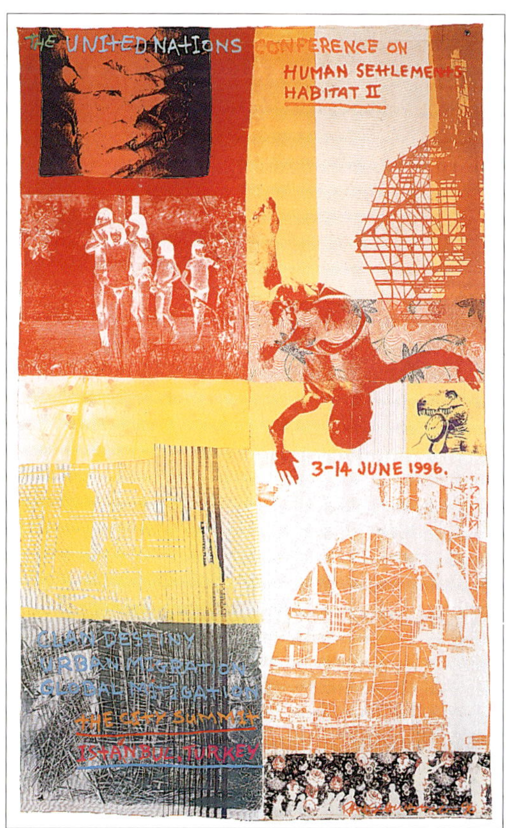

*20. Clan Destiny, by Robert Rauschenberg,
for Habitat II conference, "The City Summit,"
3–14 June 1996, Istanbul, Turkey. Offset
lithograph, 39 1/4 × 24 7/8 in.*

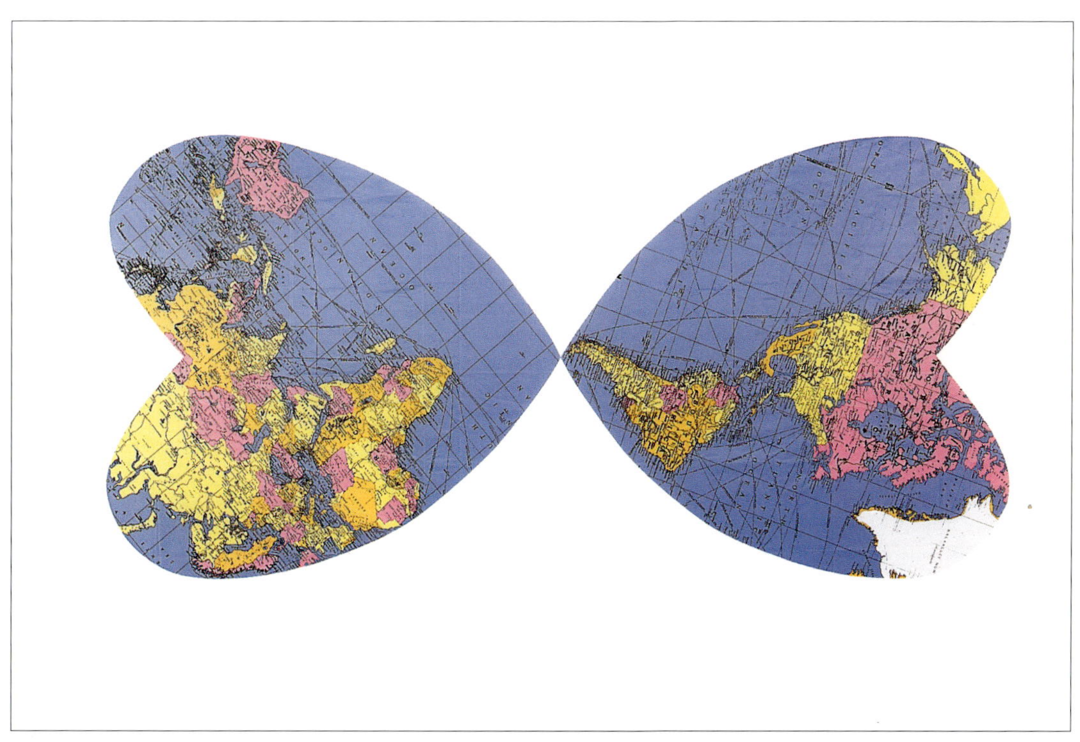

*21. Whole World (also known as Tolerance Flag), by Robert Rauschenberg,
for fiftieth anniversary of World Health Organization, 1948–1998. Fabric, 79 × 121 in.*

At UNESCO, J. C. Bernath, Michel Claude, Claude Ferrand, and Dominique Roger supplied photo illustrations. Maureen Lynch is responsible for the design of many UNDP posters, and Christian Delsol for those of the UN Population Fund.

Sources Outside the UN

Most of the posters reproduced in this volume were issued by the information departments of the UN and its subsidiary and specialized agencies. But a few were created by nongovernmental organizations in direct support of a United Nations year, conference, or other special event. The U.S. and Canadian committees for UNICEF provided several of these. Others were provided by NGOs or governmental authorities in Australia, Canada, Italy, the Scandinavian countries, Thailand, and the United States, often in direct collaboration with the UN agency concerned.

League of Nations Posters

Two of the very few posters produced by the League of Nations have been included to show the continuum over the last century of social issues that, in this new century, remain global problems (see pages 28–29). The League existed from 1920 to 1946, though it was largely inactive from the onset of World War II until it was superseded by the UN in April 1946. In its earlier years the league had some minor successes in settling disputes but was unable to prevent or significantly influence the events in Europe that led to the world conflict. It did, however, take constructive steps in support of minorities, to improve health and labor conditions around the world, and to provide aid to many refugees of World War I. The aid to refugees was carried on under the leadership of Fridtjof Nansen, the Norwegian explorer and statesman who won the Nobel Peace Prize in 1922 for his postwar relief activities. In 1931, the League honored him by creating the Nansen Office of Refugees, which won the Nobel Peace Prize in 1938. Nansen initiated an international travel document, known as the Nansen passport, for use by stateless persons.

Poster Competitions and Exhibits

Poster designers from one hundred fifty-seven member states participated in the United Nations' international disarmament poster competition. This competition took place in 1981, as a prelude to the General Assembly's second special session on disarmament held in June and July of 1982. First prize went to Gerhard Voigt of the German Democratic Republic; his poster, reproduced on page 30, was issued in six languages. Entries from Hungary, Indonesia, Peru, and the United States received honorable mentions. An outstanding exhibition of UN posters was held in 1995 in Tokyo in commemoration of the fiftieth anniversary of the world body. Children at the UN's International School submitted designs for a poster competition in 1998 relating to the UN and the millennium. A number of the most attractive posters on the theme of population were designed by teenagers for the annual UN Population Fund poster competition.

It is gratifying that many fine artists have been motivated to create posters for the United Nations. There may be no better profile of the many and varied activities of the organization in its first half-century than these signposts issued along the way. Taken together, the posters in this book are an important tribute to the United Nations and all it stands for. They are also a strong testament to the enduring value, beauty, and power of the poster as an art form and as a means of communication.

FOR A BETTER WORLD

Posters from the United Nations

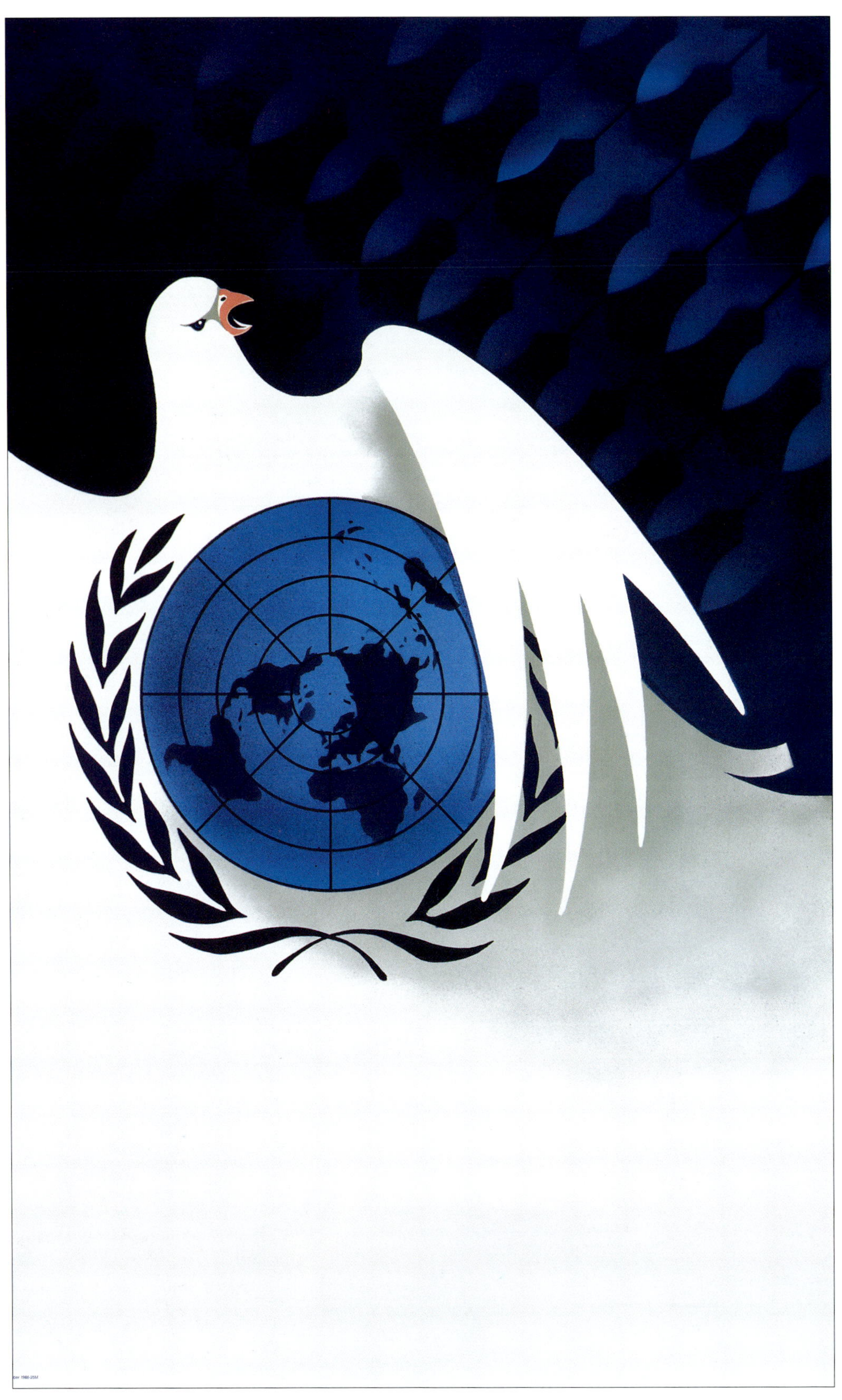

22. United Nations for a Better World, *1986, by Panamanian artist Ricardo Ernesto Jaime De Freitas, art direction by Graphic Design Section, UN Department of Public Information.*

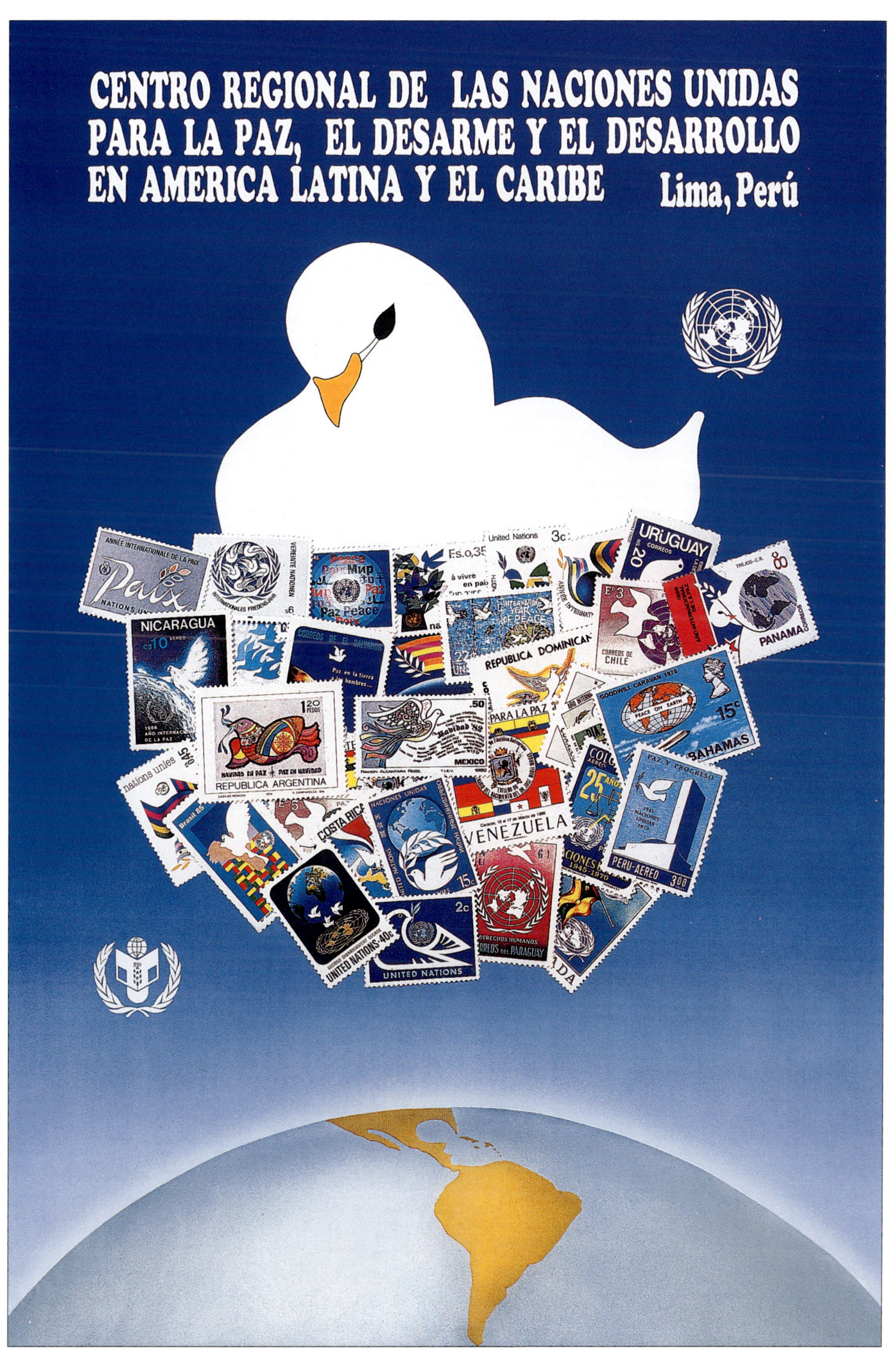

23. Stamps and Dove, *designed by Rocco Callari. A Latin American poster illustrating UN postage stamps issued by the UN Postal Administration.*

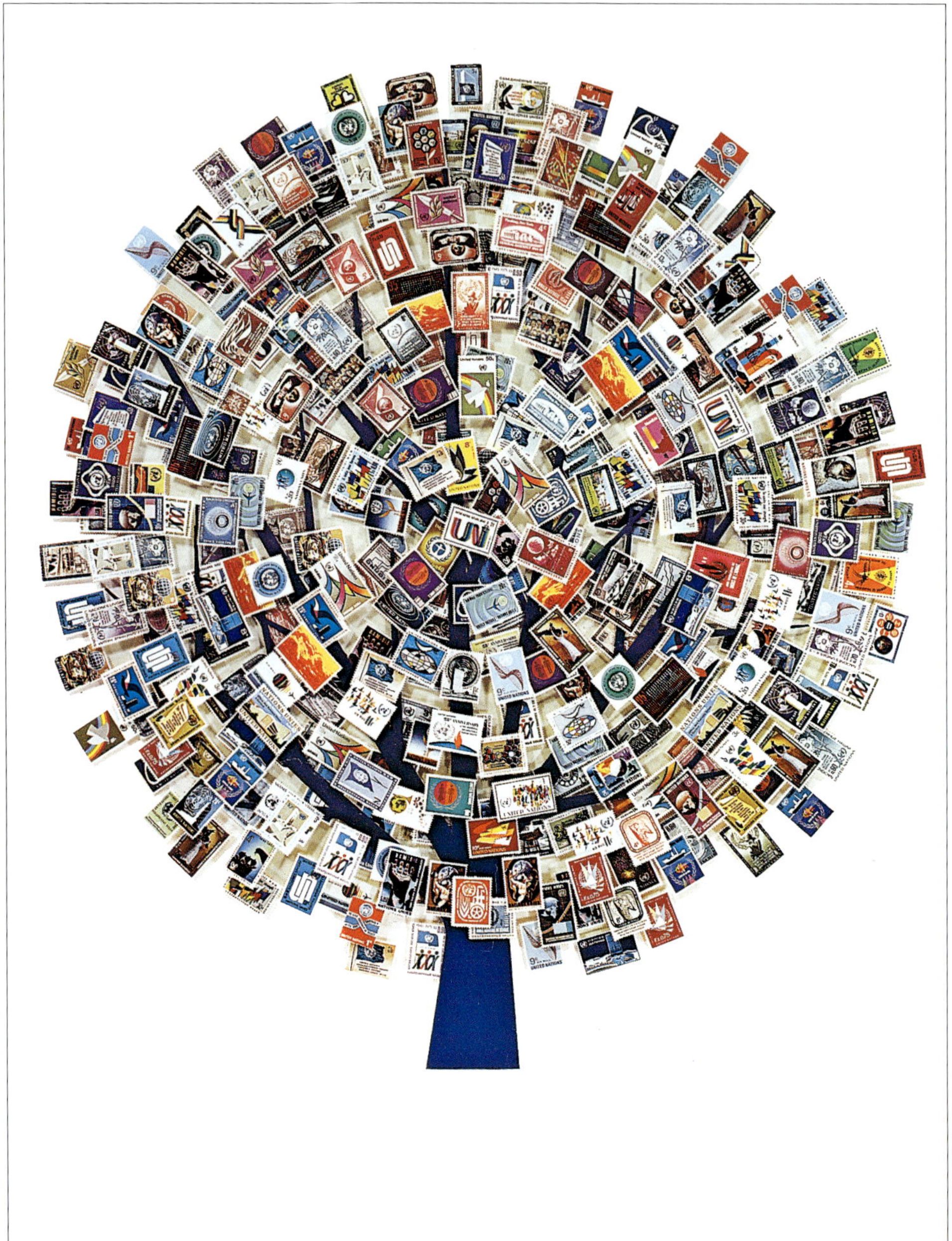

*24. UN Stamp Wheel,
designed by Rocco Callari.
Depicts a selection of the
postage stamps issued by
the UN Postal Administration.*

The **United Nations Department of Public Information (DPI)**, established in 1946, commun-
icates the complex work of the United Nations system through such outlets as the UN website, print
publications, press releases, radio and television programming, documentary videos, special events, public
tours, and library facilities. DPI's Media Division provides live television and radio news broadcasts of
major UN activities to correspondents and news organizations worldwide. The Promotion and Public Service
Division conducts public-awareness campaigns to promote UN conferences, themes, and programs through
special events. The Library and Publications Division oversees the work of the Dag Hammarskjöld Library,
which maintains a complete collection of UN documentation and provides research and reference services.
The Information Center Service coordinates sixty-nine UN information centers and eight UN offices with
information components around the world. Information about the UN is available at the UN's website:
www.un.org.

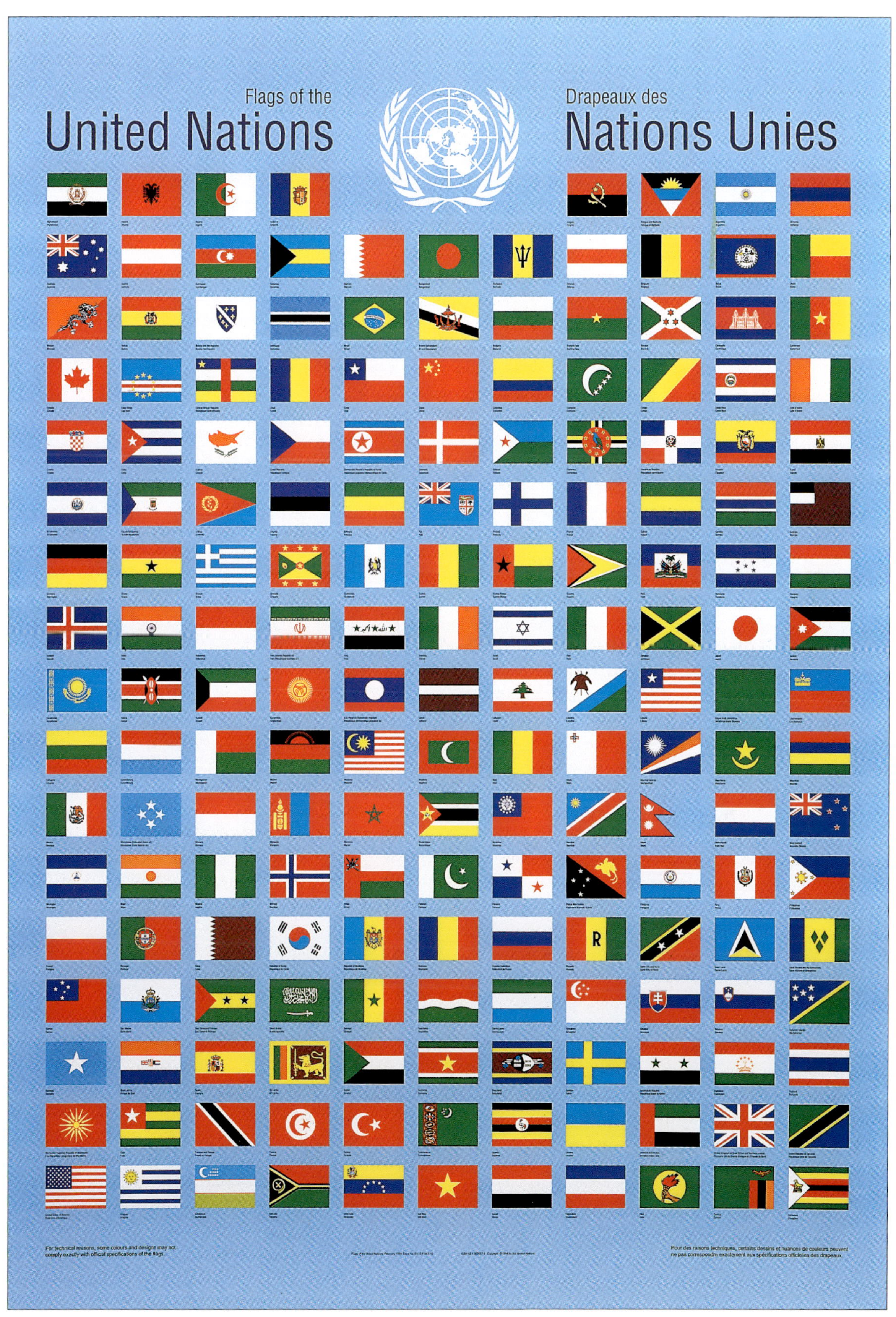

25. Flags of the United Nations, *1994. Depicts flags of one hundred seventy member states (the number has grown to 189).*

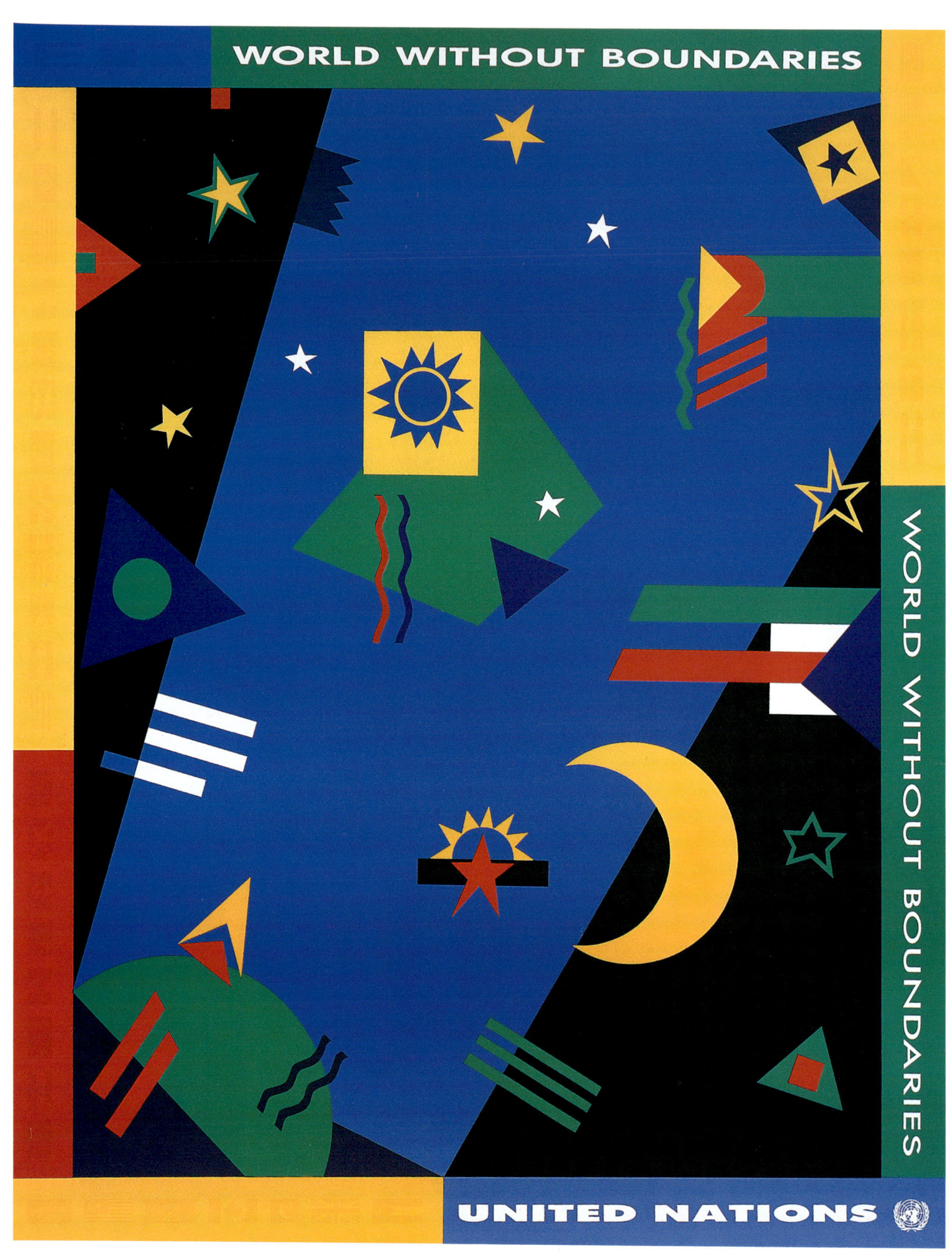

26. World Without Boundaries, *designed by Jan Arnesen, UN Department of Public Information, and Namibian artist Jo Rogge.*

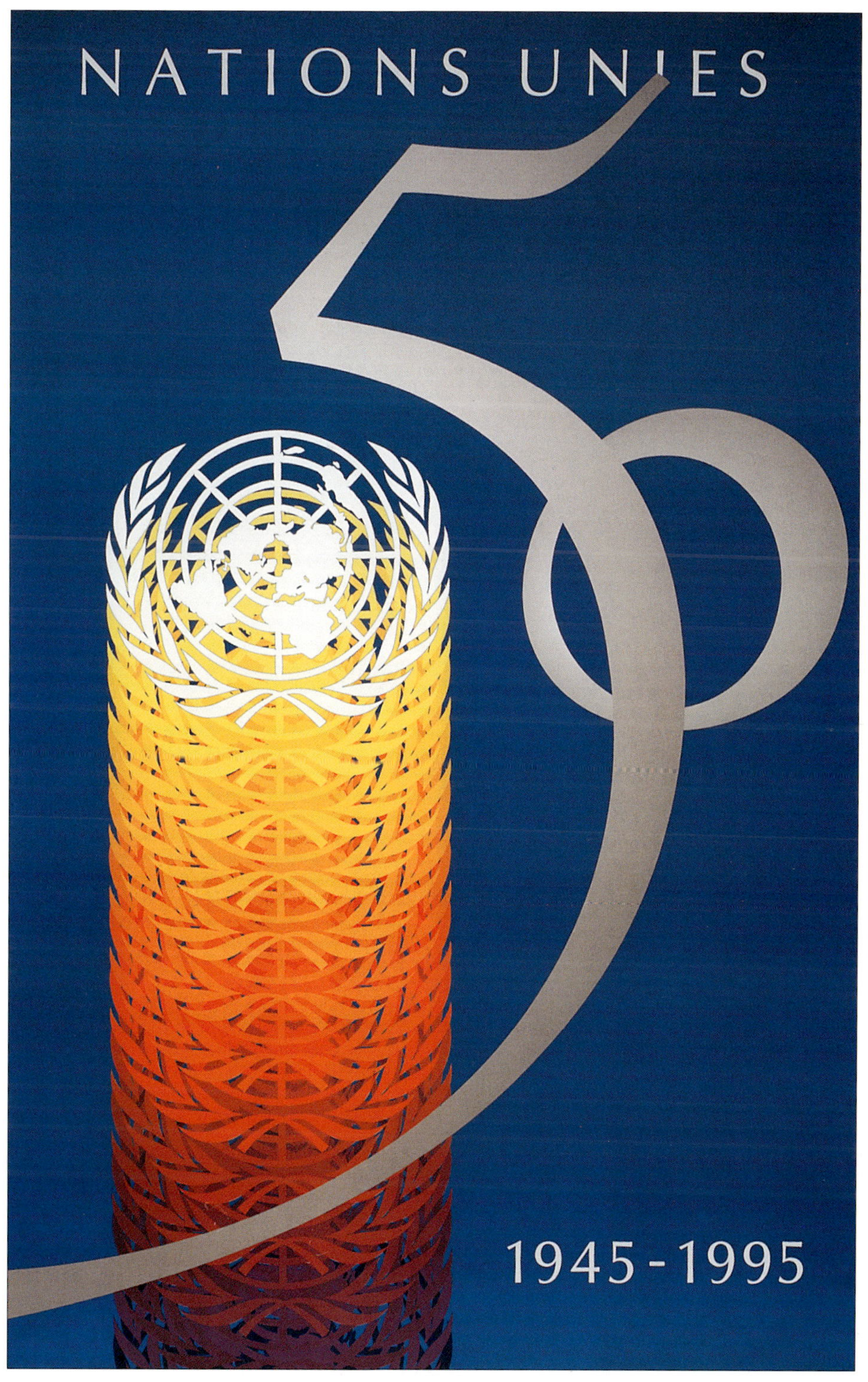

27. UN Fiftieth Anniversary, 1995, designed by José Castiñeira, Graphic Design Section, UN Department of Public Information.

United Nations Headquarters, New York serves three major groups: delegates, the secretariat, and journalists. The delegates, including the Economic and Social Council and the Trusteeship Council, convene in the General Assembly Building and the adjoining conference rooms. Most of the international UN staff facilitate meetings, collect information, and prepare reports in the Secretariat Building, where offices are provided for accredited journalists and daily briefings are held. The Security Council also meets in this building. A third building houses the extensive UN library.

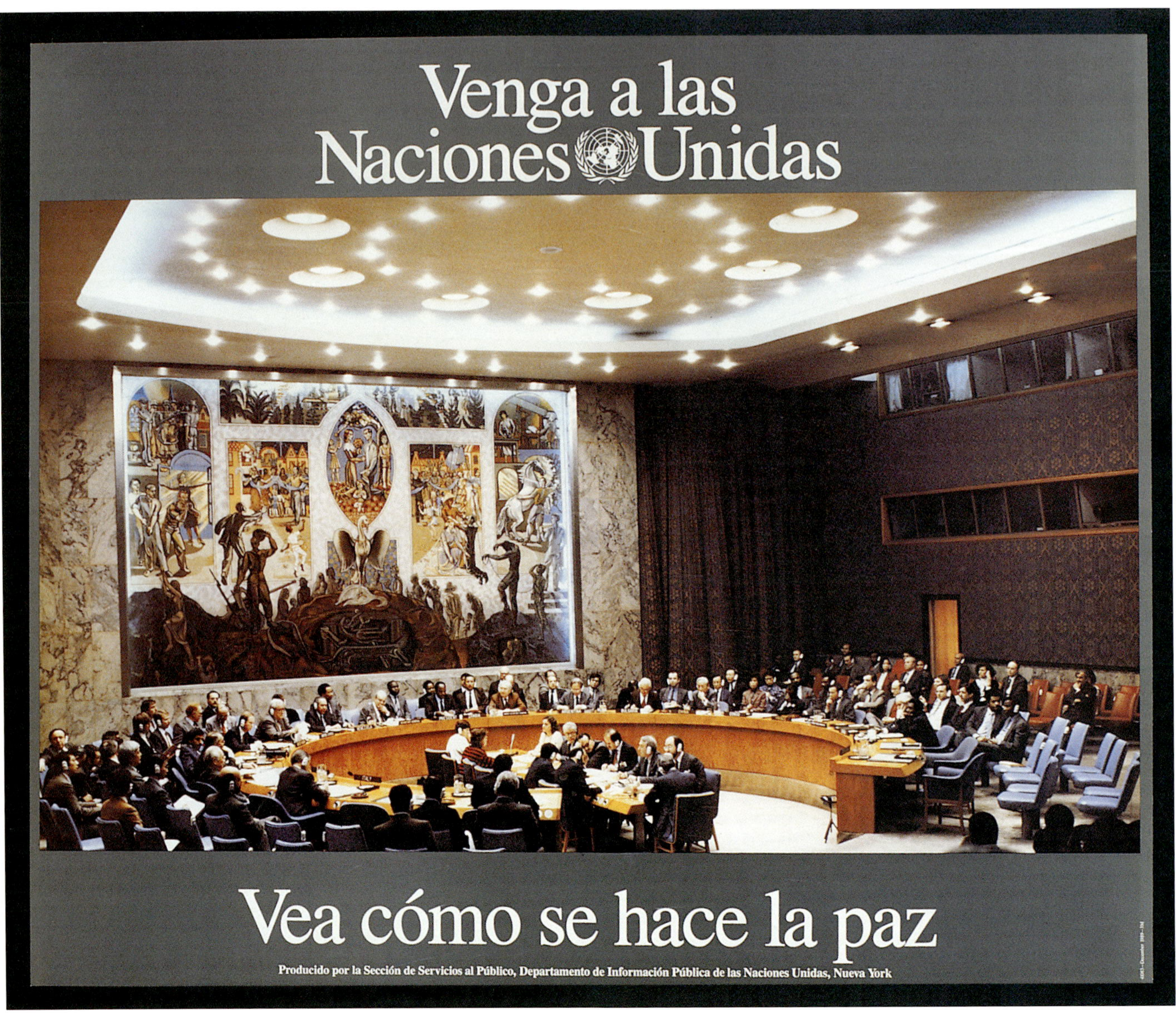

28. See Peace in the Making—Come to the UN *(Spanish version), designed by James Eschinger, Graphic Design Section, UN Department of Public Information. Depicts the Security Council in session.*

The **UN Security Council** is composed of five permanent members—China, France, the Russian Federation, the United Kingdom, and the United States—and ten members elected by the General Assembly for two-year terms. The council is responsible for maintaining international peace and security in accordance with the principles and purposes of the UN, investigating disputes that would lead to international friction or threaten peace, negotiating disputes, formulating plans for regulating armaments, imposing economic sanctions, taking military action against an aggressor, recommending to the General Assembly the appointment of the Secretary-General, and, together with the assembly, electing the judges of the international court. Member states are obliged to accept and carry out the council's decisions.

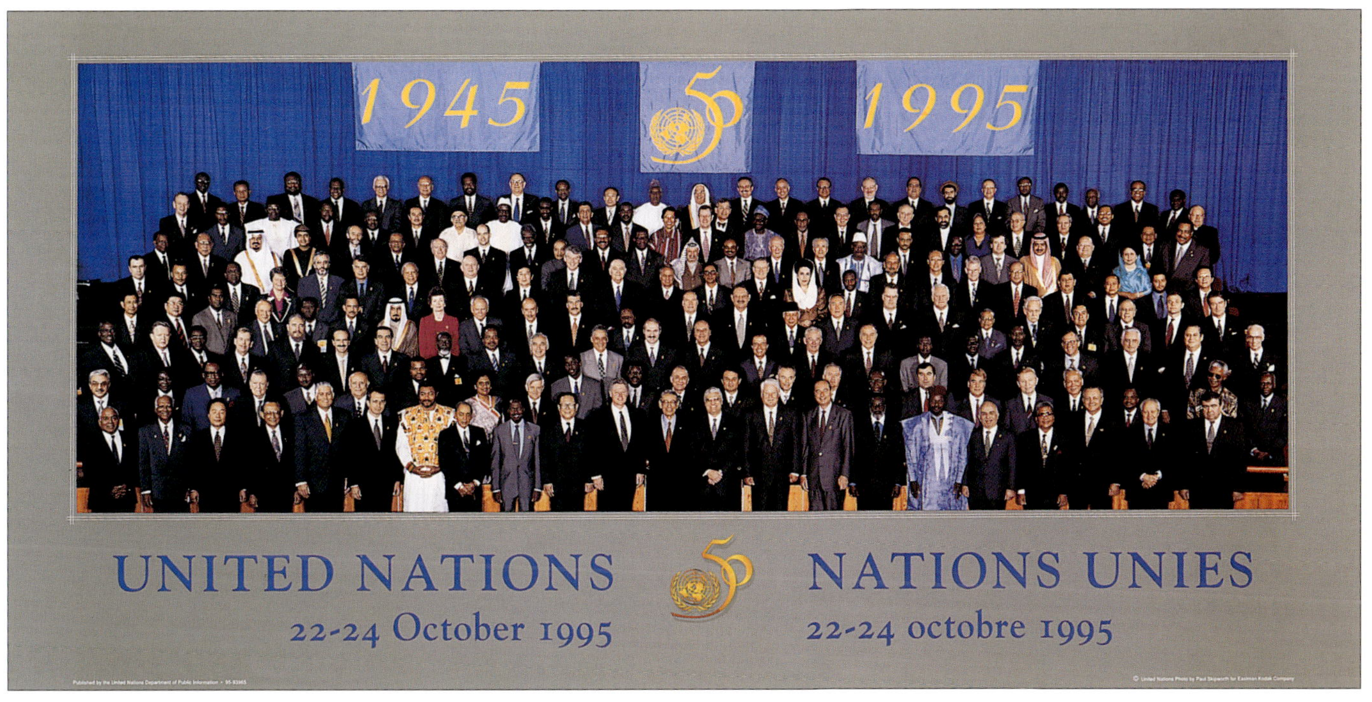

29. *UN heads of state attending the 1995 summit meeting (held on 22–24 October 1995) celebrating the fiftieth anniversary of the UN. Designed by José Castiñeira, Graphic Design Section, UN Department of Public Information. Photo by Paul Skipworth for Eastman Kodak Co.*

The **General Assembly Affairs and Conference Services**, the main deliberative organ of the UN, has the right to discuss all matters within the scope of the UN Charter, including the powers and functions of the other UN organs. All member nations of the UN are represented in the General Assembly. The General Assembly initiates studies and makes recommendations to promote international cooperation in the political, economic, social, cultural, educational, and health fields, to encourage the progressive development of international law and its codification, to monitor elections, and to further the realization of human rights and fundamental freedom for all without distinction as to race, sex, language, or religion.

MINORITIES

After the War many states signed Treaties, or made Declarations to the League in regard to their racial, religious and linguistic minorities. The fulfilment of the obligations thus contracted was placed under the guarantee of the League.

Each member of the Council has the right to bring to the attention of the Council any infraction or danger of infraction of these obligations.

Differences of opinion as to questions of law or fact arising out of these treaties or declarations can be referred to the Permanent Court of International Justice.

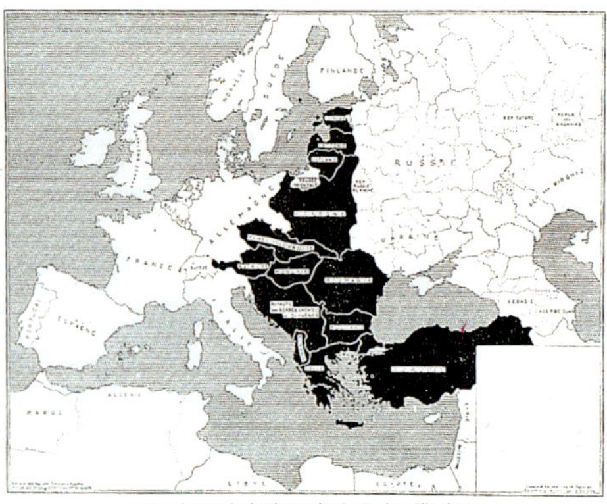

Map of States having international minority obligations.

PROCEDURE IN MINORITIES QUESTIONS

is laid down by the Council. Each petition, if accepted as conforming with certain conditions, is submitted, together with the observations of the interested government, to the President of the Council, who, with the assistance of two other members, (the "Committee of Three"), decides whether the petition :

(1) shall be dimissed,

(2) can be settled by the Committee without formal decision,

(3) shall be referred to the Council, which may take such action as it deems best.

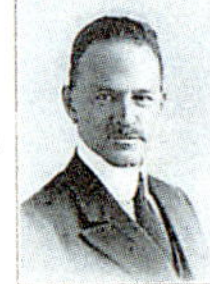

Racial and Linguistic Minorities under the protection of the League :

Albanians	Hungarians	Ruthenian-Ukrainians
Armenians	Italians	Serbs. Croats and Slovenes
Bulgars	Jews	Slavs (Others)
Czechoslovaks	Latvians	Swedes
Esthonians	Lithuanians	Turks and Tartars
Germans	Poles	
Greeks	Roumanians	
Gypsies	Russians	

Information Section League of Nations Secretariat, Geneva, Autumn 1928.

The **League of Nations** was formed in 1920 to preserve peace, seek settlement of international disputes, and facilitate international cooperation in furthering the moral and material welfare of humanity. A predecessor to the UN, the league was created by the signatories of the Treaty of Versailles—which brought World War I to an end. It consisted of an assembly, council, and secretariat. In fulfillment of part of its mandate, the League established two offices that provided humanitarian assistance: the Nansen International Office for Refugees and the Minorities Section of the League Secretariat. The League was dissolved in 1946, following World War II.

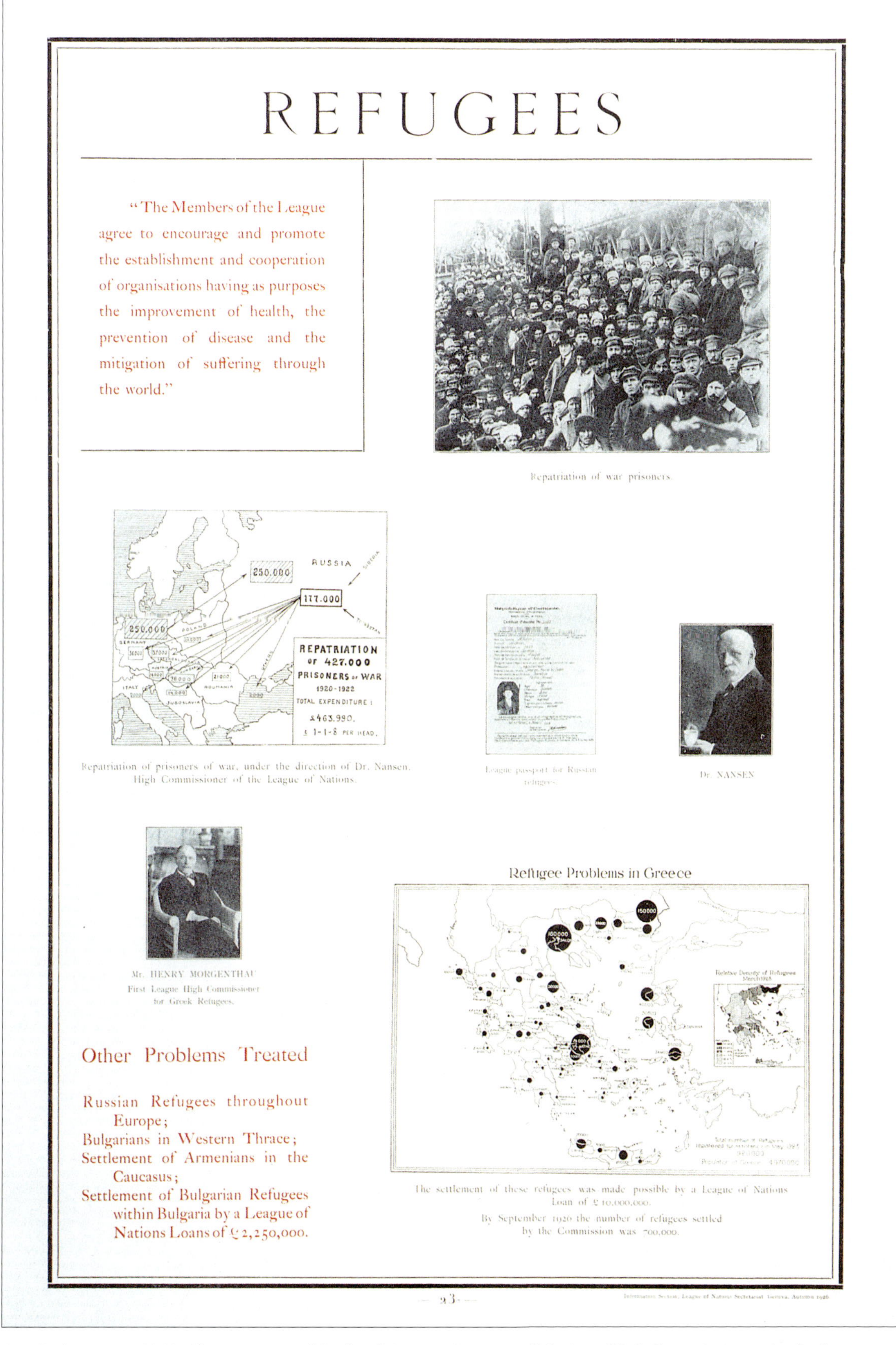

31. *Refugees, c. 1940. Shows image of Fridtjof Nansen, League of Nations High Commissioner for Refugees (League of Nations poster).*

32

United Nations General Assembly
Second Special Session on Disarmament
May 1982

33

UNITED NATION — GENERAL ASSEMBLY
SECOND
SPECIAL
SESSION
on
disarmament
'82

34

ASAMBLEA GENERAL DE LAS NACIONES UNIDAS
SEGUNDO PERIODO EXTRAORDINARIO DE SESIONES DEDICADO AL DESARME / MAYO DE 1982

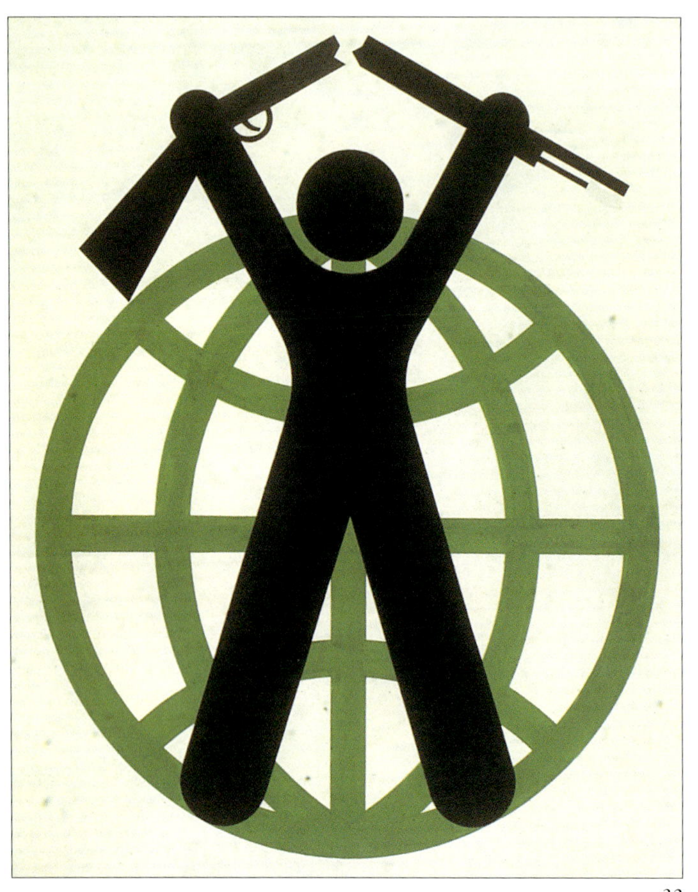

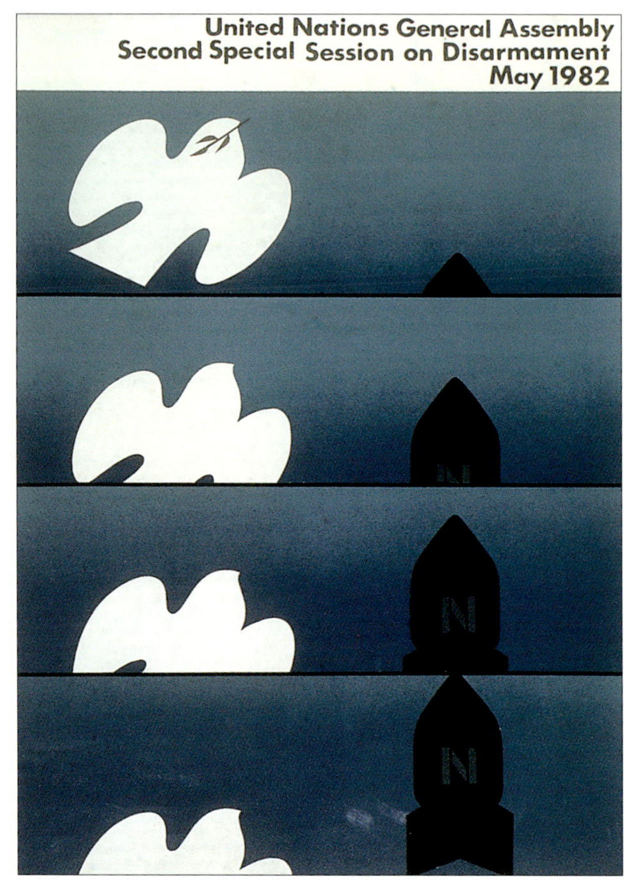

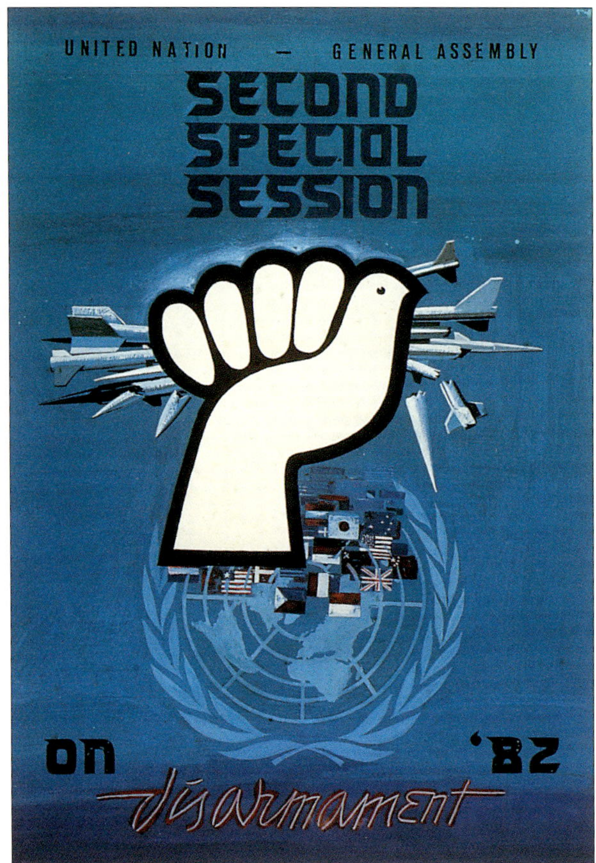

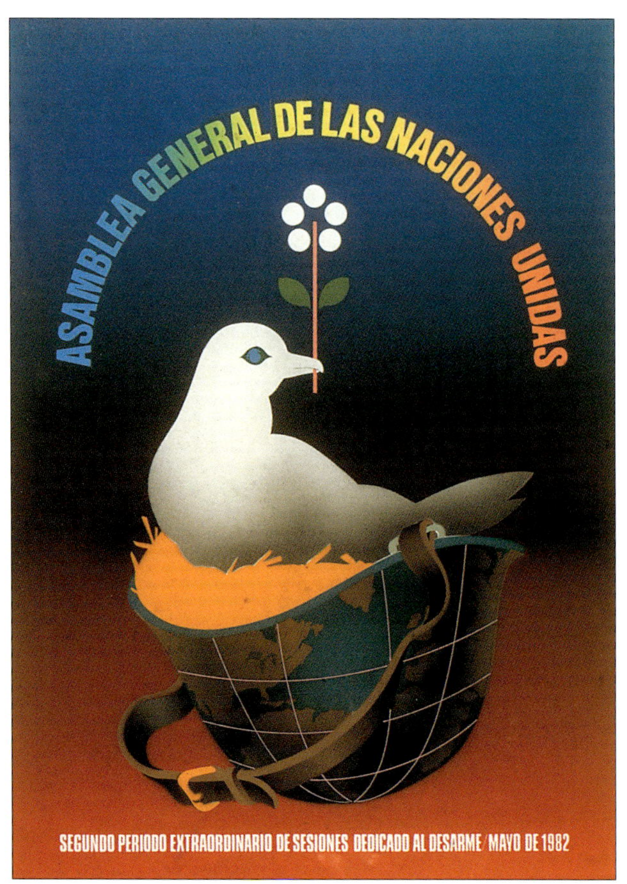

35

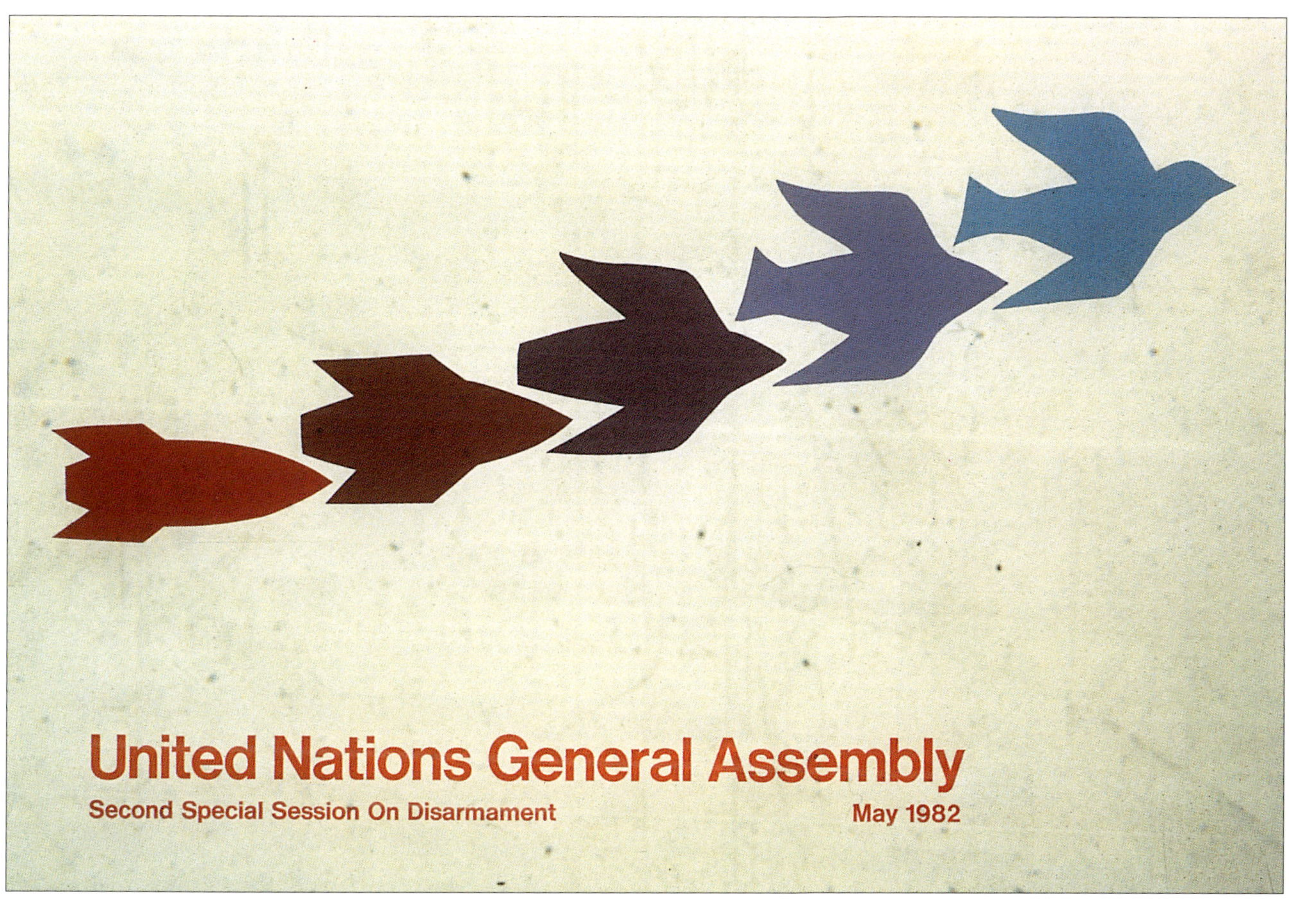

32–36. *One hundred fifty-seven UN member states submitted poster designs for an international poster competition on disarmament in 1981. The winning poster, by German artist Gerhard Voigt (32), was used to help promote the UN General Assembly's second special session on disarmament, 7–9 June 1982. Honorable mentions were also awarded to posters submitted by artists from Peru, the United States, Indonesia, and Hungary.*

36

The **United Nations Department for Disarmament Affairs** has focused attention on multilateral disarmament and arms limitation. Among the department's highest priorities is to reduce and eventually eliminate weapons of mass destruction. The scope of international deliberations and negotiations on disarmament has changed in recent years; many nations have begun to more closely consider threats related to the excessive and destabilizing accumulation of conventional armaments, the proliferation of small arms and light weapons, and the humanitarian crisis caused by the massive deployment of land mines in conflict areas.

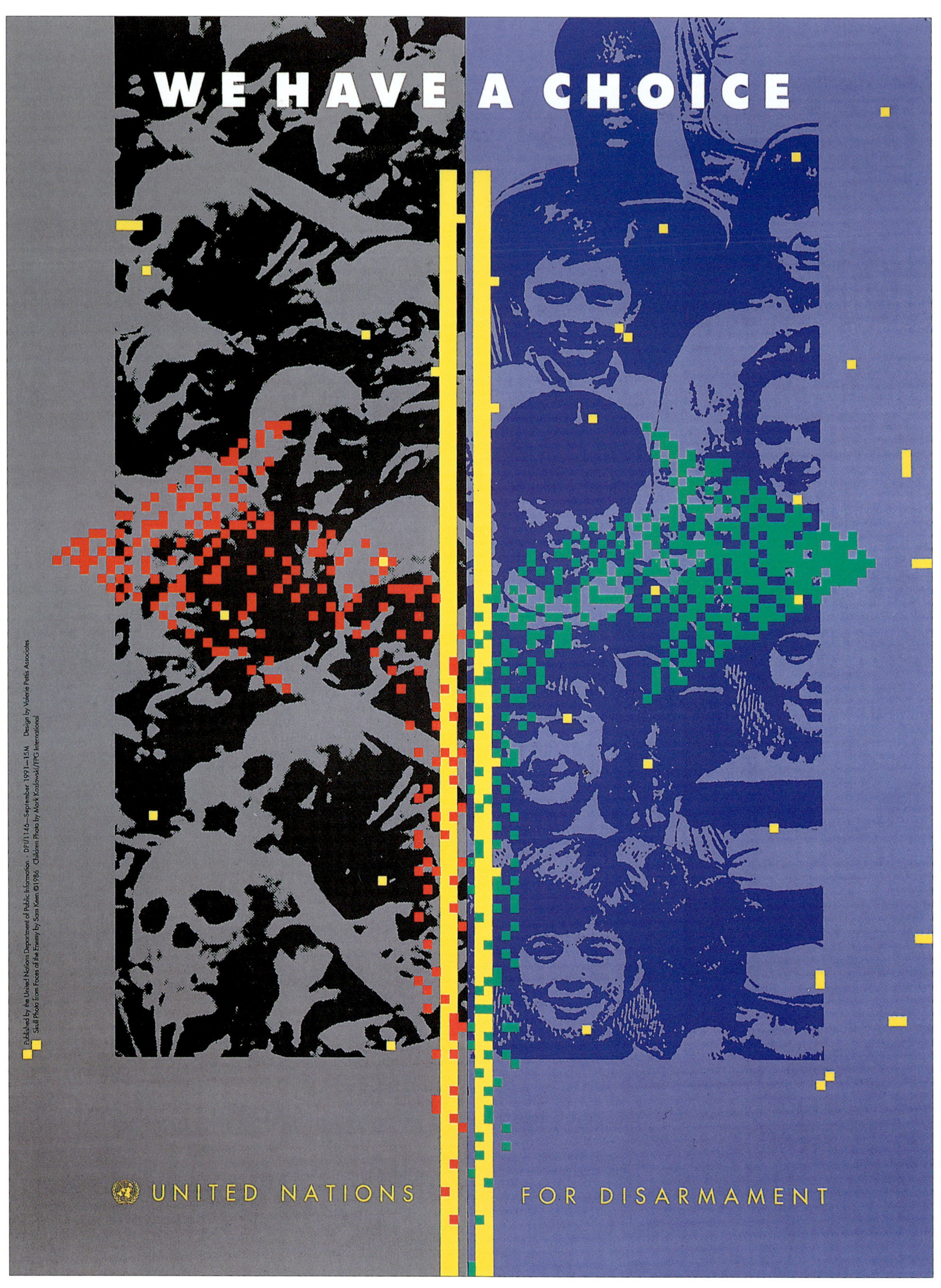

37. We Have a Choice, *September 1991, art by Valerie Pettis Associates, art direction by Jan Arnesen, UN Department of Public Information. Photo of skull from* Faces of the Enemy *by Sam Keen, 1986. Photo of children by Mark Kozlowsky, F.P.G. International.*

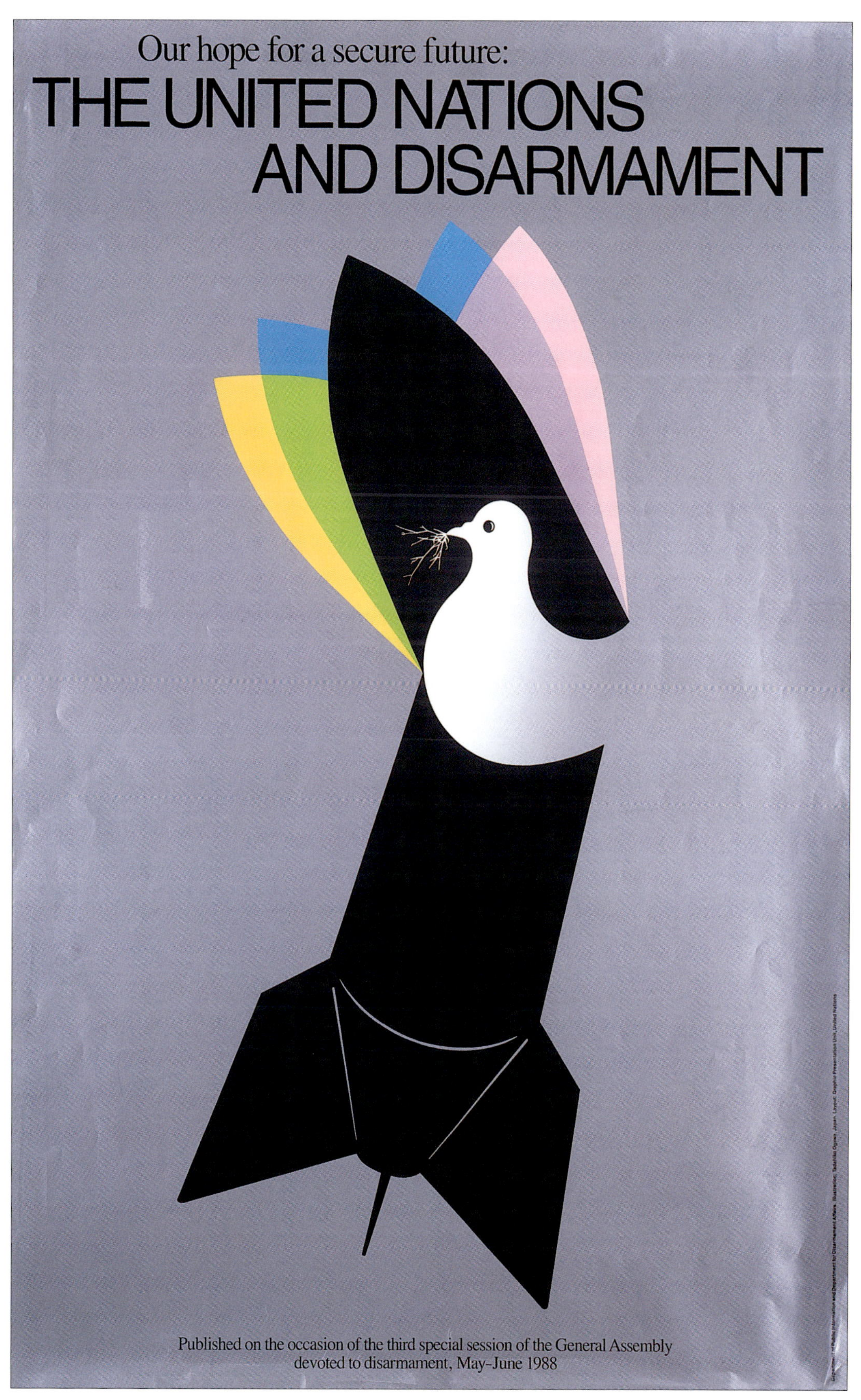

38. Our Hope for a Secure Future, *1988, illustration by Tadahiko Ogawa, layout by UN Graphic Design Section and Department for Disarmament Affairs. Commemorates a special session of the General Assembly devoted to disarmament.*

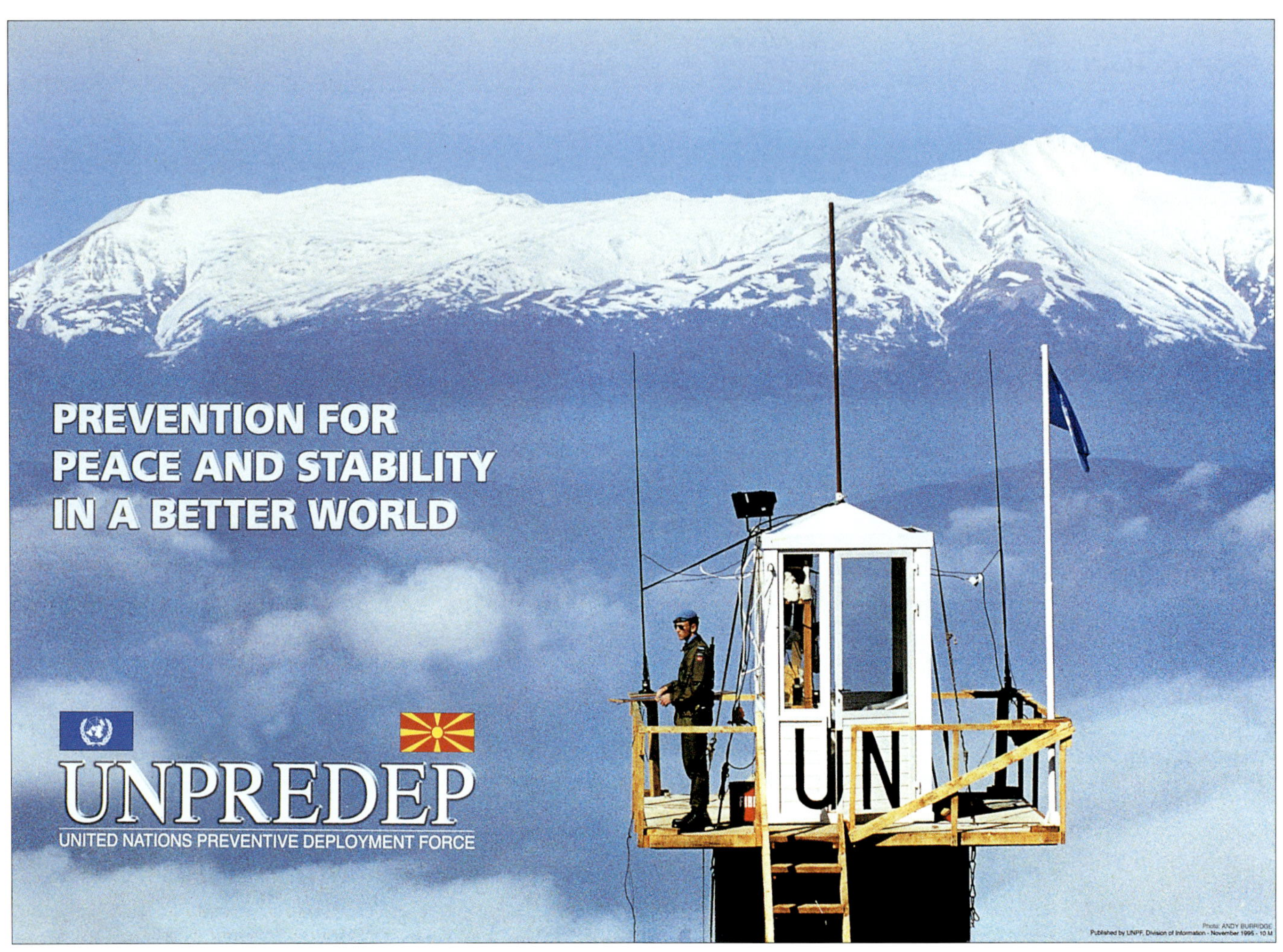

39. Prevention for Peace and Stability in a Better World, *November 1995. Surveillance by a blue-helmeted peacekeeper from a watchtower (UN Preventive Deployment Force and UN Department of Public Information poster). Photo by Andy Burridge.*

United Nations Peacekeeping Operations are authorized by the Security Council; they are designed to advance international peace and security. Peacekeeping was pioneered by the UN in 1948, with the establishment of the United Nations Truce Supervision Organization in the Middle East. Operations may involve military observers, peacekeeping forces, and civilian police. The Department of Peacekeeping Operations was created in 1992 to provide executive direction, management, and logistical support to UN peacekeeping operations worldwide.

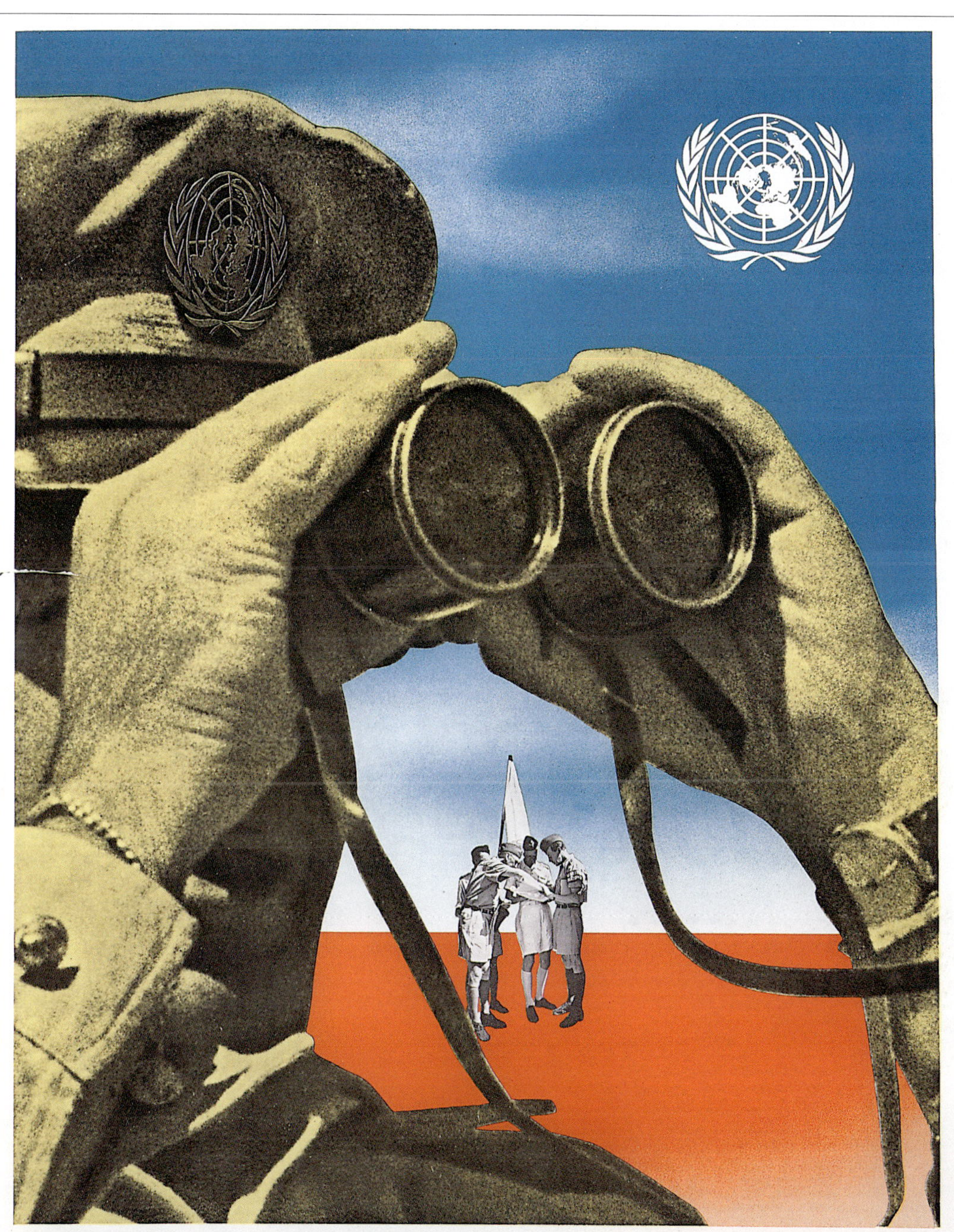

40. Vigile pour la paix *(Spyglasses for Security), c. 1950 (French version), designed by Ole Hamann, from peacekeeping series (UN Department of Public Information poster).*

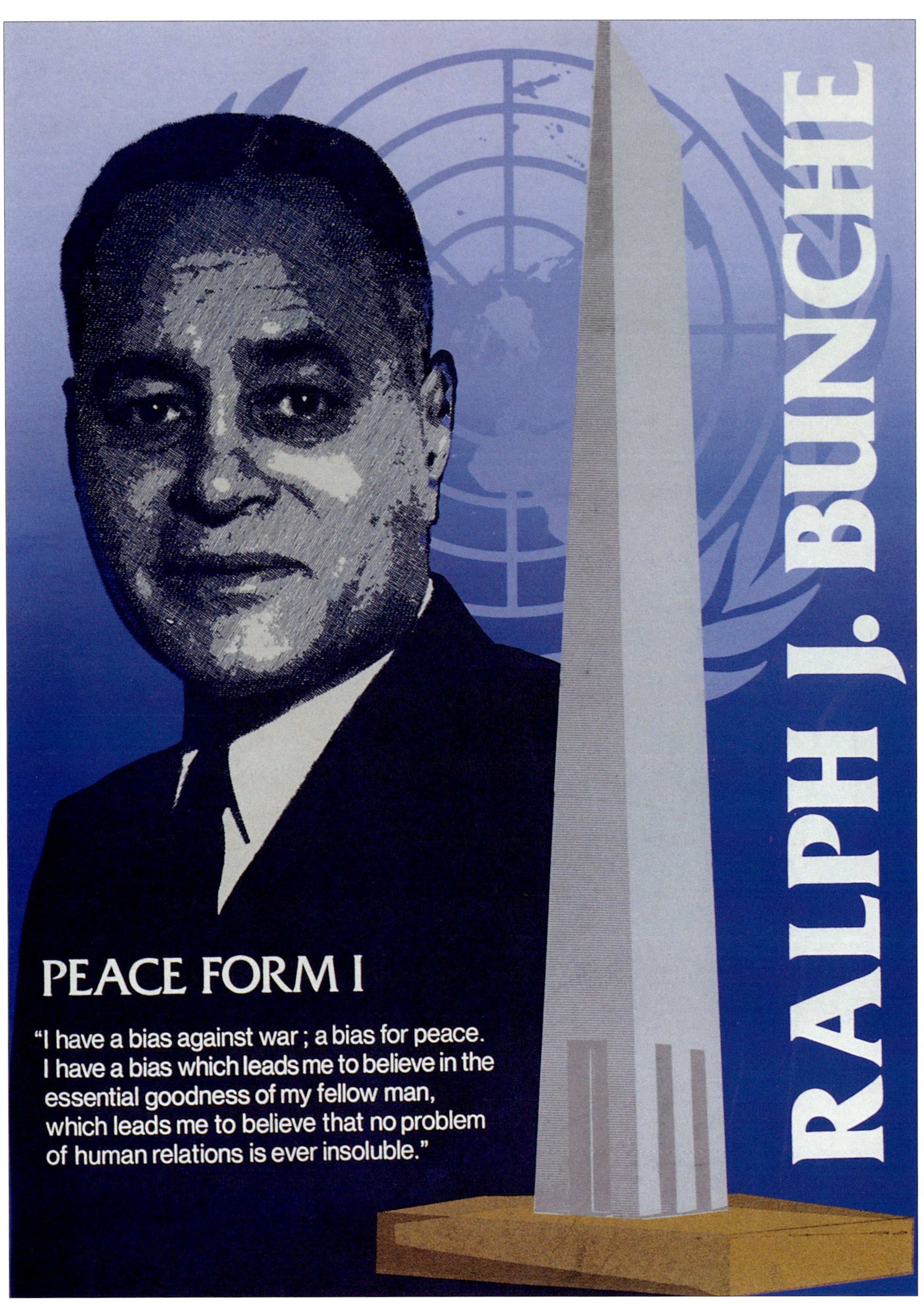

41. *Peace Form I, by Daniel LaRue Johnson. Honors Ralph J. Bunche, Under-Secretary-General of the UN and Nobel Peace Prize laureate (1950). Bunche's skill as a mediator in the Middle East contributed greatly to the negotiation of the four armistice agreements that ended the 1948 war and resulted in recognition of the state of Israel. The steel monument is sited opposite the UN Secretariat Building on First Avenue in New York City.*

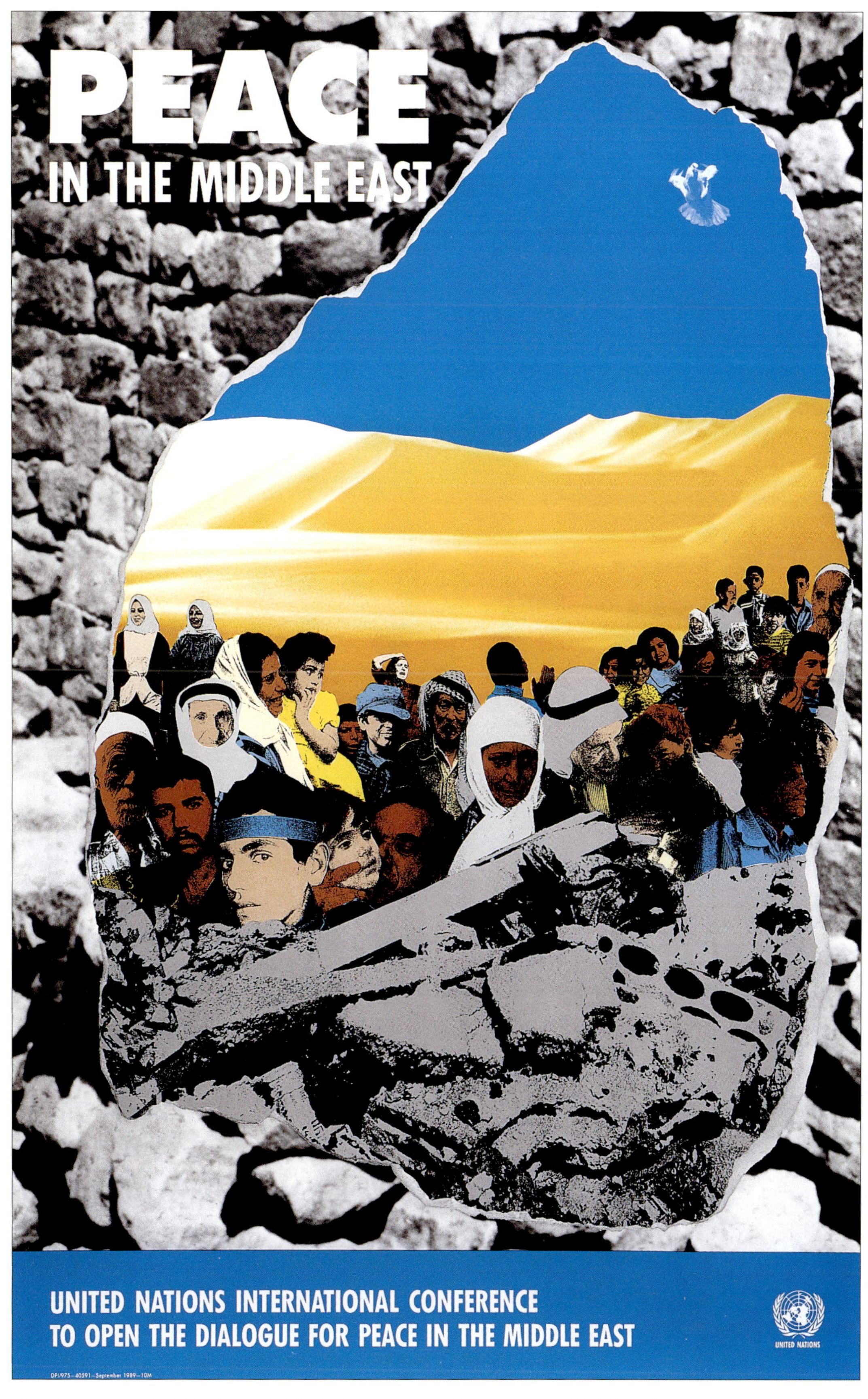

42. Peace in the Middle East, *1989, designed by UN Department of Public Information.*

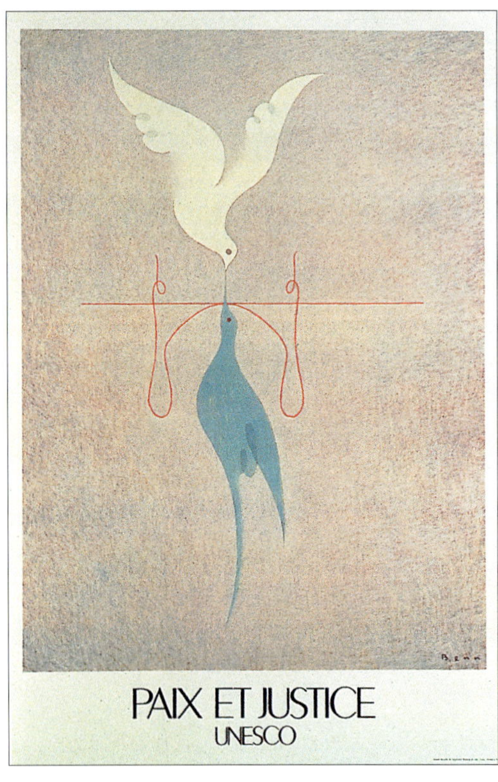

43. Peace and Justice, *1979 (French version), by Benn (UNESCO poster).*

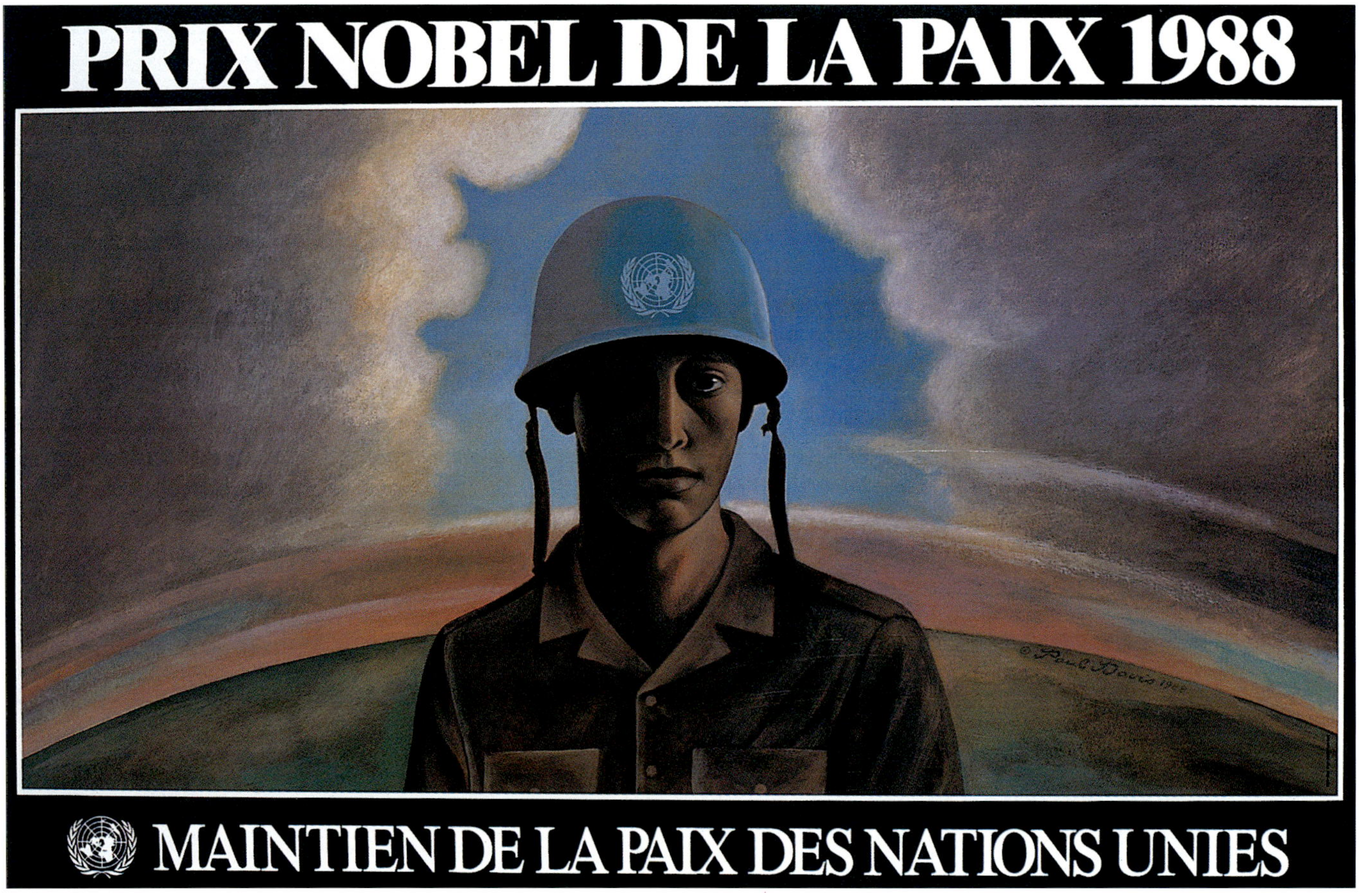

44. The Blue Helmets, 1988, *illustration by Paul Davis, design by Jan Arnesen, UN Department of Public Information. Commemorates UN's 1988 Nobel Peace Prize award for peacekeeping operations.*

The Quest for Peace
A Universal Undertaking

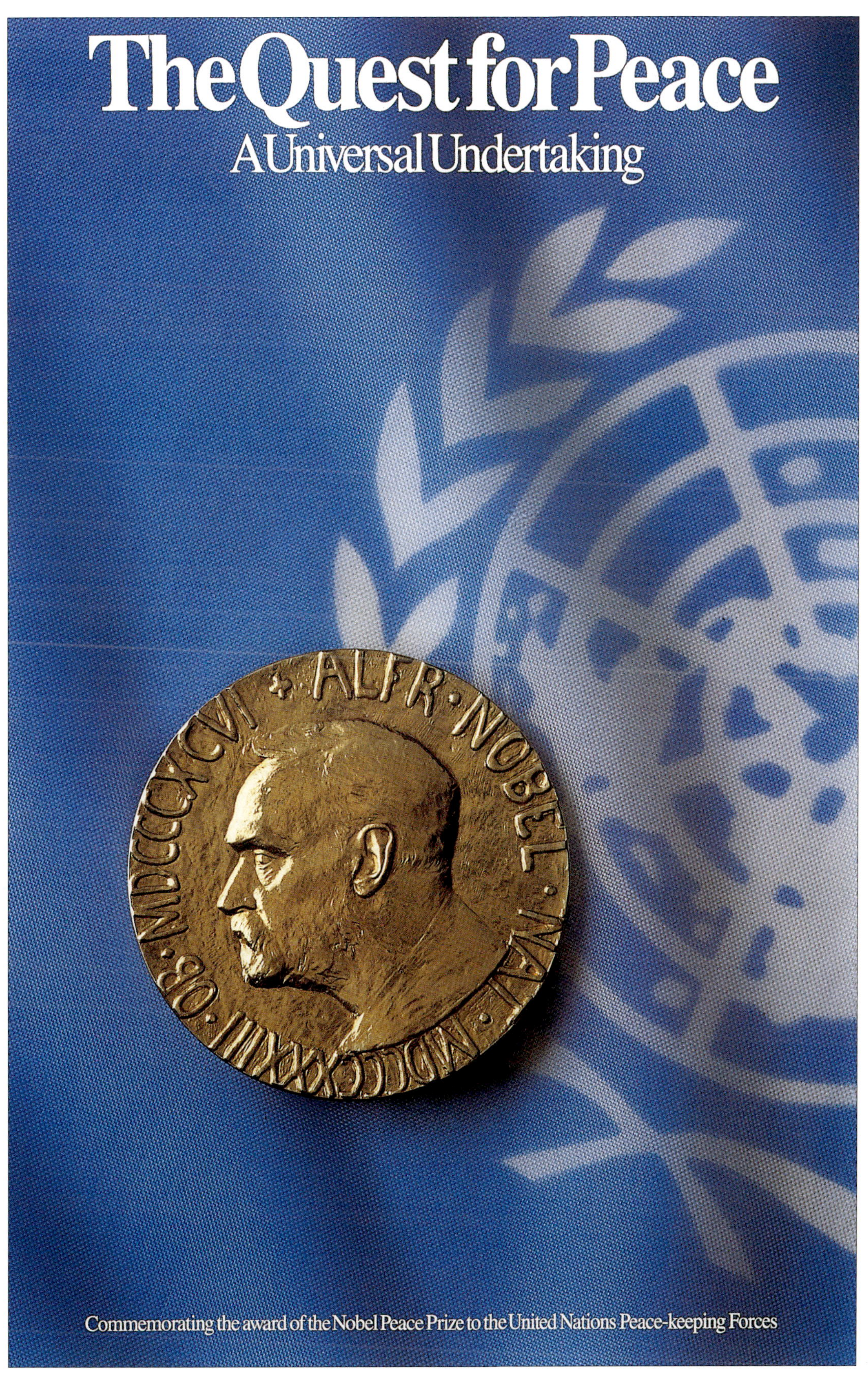

45. The Quest for Peace, *concept and design by James Eschinger, Graphic Design Section, UN Department of Public Information. Medallion with head of Alfred Bernhard Nobel on blue background; commemorates UN's 1988 Nobel Peace Prize award. Photo by Robert Zuckerman, Inc.*

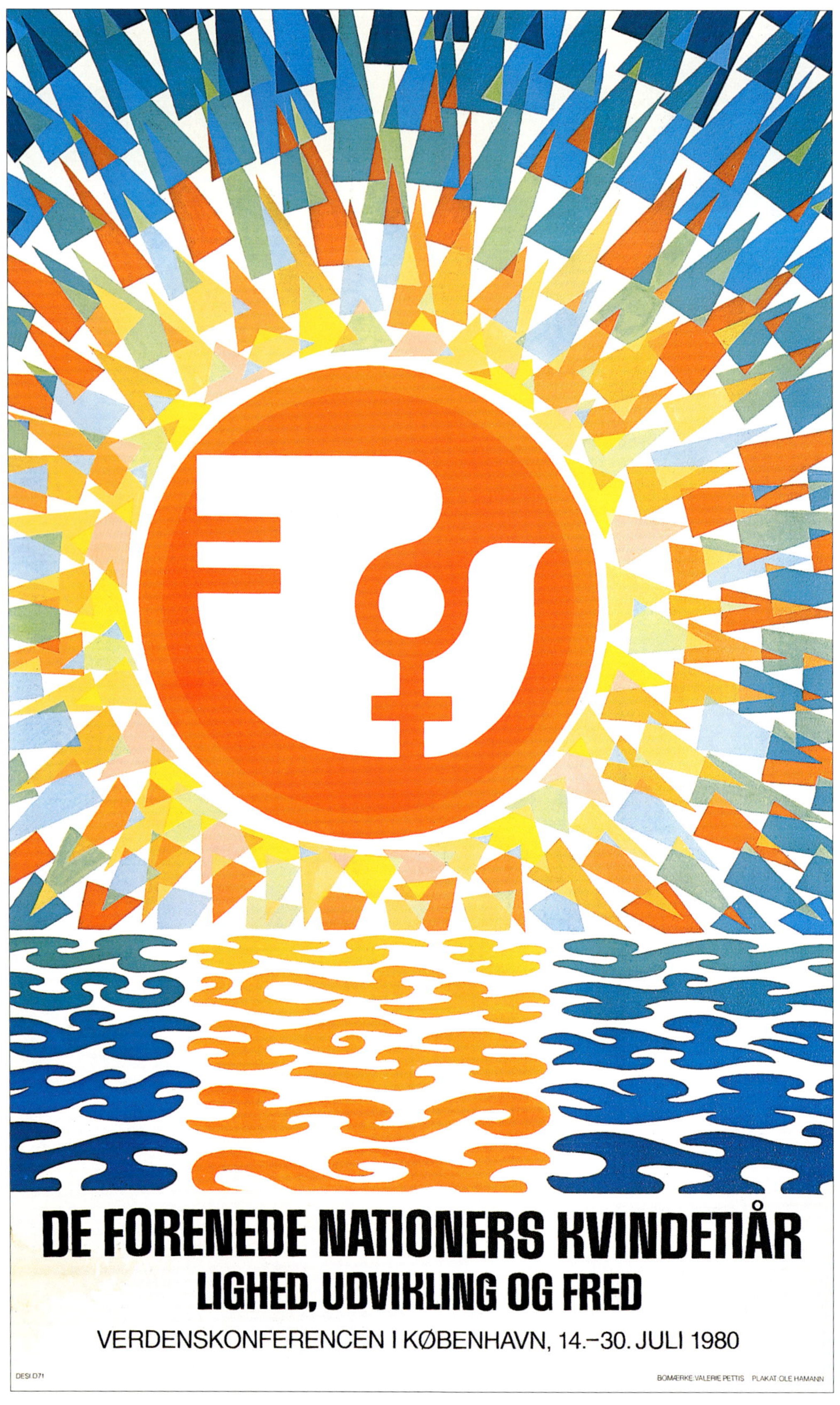

48. Decade for Women, 1980–1990 *(Danish version), design by Ole Hamann, symbol by Valerie Pettis, for world conference in Copenhagen, 14–30 July 1980.*

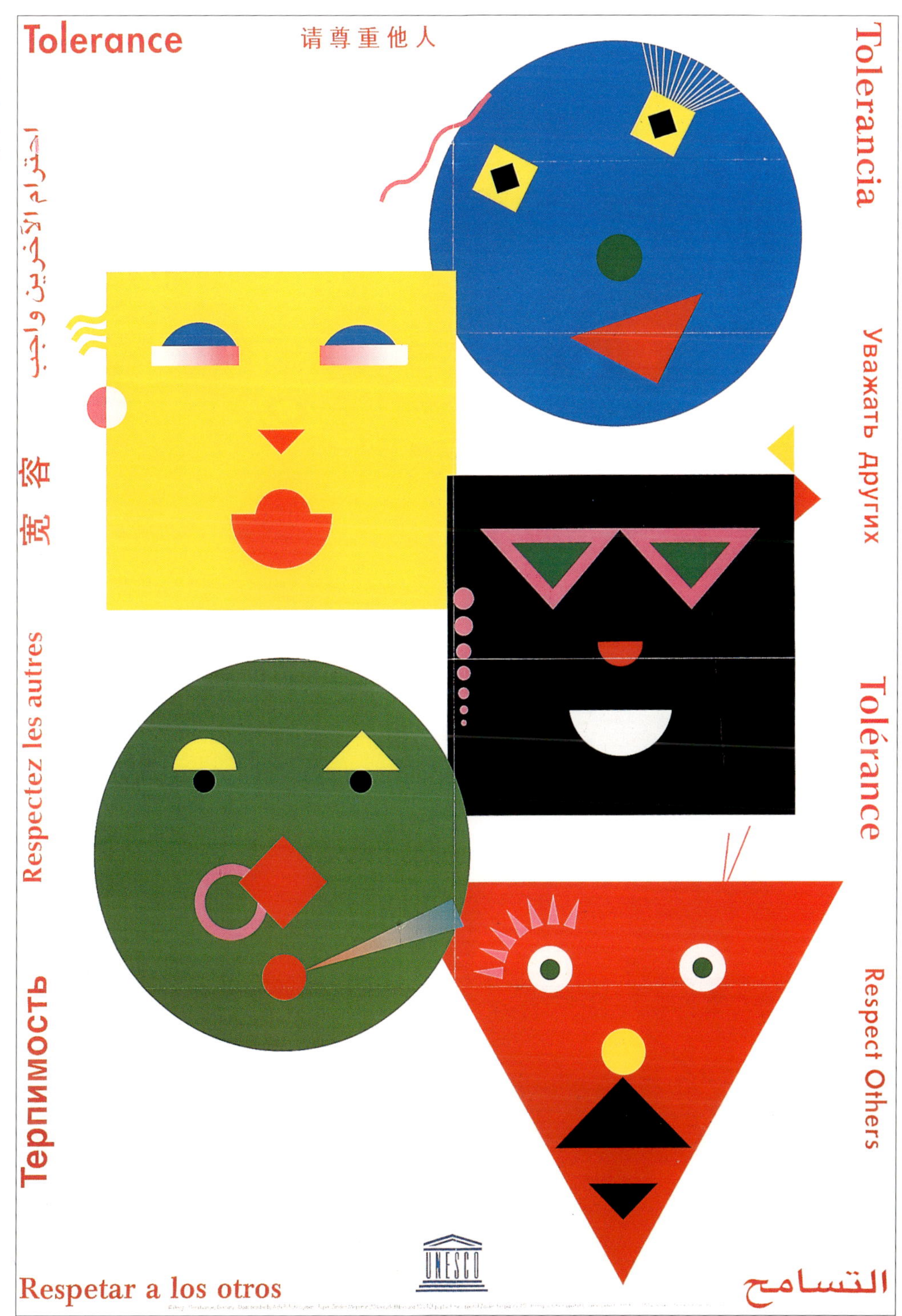

49. *Tolerance: Respect Others, designed by German artist Helmut Langer (UNESCO poster observing International Day for Tolerance).*

The **Office of the High Commissioner for Human Rights (OHCHR), Geneva** is charged with promoting and protecting the enjoyment of civil, cultural, economic, political, and social rights. Established in 1993, OHCHR prepares reports and undertakes research at the request of the General Assembly and other policy-making bodies; cooperates with governments and international, regional, and nongovernmental organizations for the promotion and protection of human rights; and acts as the secretariat for the many meetings held by UN human-rights bodies.

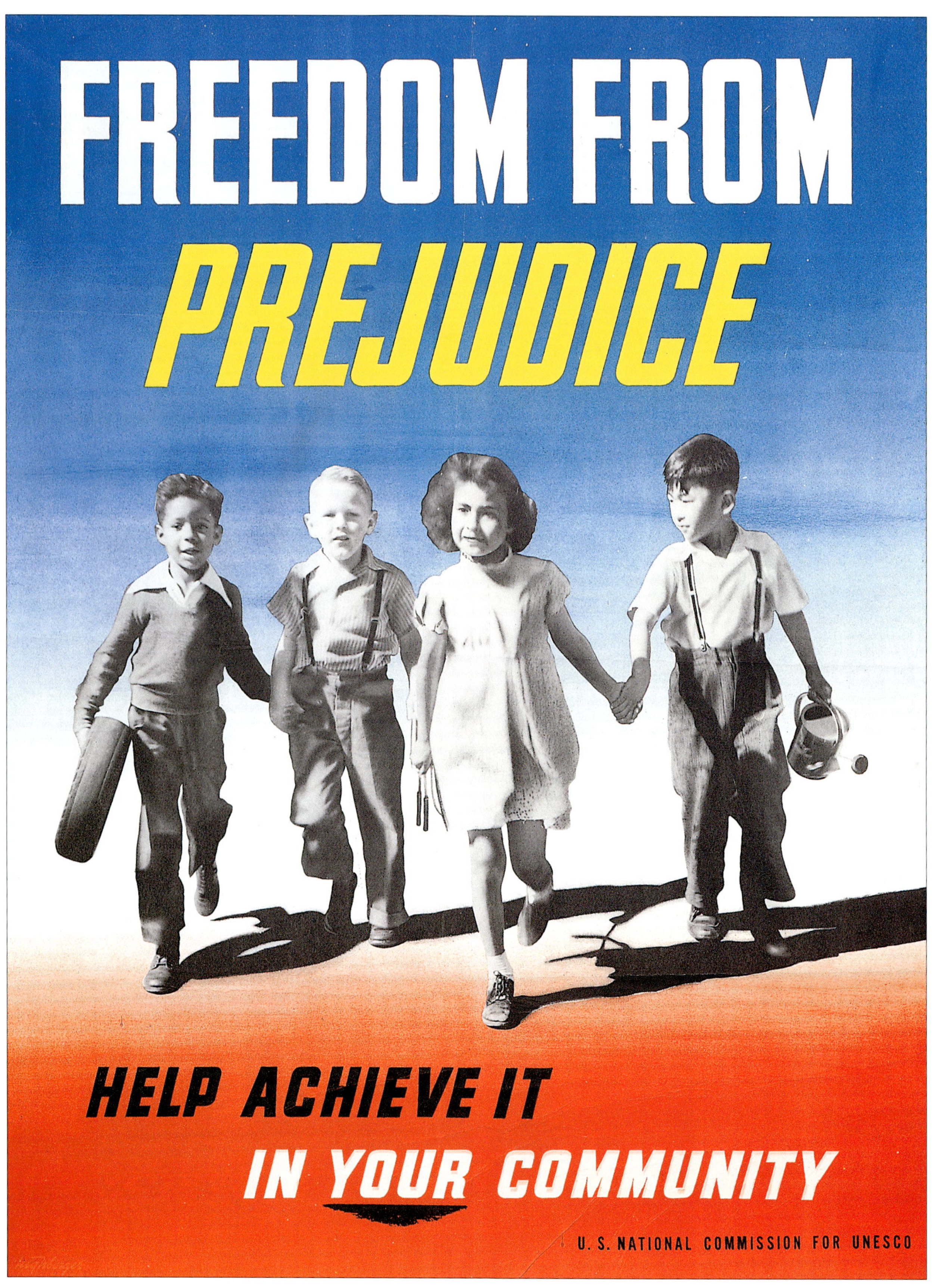

50. Freedom from Prejudice, *by Highberger.*

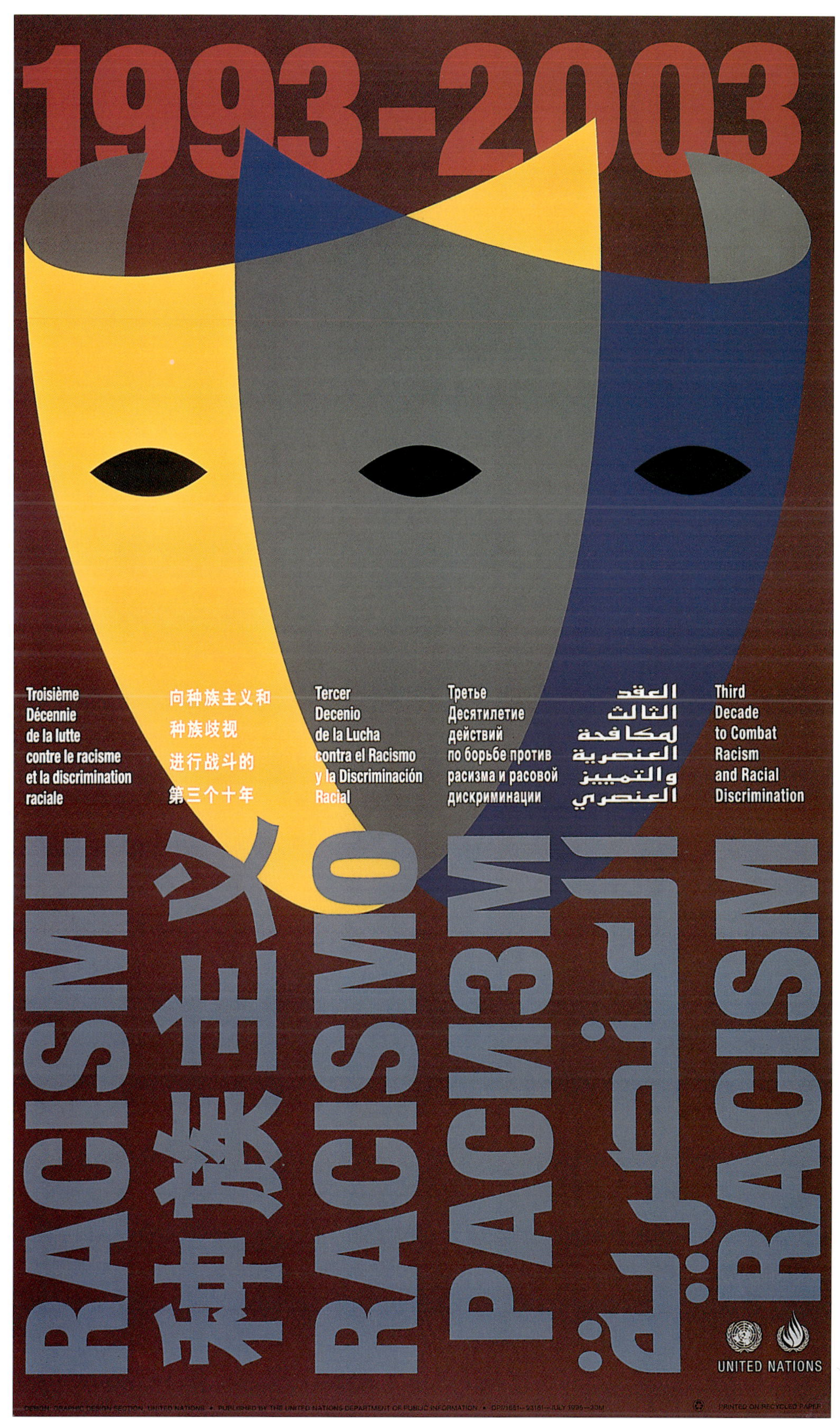

51. Racism, *July 1995, designed by José Castiñeira, art direction by Jan Arnesen, UN Department of Public Information, for "Third Decade to Combat Racism and Racial Discrimination, 1993–2003."*

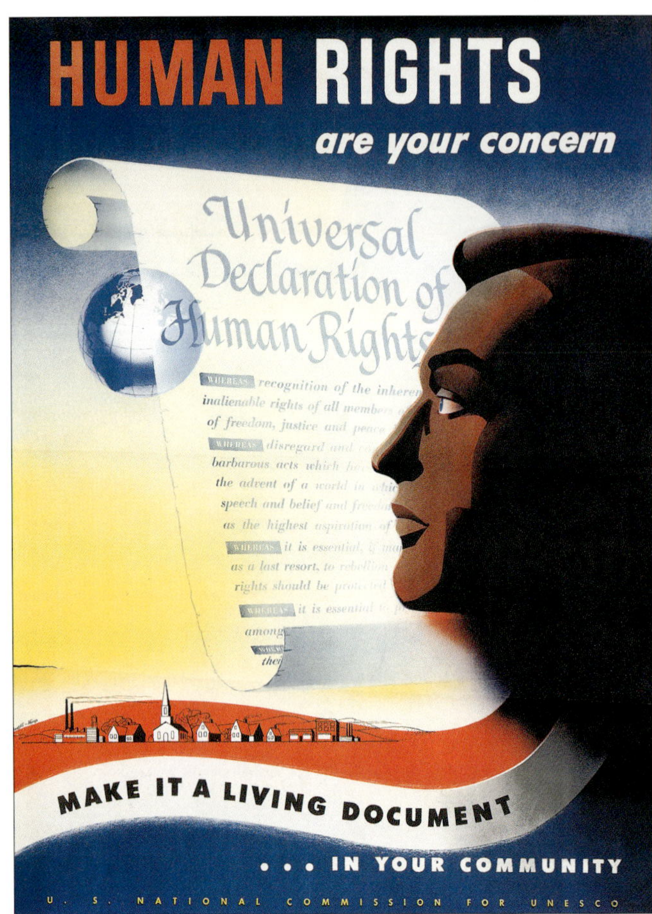

52. Human Rights Are Your Concern, *by Bausili-Hirose. Pronouncement in support of Universal Declaration of Human Rights.*

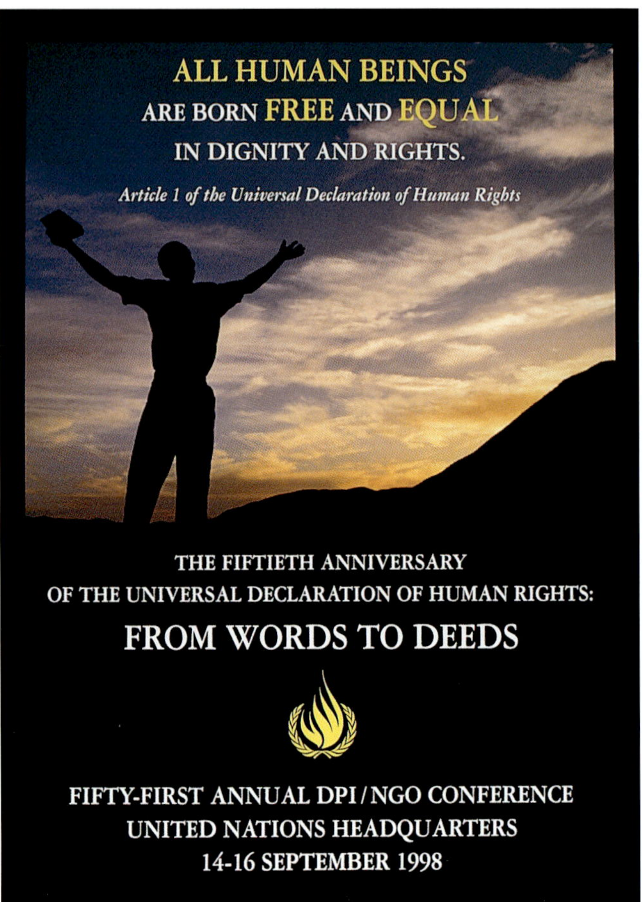

53. All Human Beings are Born Free and Equal in Dignity and Rights, from Words to Deeds, *design by Jan Arnesen, UN Department of Public Information, for Fifty-First Annual UN Department of Public Information NGO Conference, 14–16 September 1998. Commemorates fiftieth anniversary of Universal Declaration of Human Rights. Photo by Les Stone (Magnum).*

54. People Only Live Full Lives in the Light of Human Rights, *1988 (French version), concept by Galer and MacMillan Communications, Inc., illustration by Graphic Design Section, UN Department of Public Information, designed by José Castiñeira. Commemorates fortieth anniversary of Universal Declaration of Human Rights.*

55. Vigilance for Human Rights *(Spanish version), by Prodere Edinfodae, Asociación Hombres des Maiz. Men voting in Latin America.*

Flambeau pour une vie de plein épanouissement: Les droits de l'homme
LES DROITS DE L'HOMME
Publié à l'occasion du 40ᵉ anniversaire de la Déclaration universelle des droits de l'homme • 1948-1988

54

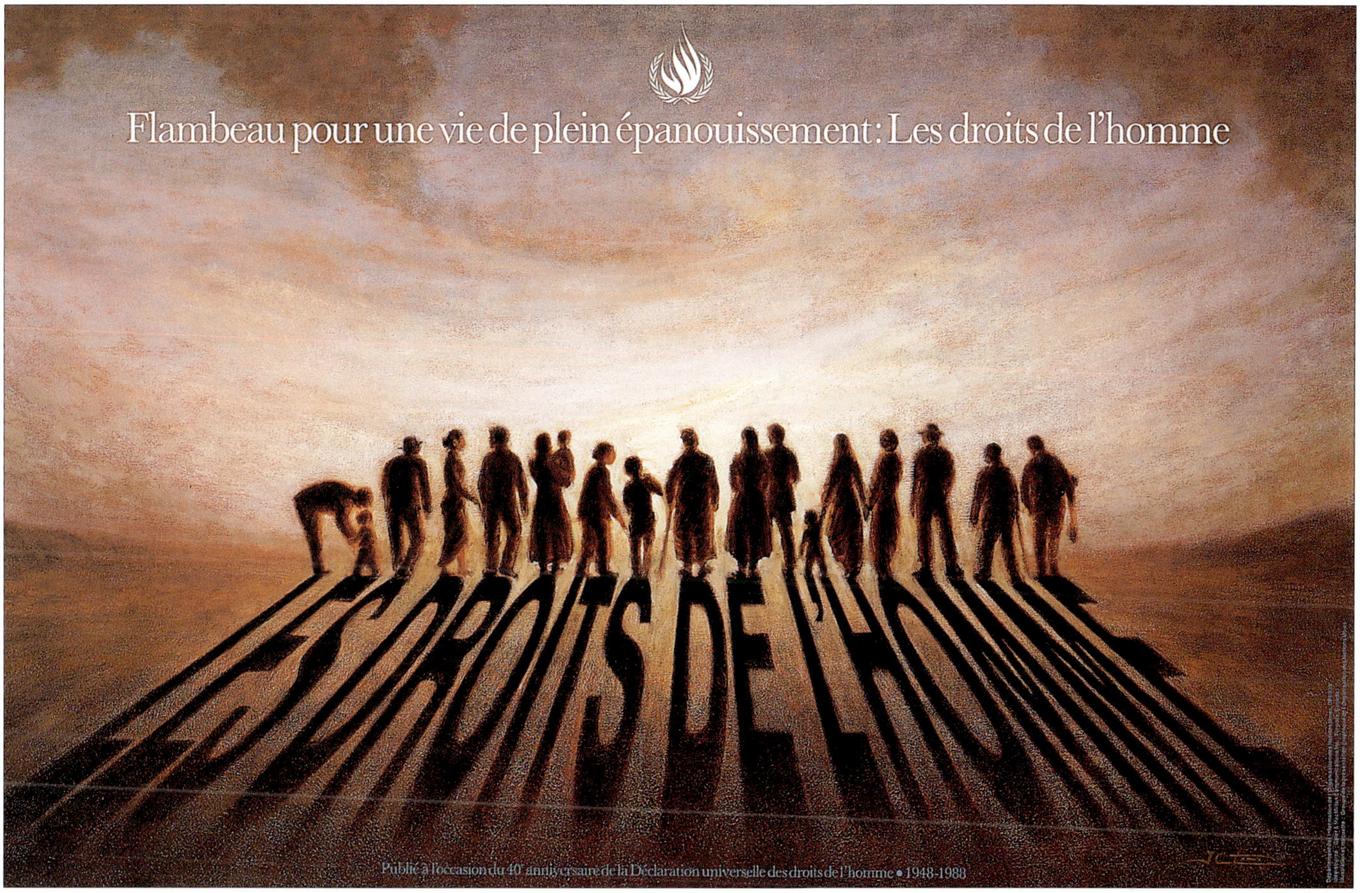

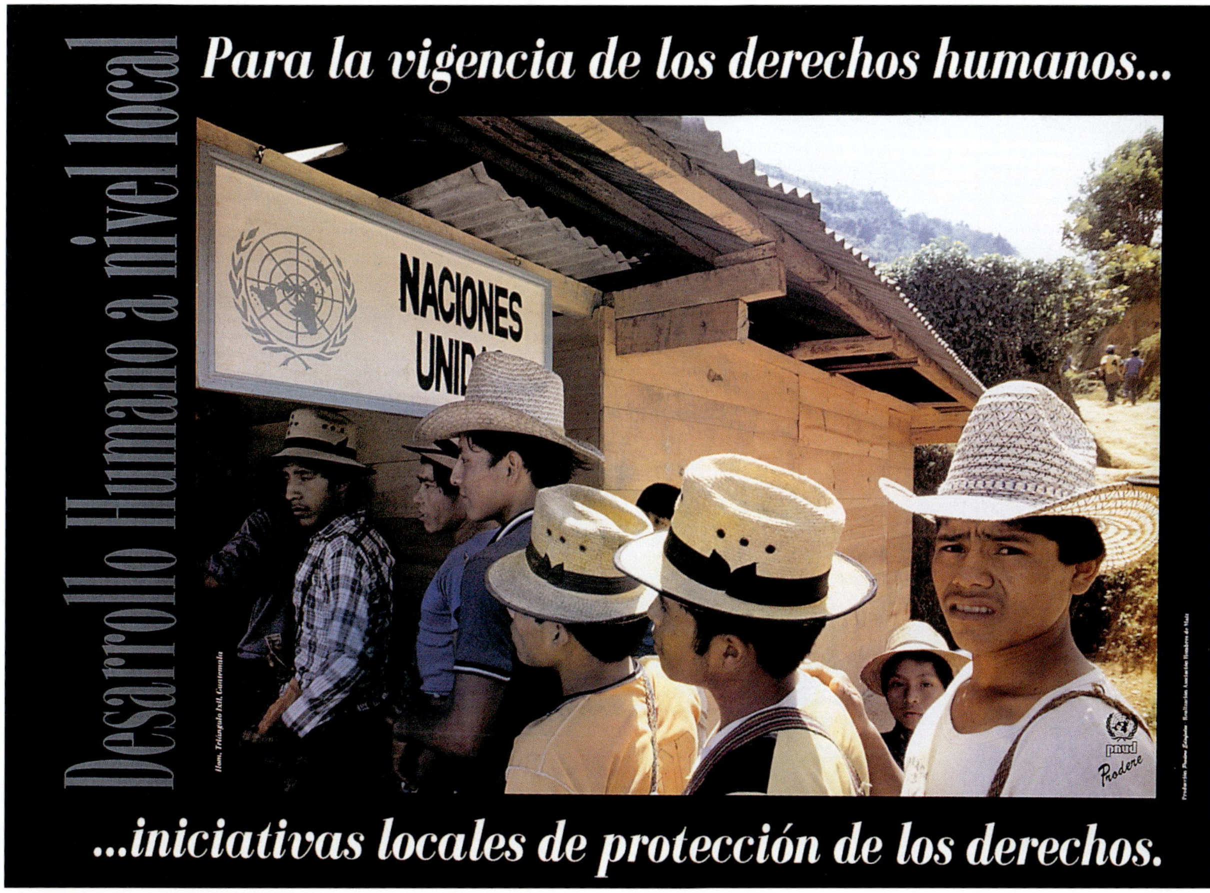

Para la vigencia de los derechos humanos...
Desarrollo Humano a nivel local
NACIONES UNIDAS
...iniciativas locales de protección de los derechos.
Hom. Triángulo Jail, Guatemala
pnud
Prodere

55

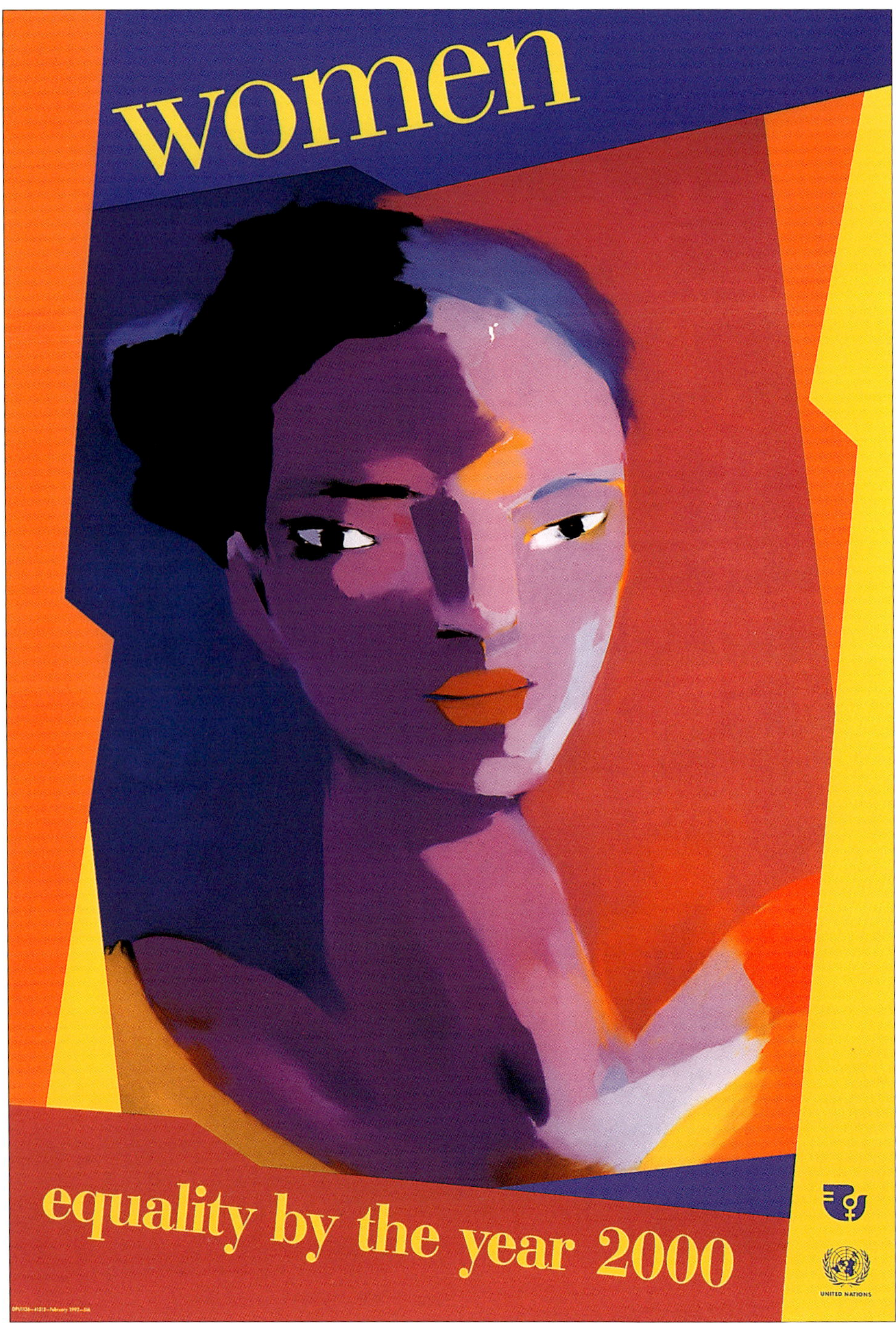

56. Equality by the Year 2000, February 1992, illustration by Patty Dryden; designed by Karen Kelleher, Jan Arnesen, and Tom Stone, UN Department of Public Information.

The **United Nations Development Fund for Women (UNIFEM), New York** promotes the economic and political empowerment of women in developing countries. UNIFEM works in three key program areas of strategic importance to women: strengthening women's economic capacity as entrepreneurs and producers, engendering governance and leadership that increase women's participation in decision-making processes, promoting women's human rights, eliminating all forms of violence against women, and transforming development into a more equitable process. Since the Fourth World Conference on Women in Beijing (1995), UNIFEM has worked to support implementation of the Beijing platform for action, which is aimed at enhancing women's empowerment on all issues concerning their lives.

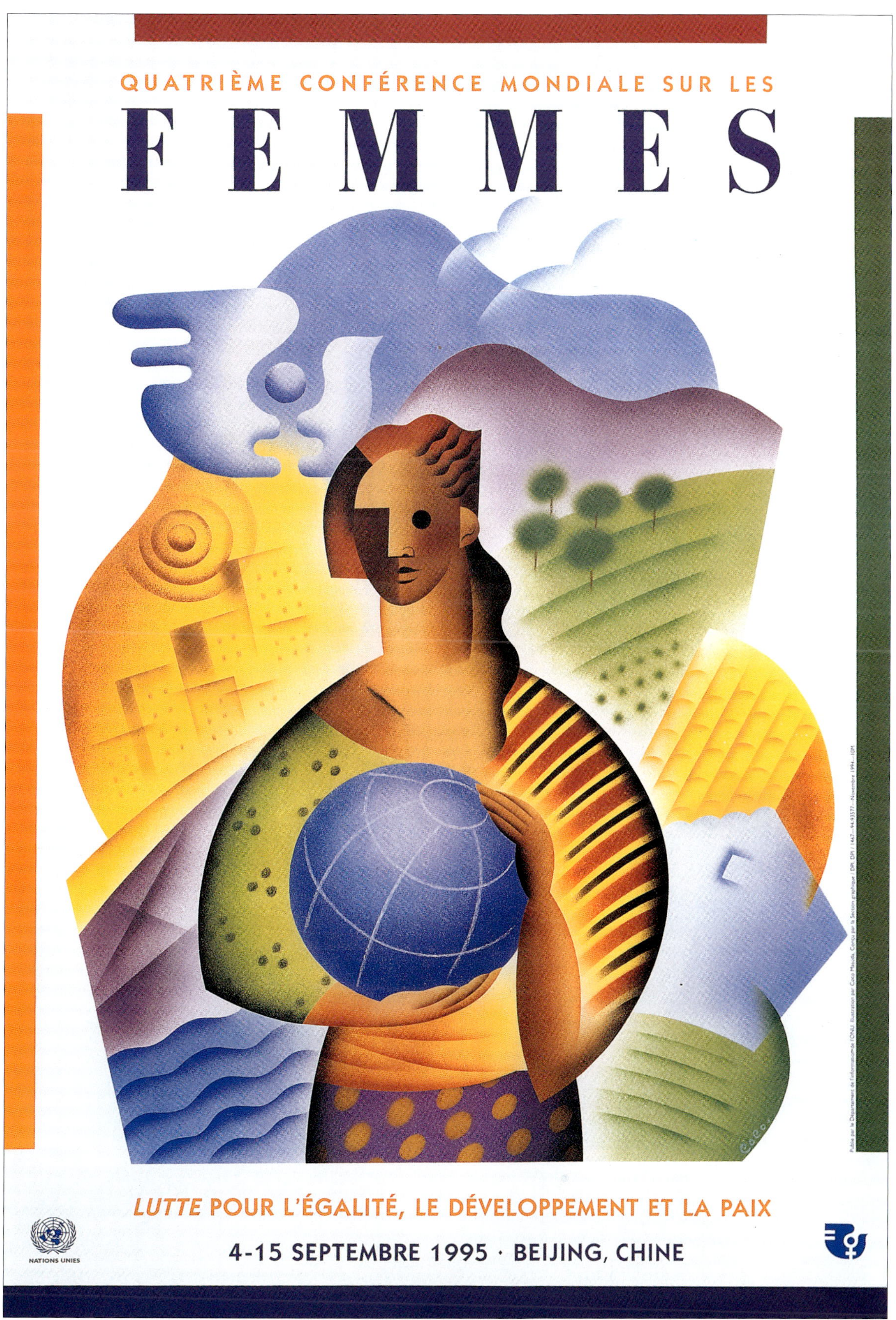

57. Women, 1994, *illustration by Coco Masuda, design by Jan Arnesen, UN Department of Public Information. Poster for Fourth World Conference on Women, Beijing, 4–15 September 1995.*

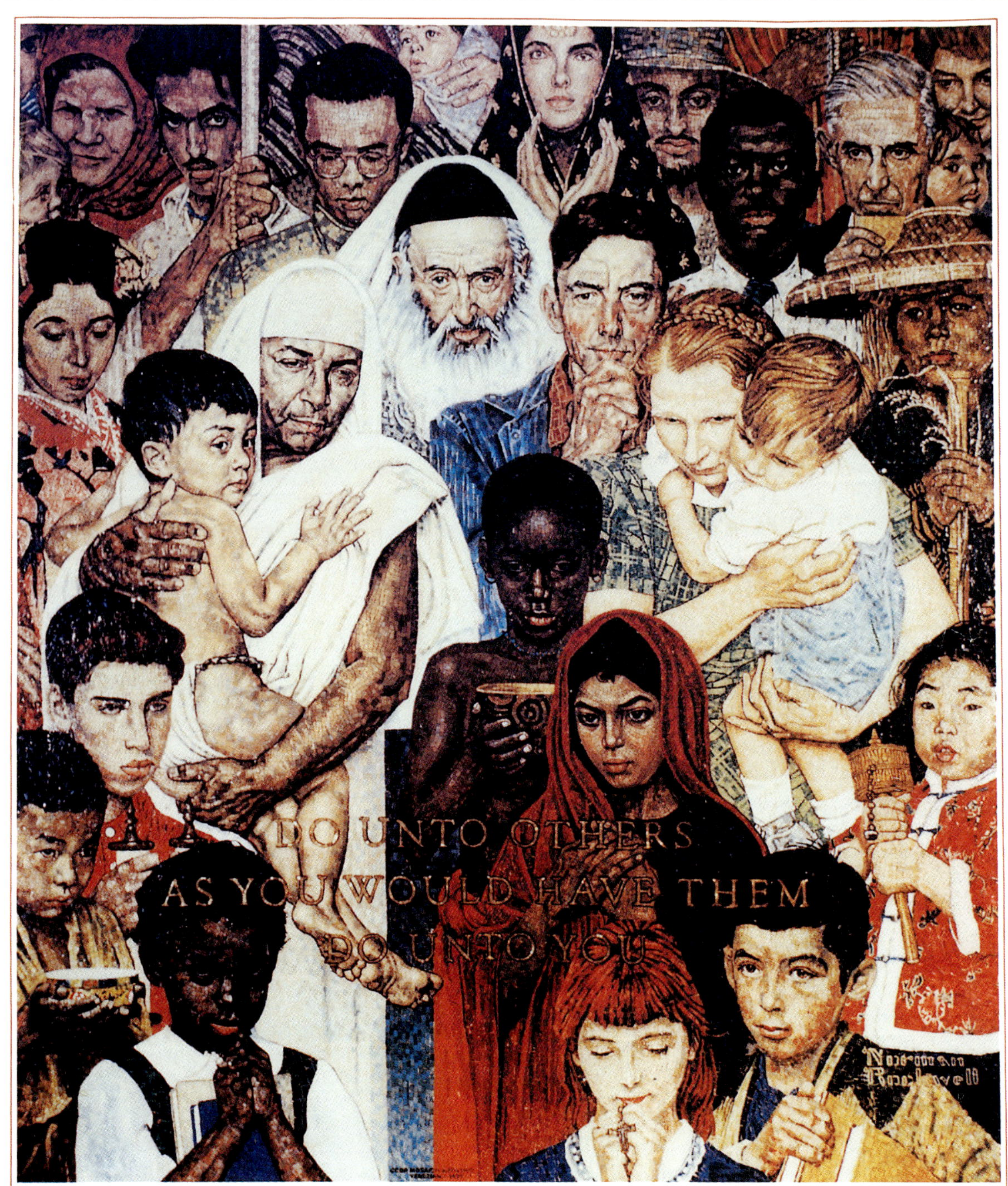

THE GOLDEN RULE
by NORMAN ROCKWELL

Mosaic at United Nations Headquarters, New York

60. The Golden Rule, *based on a large mosaic by Norman Rockwell given to the UN by the United States in 1985. Original painting is in the Rockwell Museum, Stockbridge, Massachusetts. Adapted by Patricia Doelger, Graphic Design Section, UN Department of Public Information.*

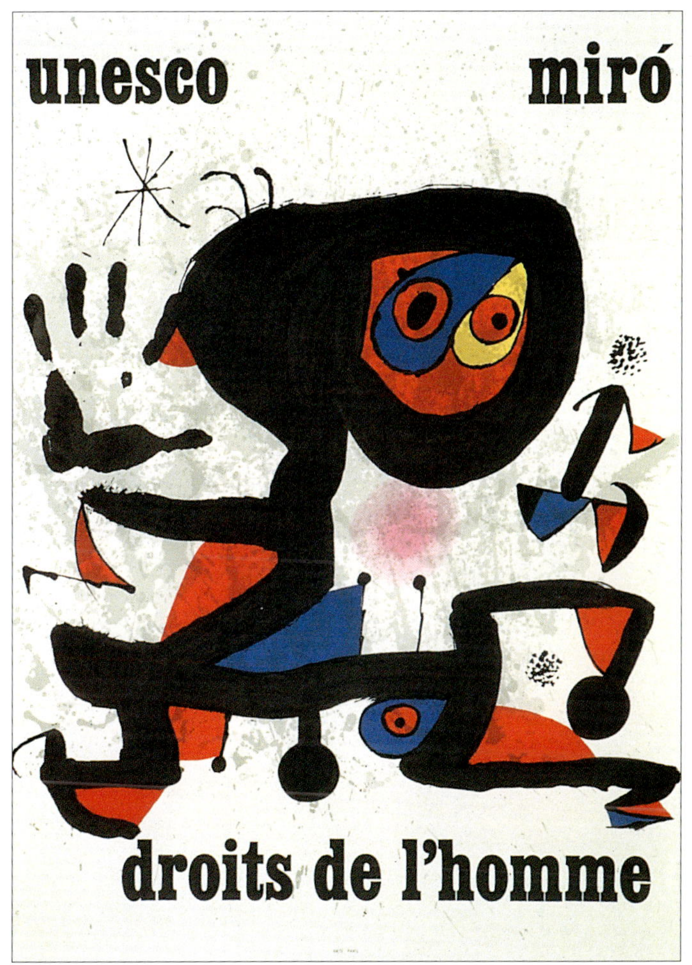

61. Anniversary of the Universal Declaration of Human Rights, *1978, art by Joan Miró (UNESCO poster).*

UNESCO

AÑO INTERNACIONAL
DE LA PAZ 1986

62. International Year of Peace, *1986, by Portuguese artist Vieira da Silva (UNESCO poster)*

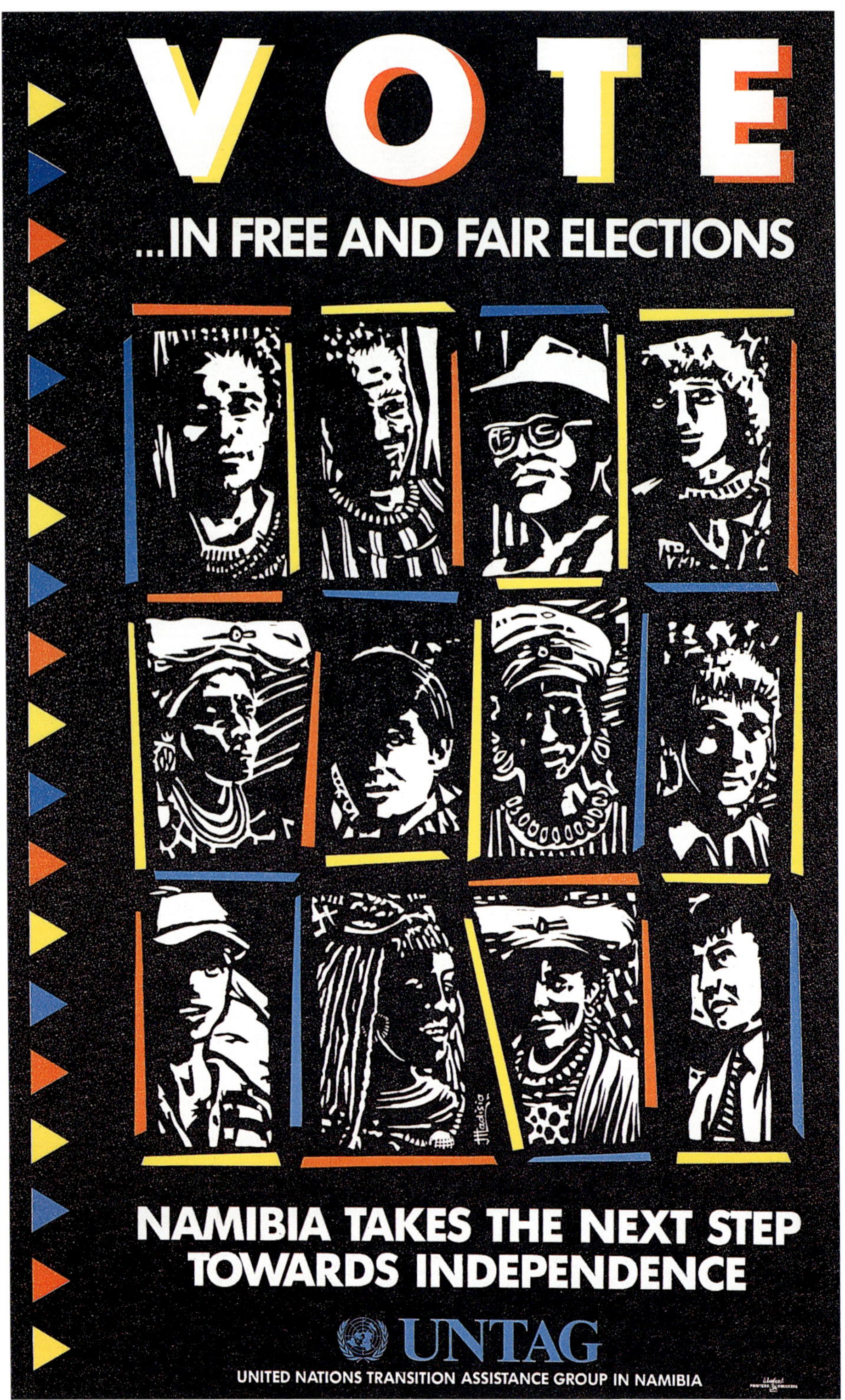

63. Vote in Free and Fair Elections, illustration by Namibian artist Joseph Madisia, design by Jan Arnesen. Instructions for UN-supervised Namibia election, 1989–90 (UN Transition Assistance Group poster).

The **United Nations Transition Assistance Group (UNTAG) in Namibia** supervised the 1989–1990 Namibian elections in which blacks were permitted to vote for the first time. Until then, the territory—known as Southwest Africa—had been administered by South Africa under the tight fist of that country's apartheid regime. The elections led to independence for the new nation of Namibia and were the precursors to elections in South Africa.

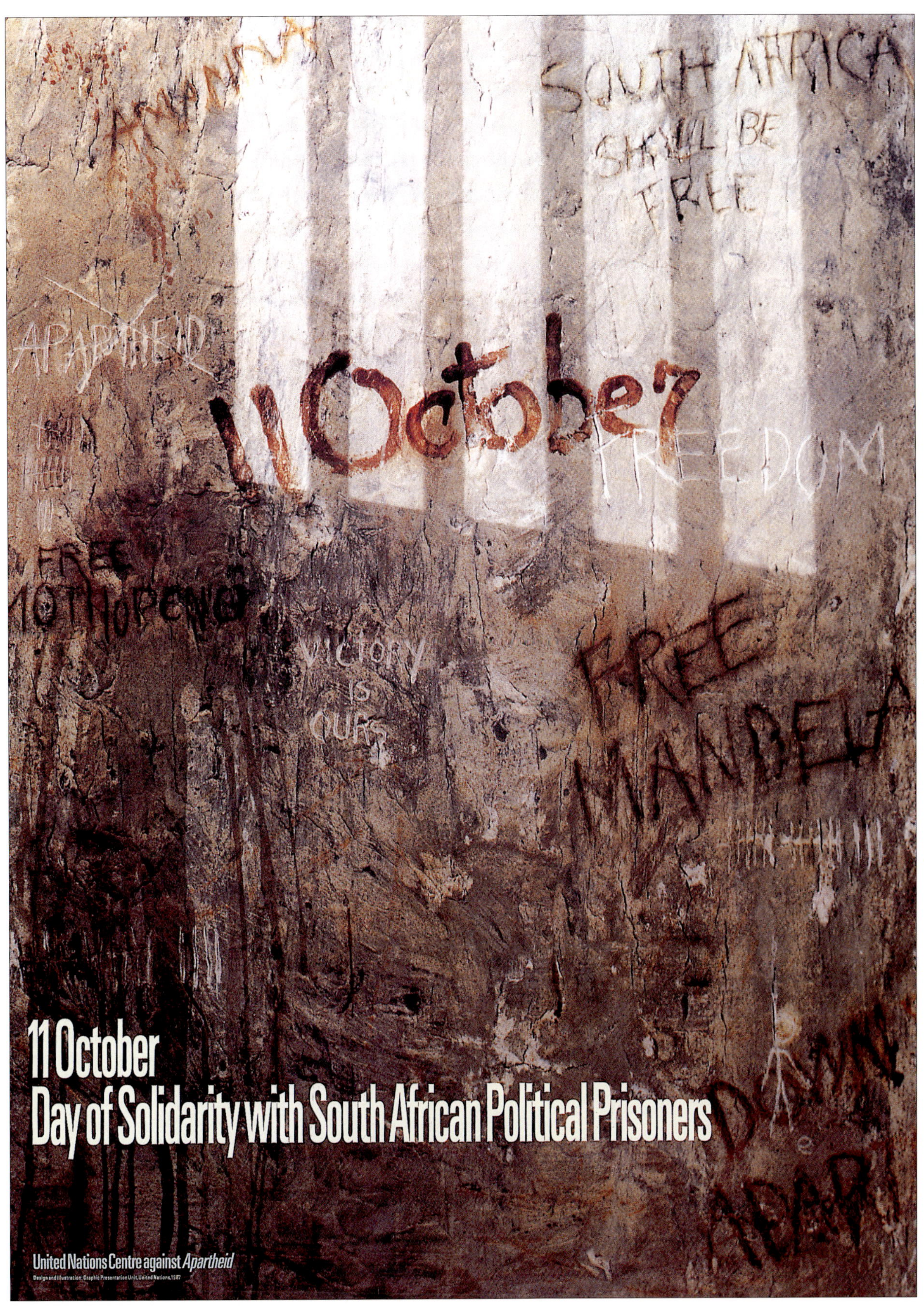

64. Day of Solidarity, *11 October 1987, art by José Castiñeira, Graphic Design Section, UN Department of Public Information (UN Centre Against Apartheid poster). This poster won an award from the American Institute of Graphic Arts.*

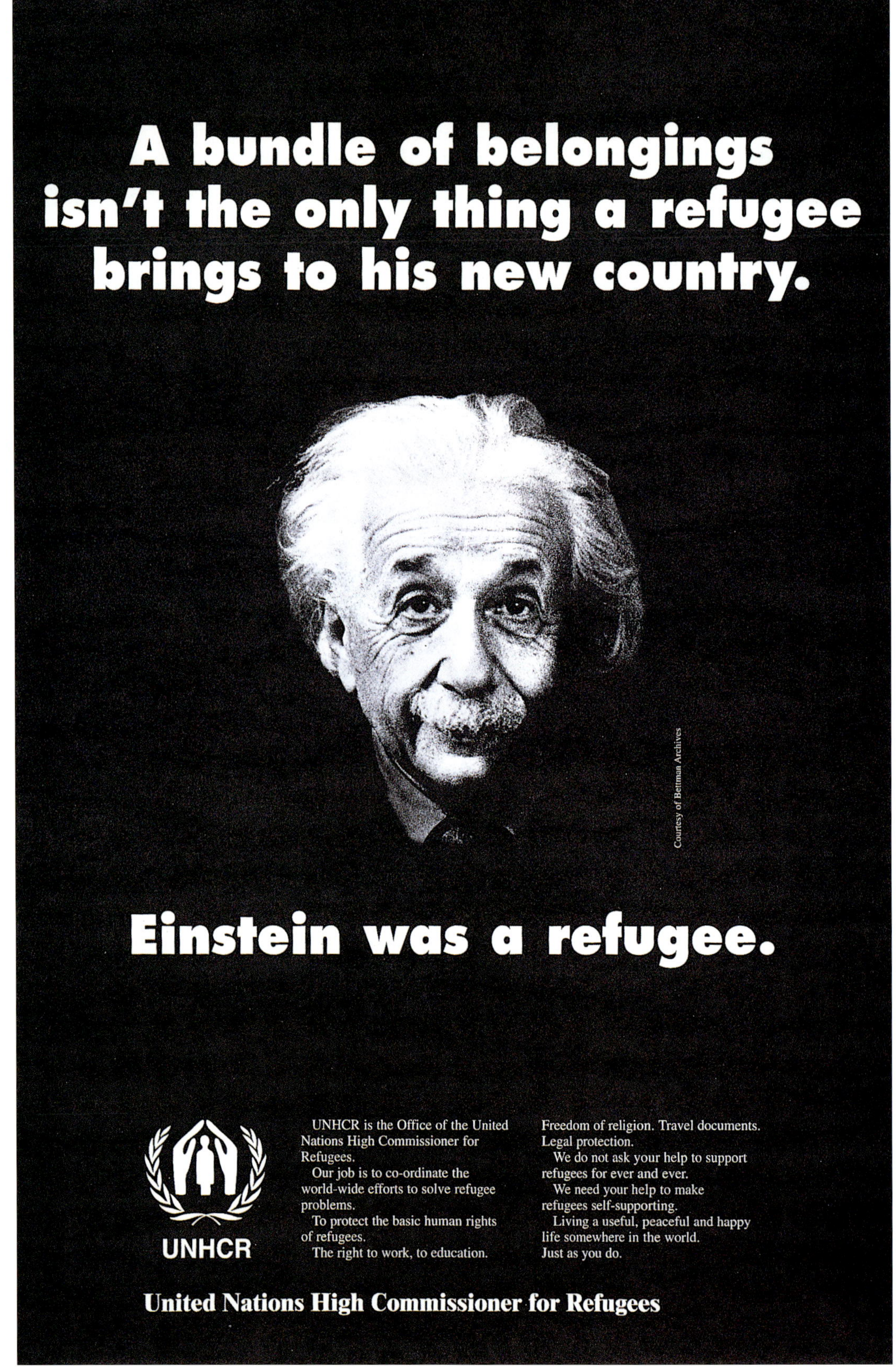

71. A Bundle of Belongings Isn't the Only Thing a Refugee Brings to His New Country *(UN High Commissioner for Refugees poster). Photo of Einstein by Phillippe Halsman, courtesy of Bettmann Photo Archives.*

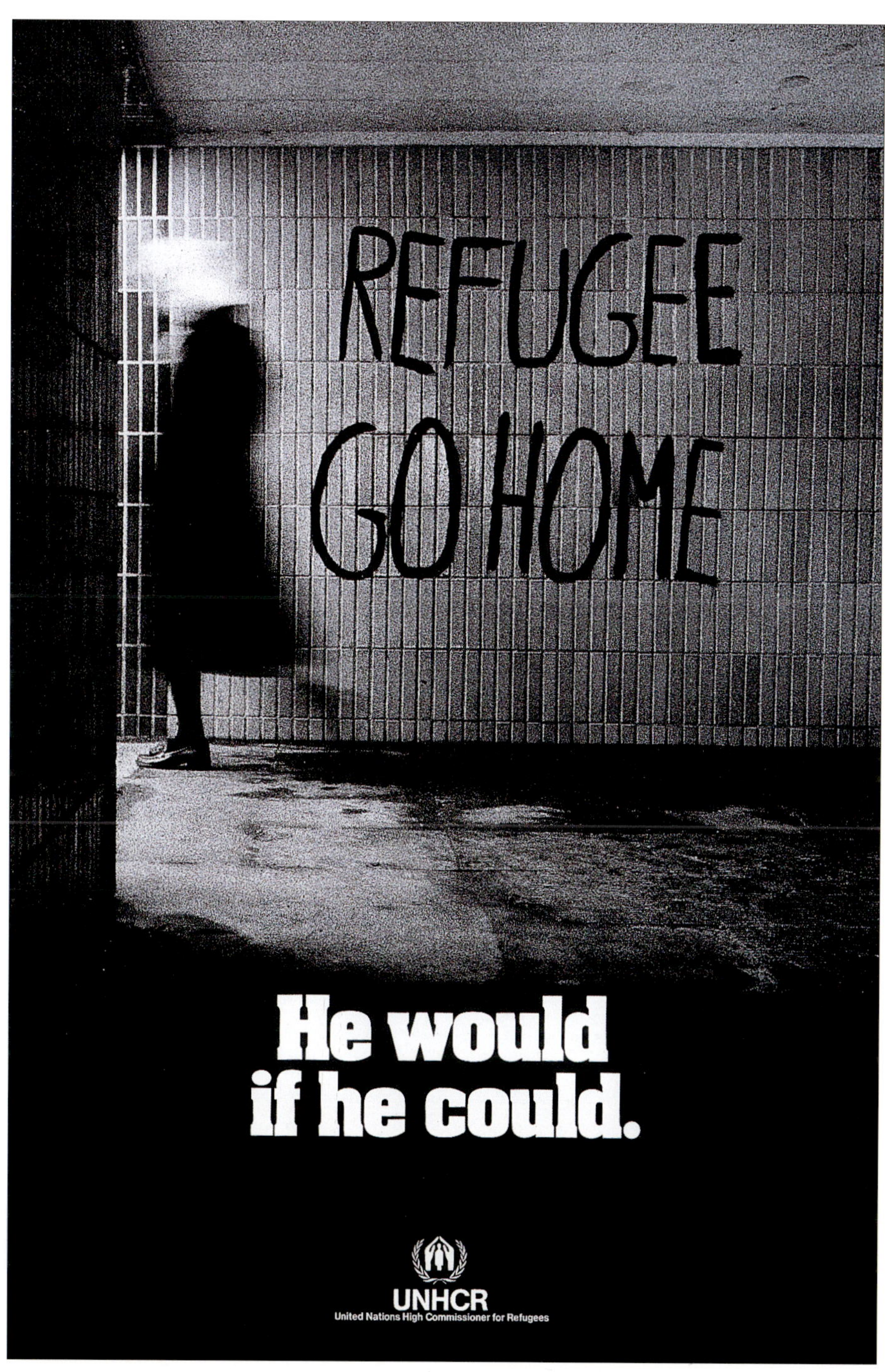

The **Office of the United Nations High Commissioner for Refugees (UNHCR), Geneva**—a successor agency to the International Refugee Organization—was created by the General Assembly in 1951 to help the more than 20 million refugees in the world; in its 1998 report, the UNHCR claimed to have helped more than 30 million people. The principal function of this humanitarian organization has been to protect refugees, seek durable solutions to their plight, and furnish them with material assistance. These goals are accomplished through voluntary repatriation, integration in countries of first asylum, or resettlement in a third country. UNHCR has offices in one hundred twenty-two countries. It is advised by a fifty-three member executive committee.

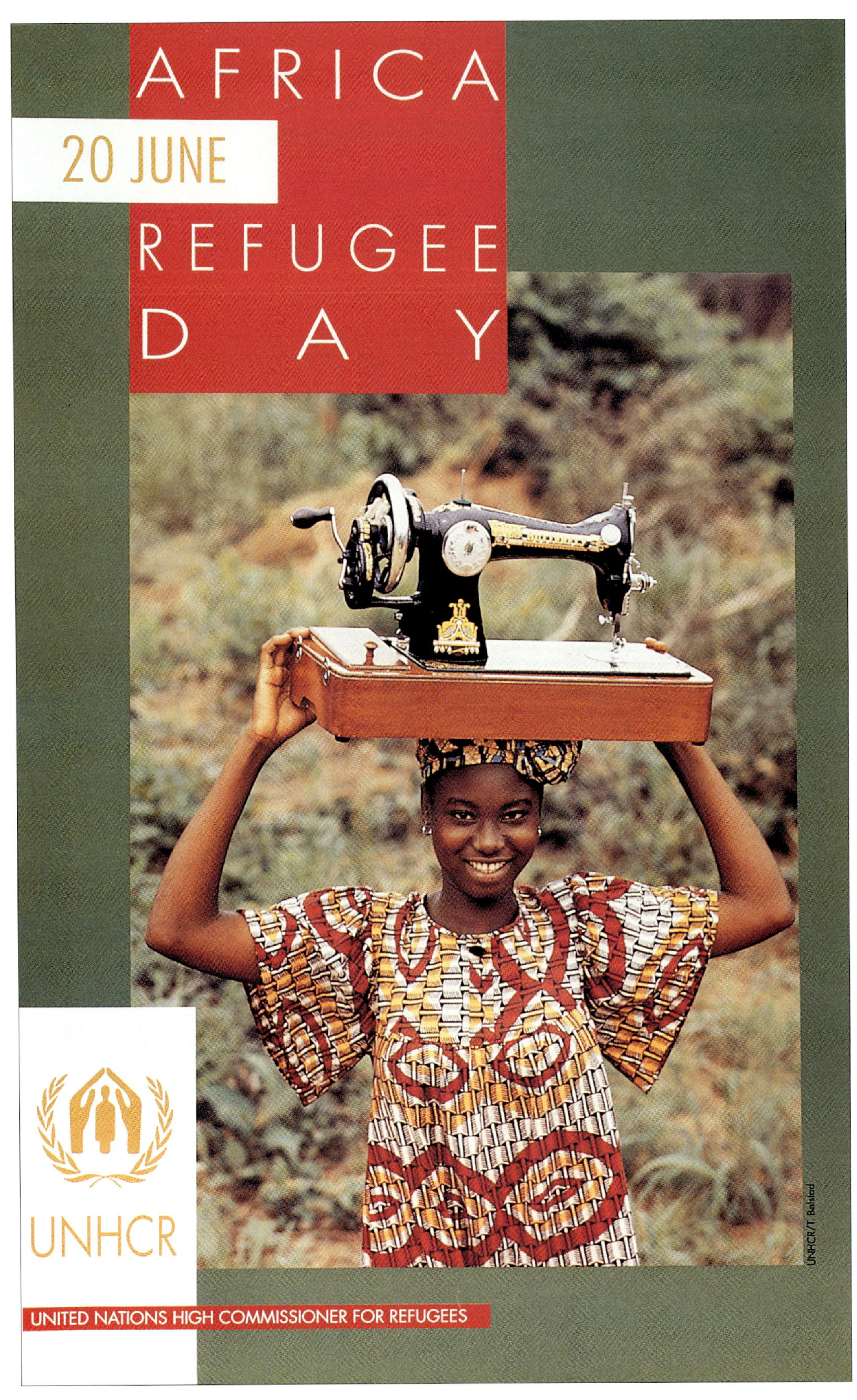

73. Poster for Africa Refugee Day, *20 June. Woman in colorful dress balances a sewing machine on her head (UN High Commissioner for Refugees poster). Photo by T. Bolstad.*

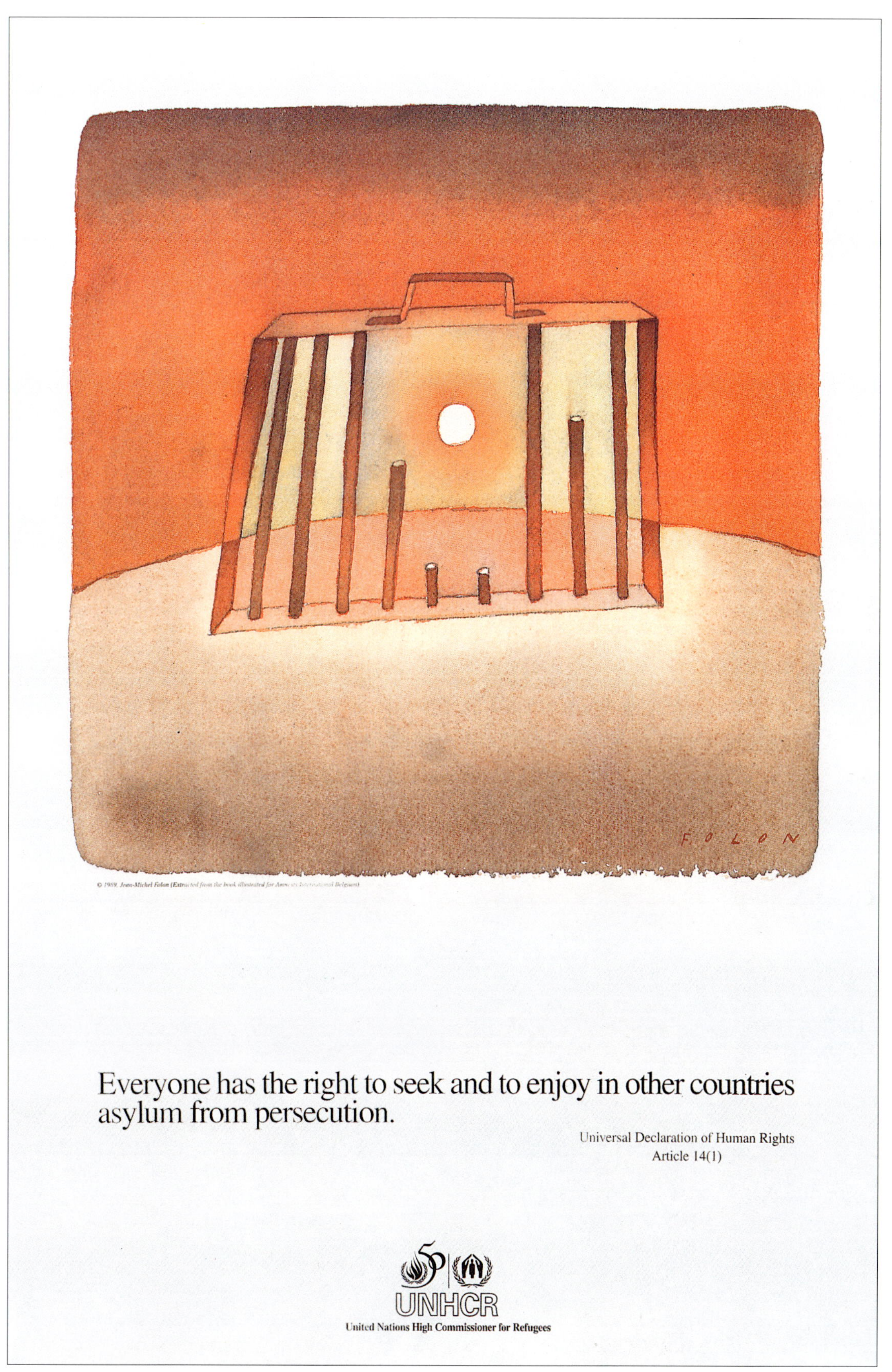

74. Right to Protection, *1989, art by Jean-Michel Folon (UN High Commissioner for Refugees poster).*

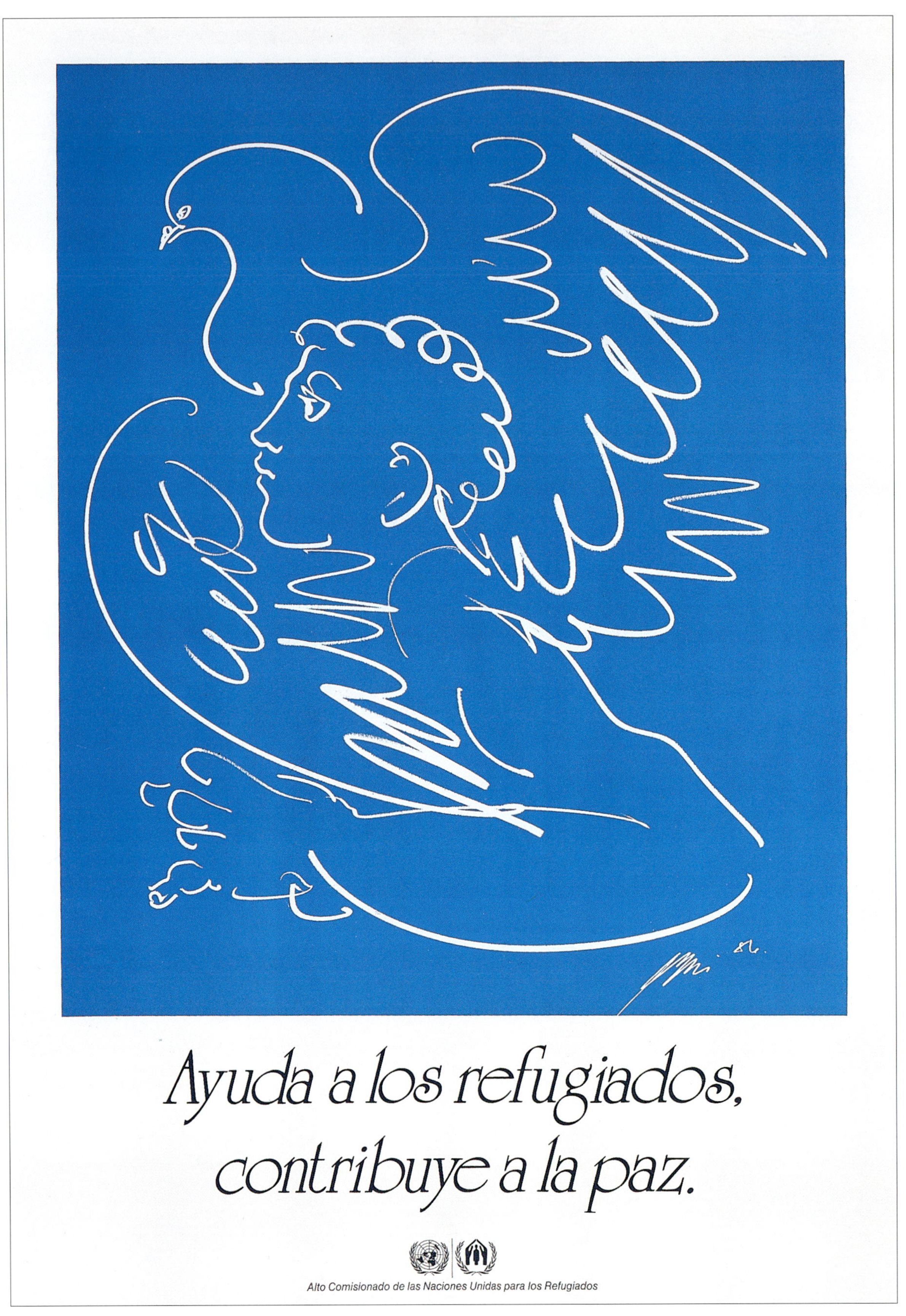

75. Aiding Refugees Contributes to Peace, 1986 (Spanish version), illustration by Hans Erni (UN High Commissioner for Refugees poster).

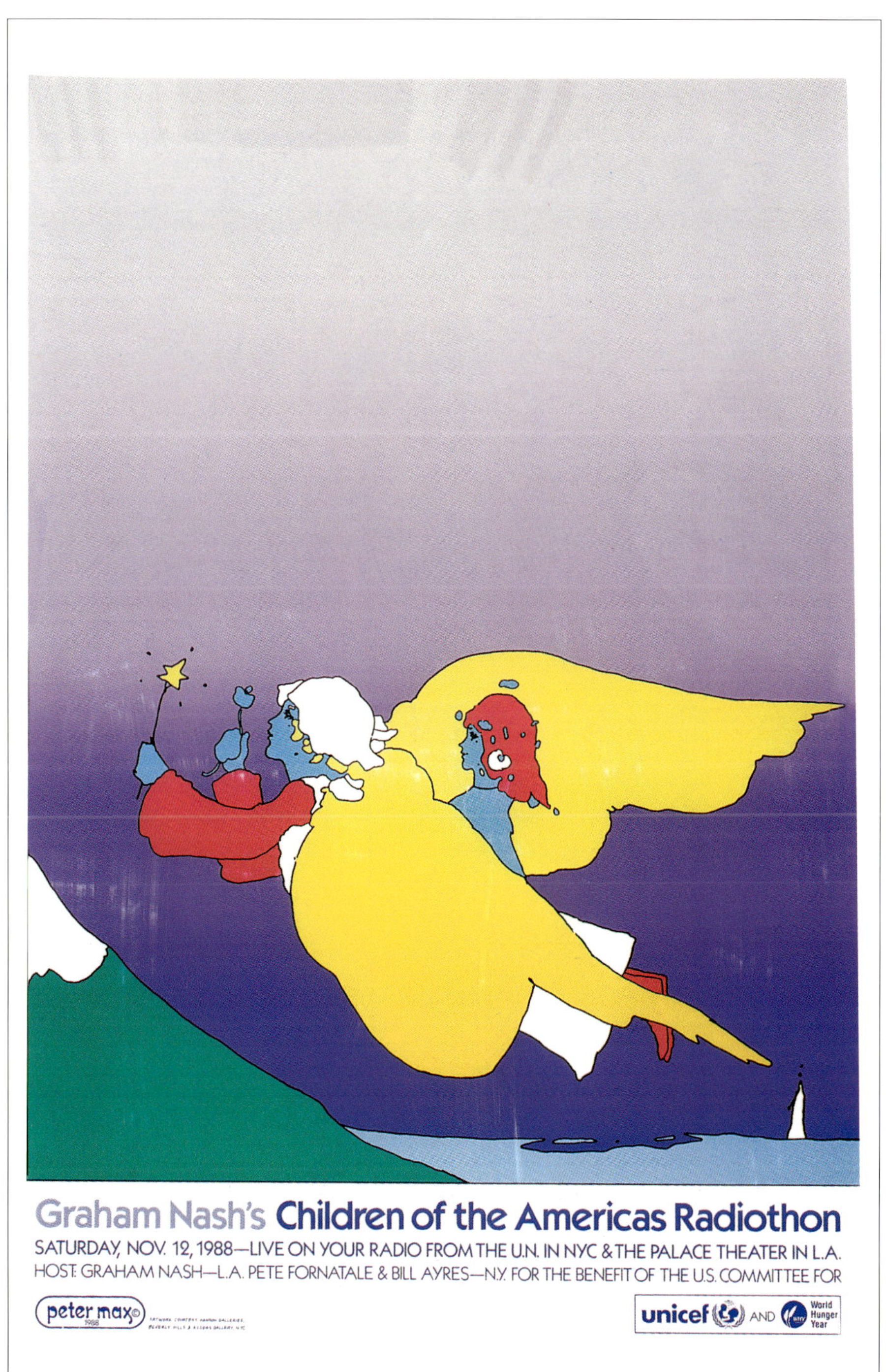

76. Poster by artist Peter Max, for Children of the Americas Radiothon, 12 November 1988 (UNICEF poster).

The **United Nations Children's Fund (UNICEF), New York** is the only UN organization dedicated exclusively to children. Created by the General Assembly in 1946, UNICEF's programs aim to improve the lives of children everywhere, particularly those in developing countries. The low-cost, community-based programs address primary health care, nutrition, basic education, water and environmental sanitation, gender isuues, and development. UNICEF promotes the full implementation of the Convention on the Rights of the Child, adopted unanimously by the General Assembly in 1989. UNICEF publishes the annual report, *The State of the World's Children.*

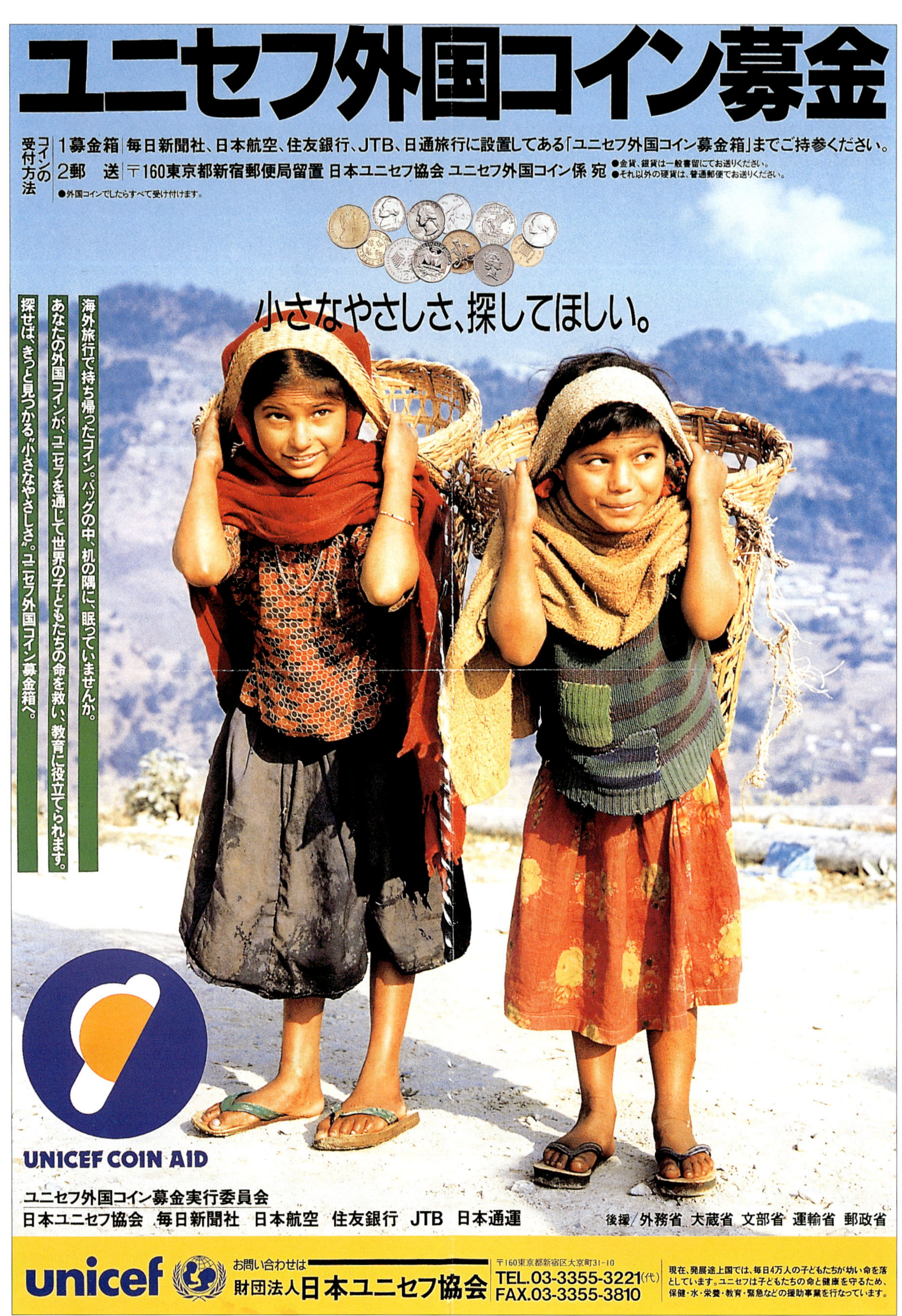

79. Change for Good (UNICEF poster). *Spare change is collected by UNICEF from travelers in various foreign currencies.*

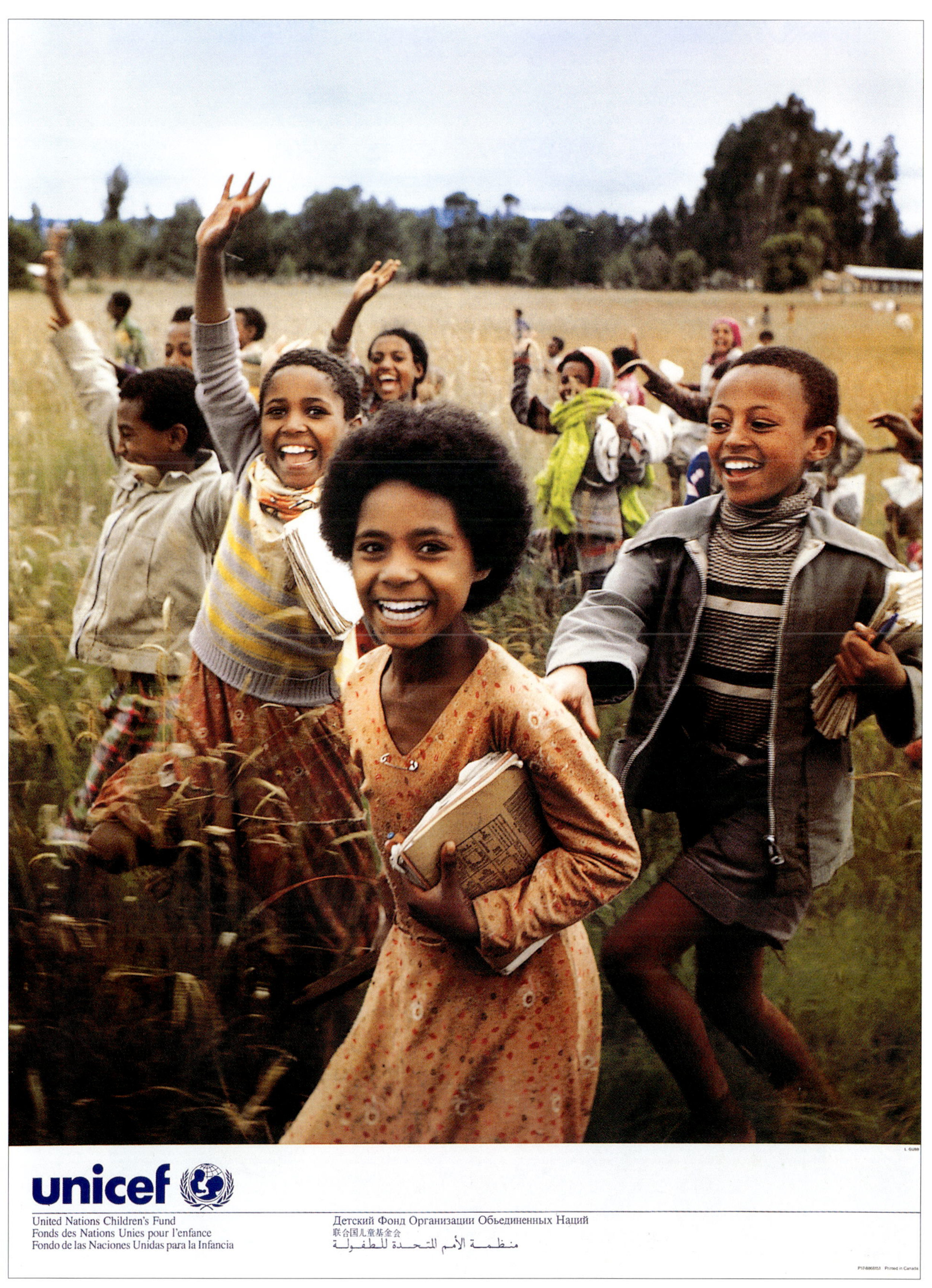

80. Children in Africa, *Canadian Committee for UNICEF and World Food Programme. Photo by Louise Gubb.*

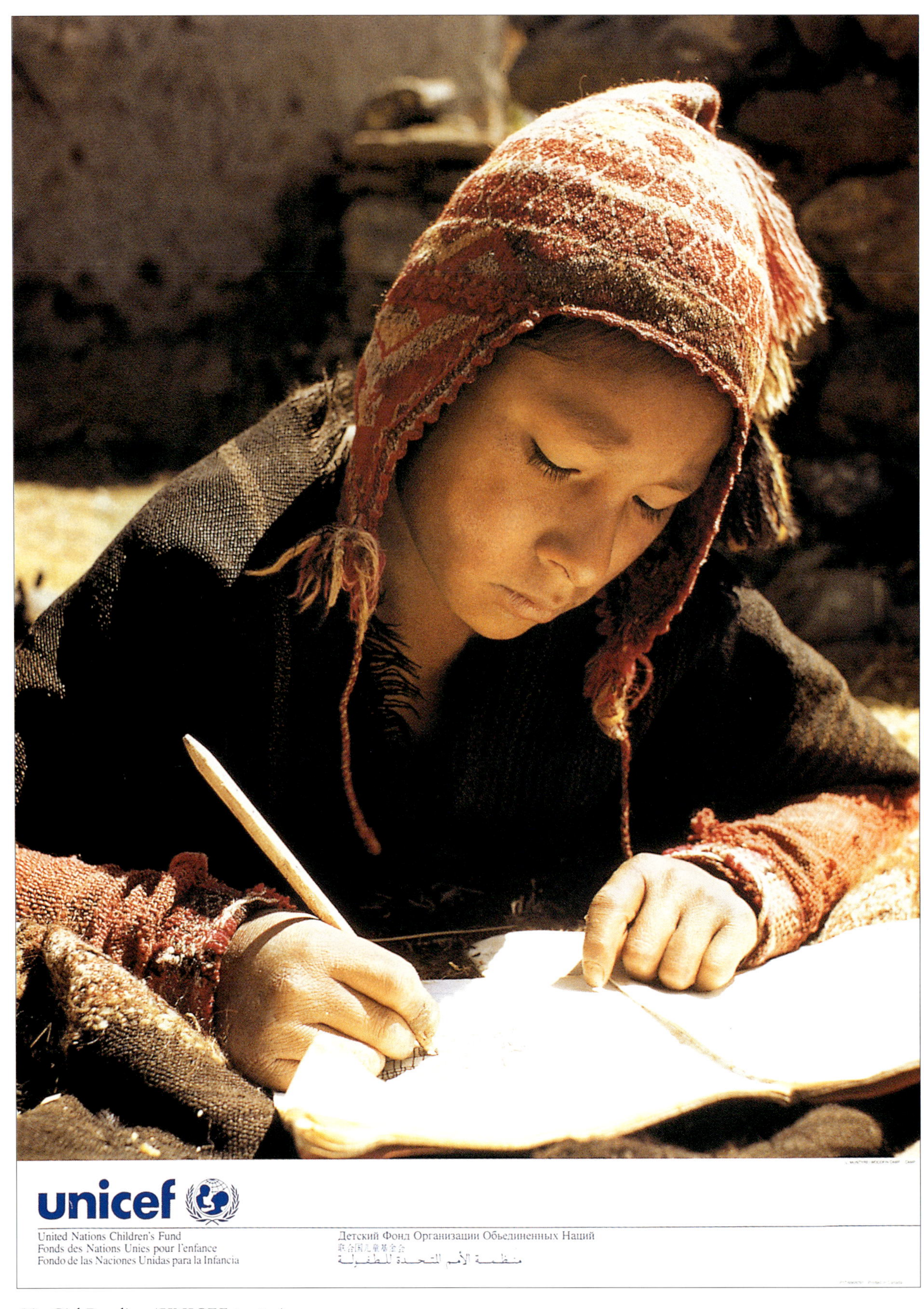

83. Girl Reading (*UNICEF poster*).

What Would You Like to be When You Grow Up?

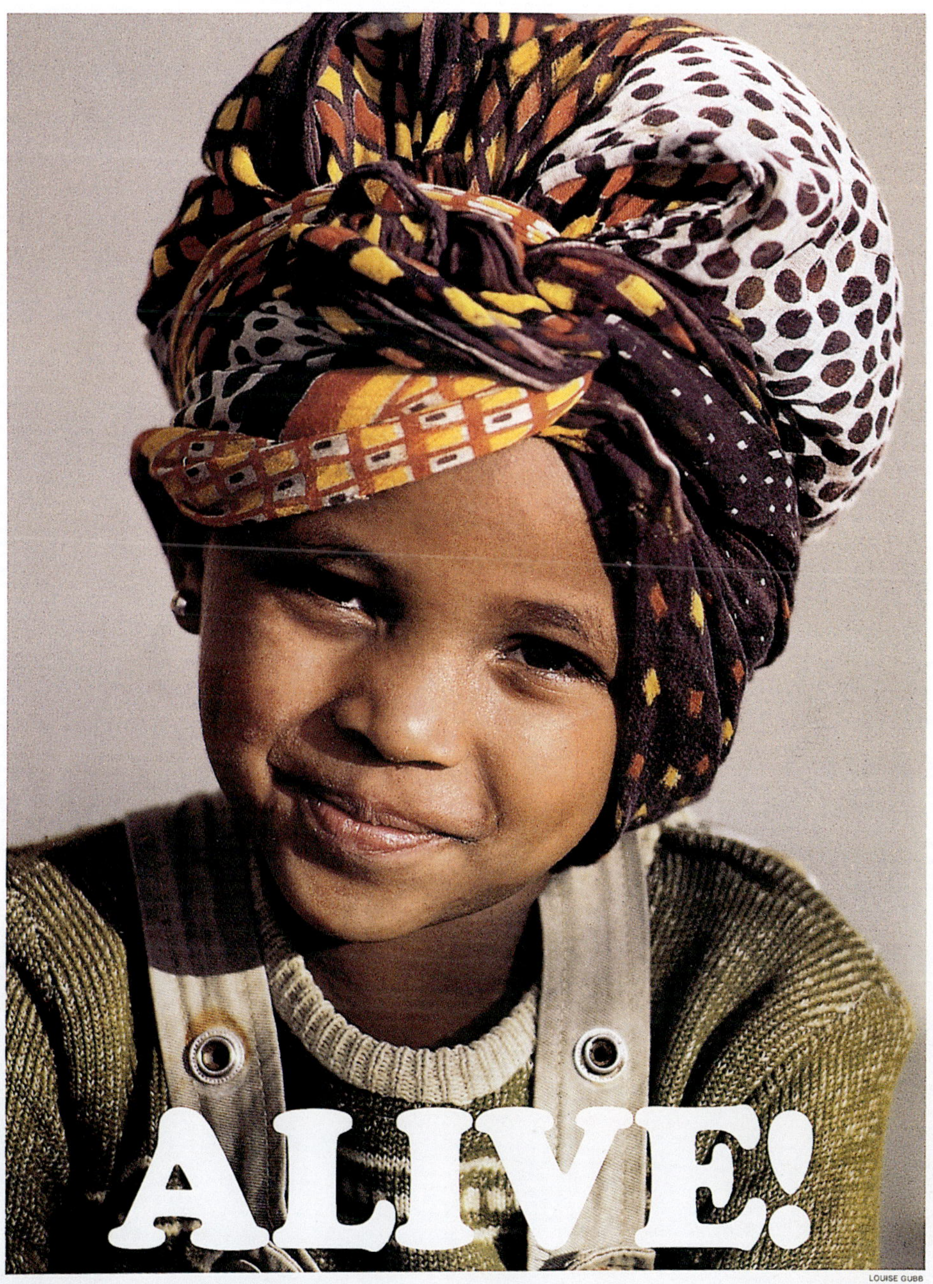

84. What Would You Like to be When You Grow Up? *from the* Alive *series (UNICEF poster). Photo by Kal Muller, Woodfin Camp & Associates.*

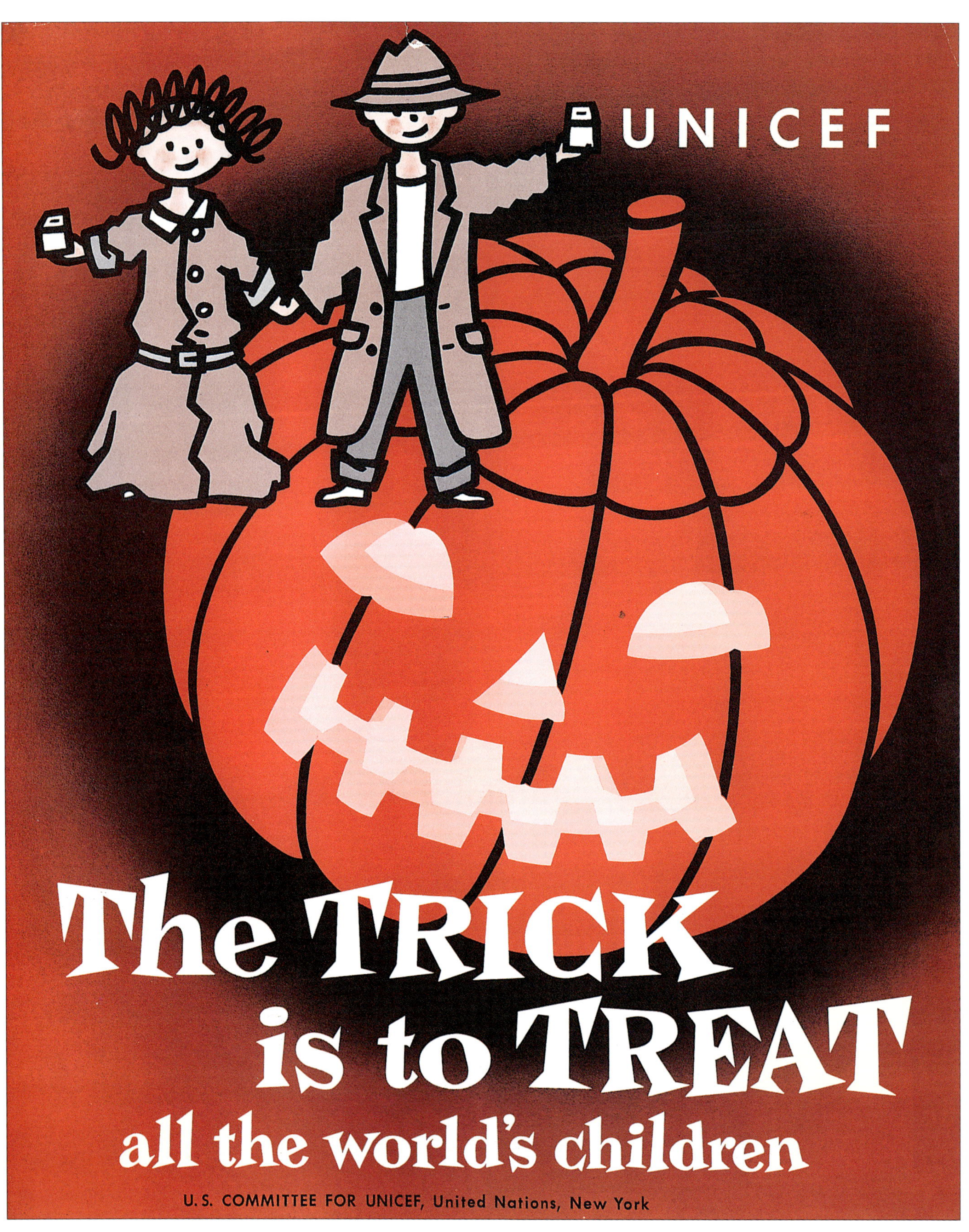

85. The Trick is to Treat. UNICEF *harvests money at Halloween to help support programs for children in more than one hundred forty countries.*

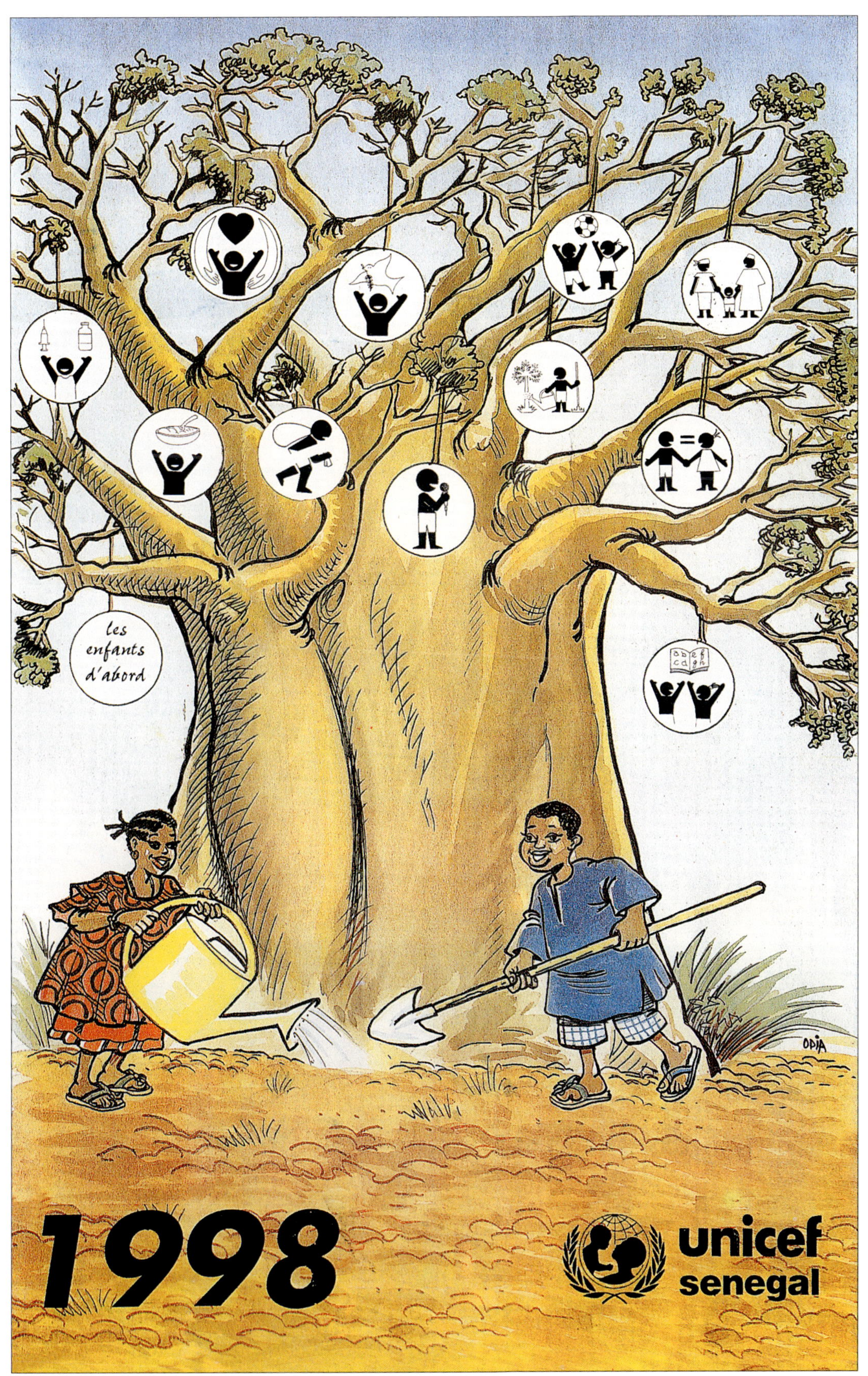

86. *UNICEF 1998 calendar poster with indigenous art from Senegal.*

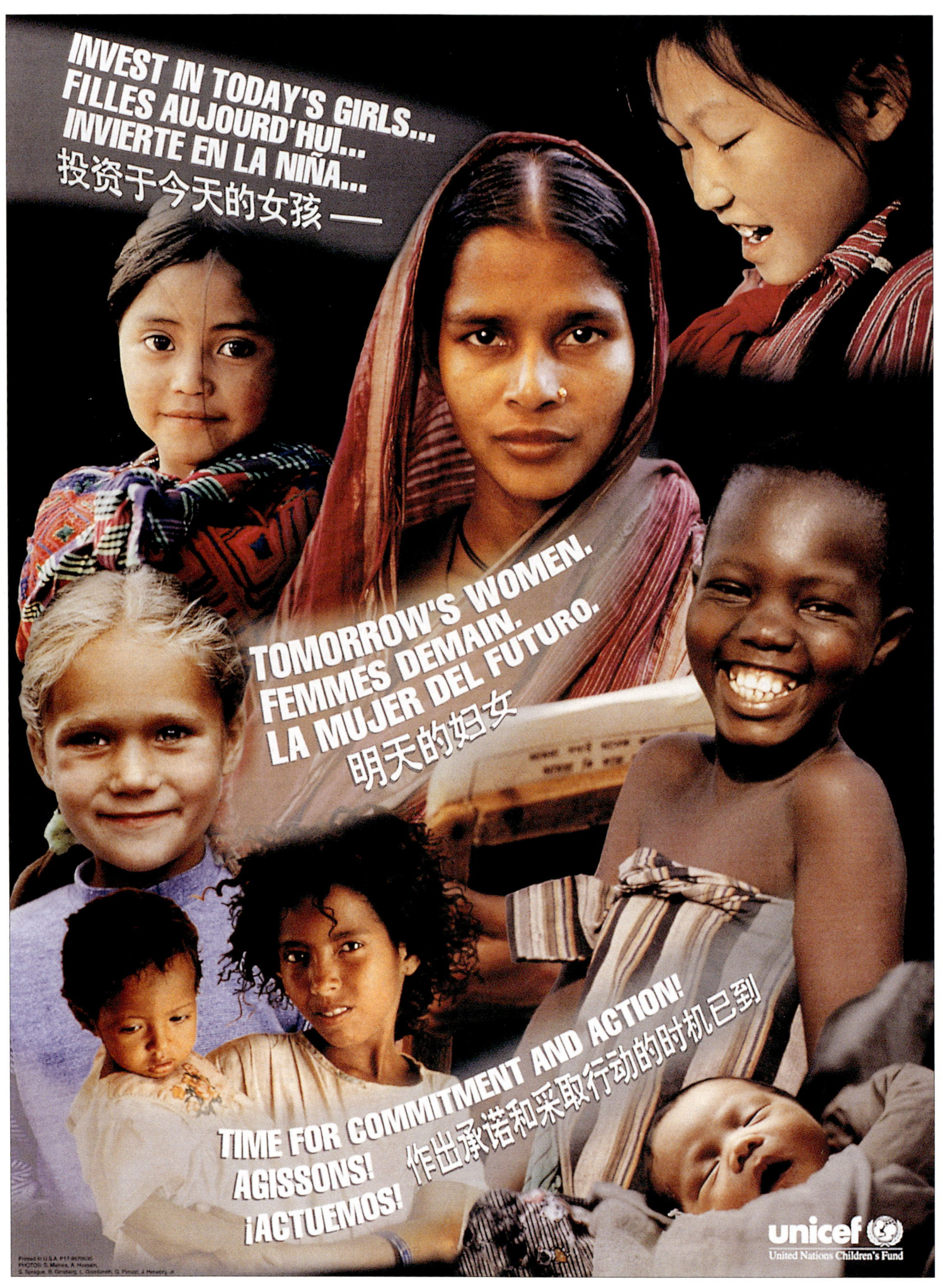

87. Invest in Today's Girls—Tomorrow's Women. *(UNICEF poster). Photos by S. Mames, A. Hossain, S. Sprague, B. Ginsberg, L. Goodsmith, G. Pirozzi, G. Henebry Jr.*

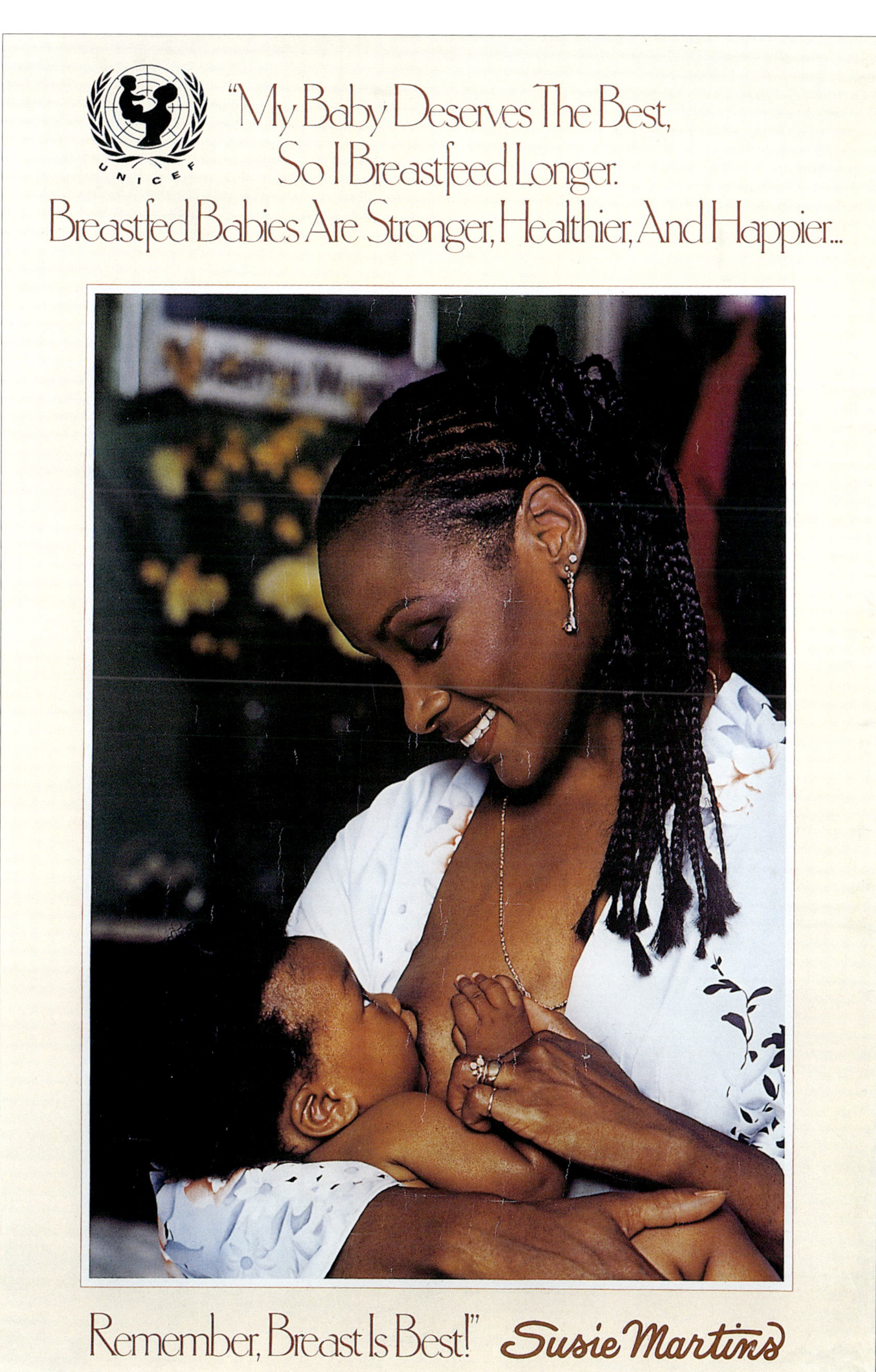

88. Breast is Best, *Susie Martins program to promote breastfeeding (UNICEF poster).*

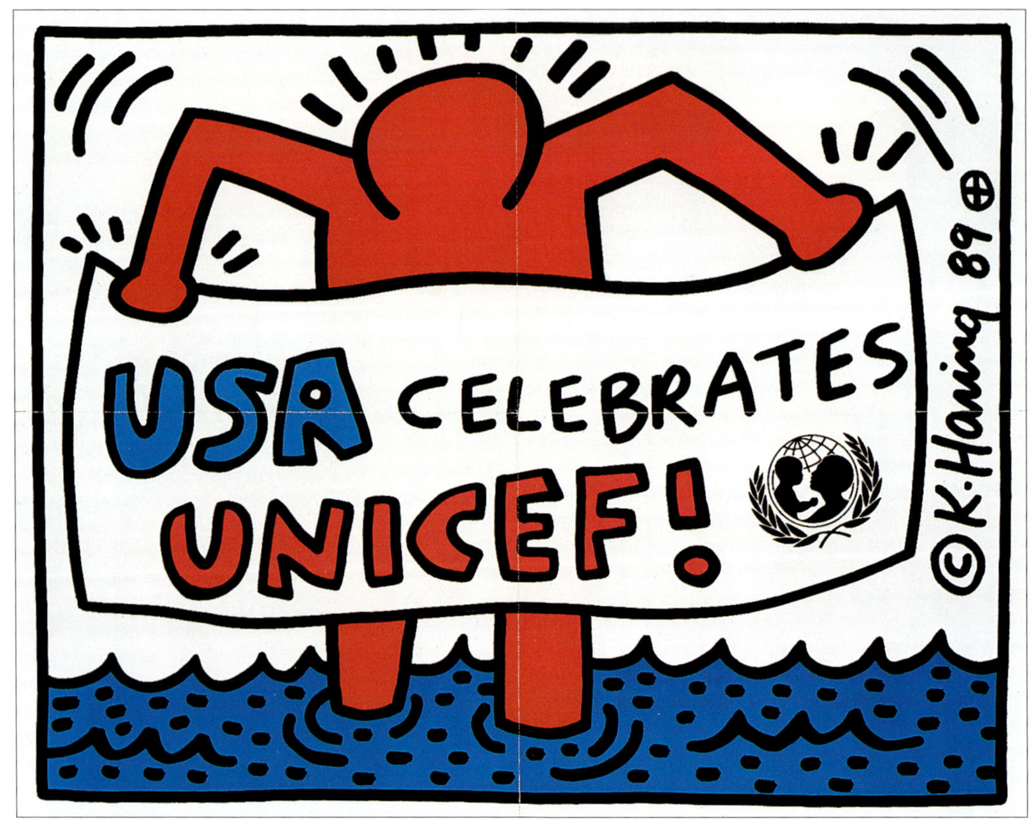

89. USA Celebrates UNICEF, *1989, art by Keith Haring.*

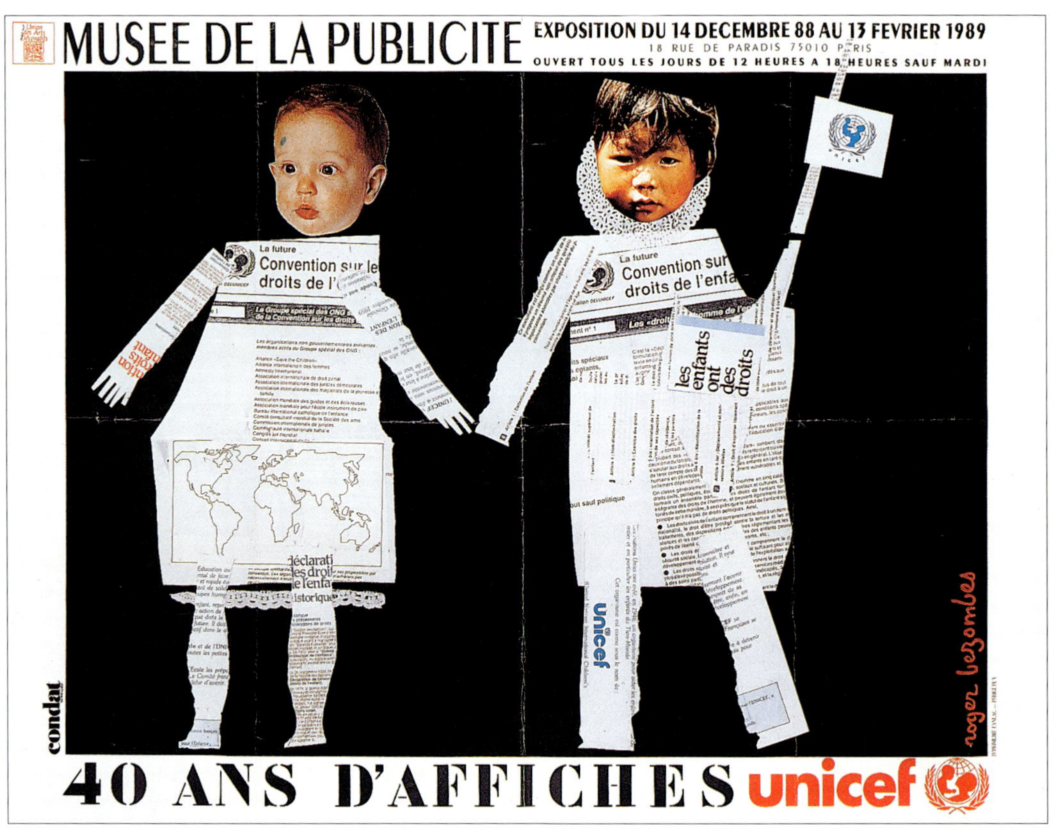

90. Paper Dolls, *1986. Celebrates UNICEF's fortieth anniversary.*

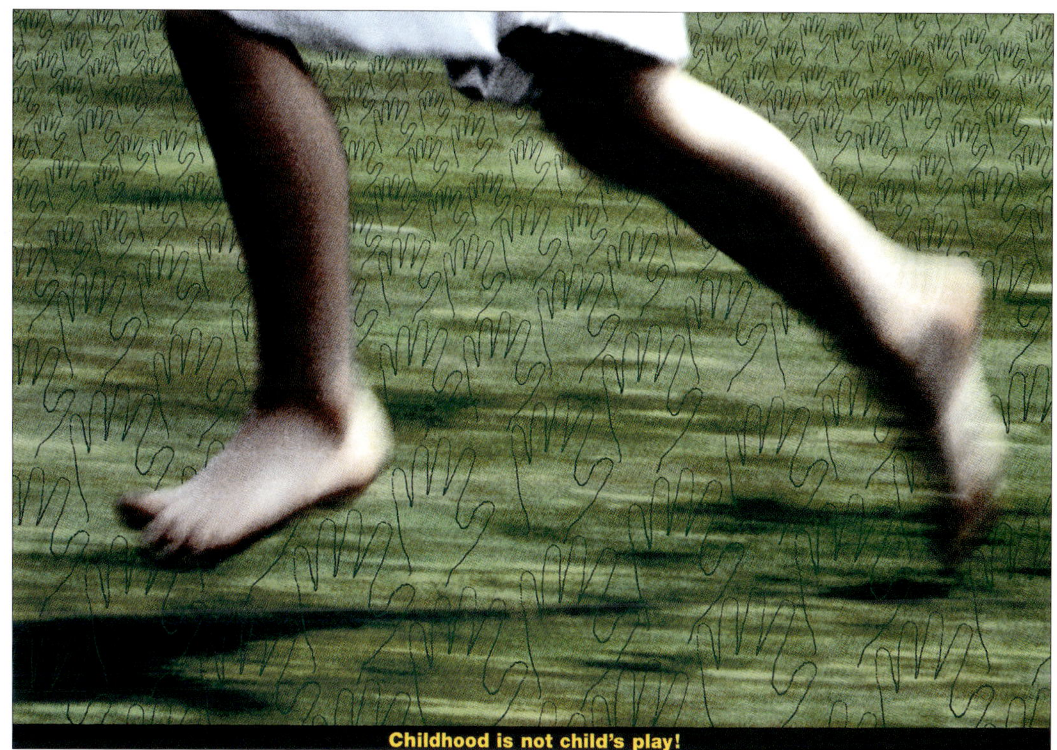

91

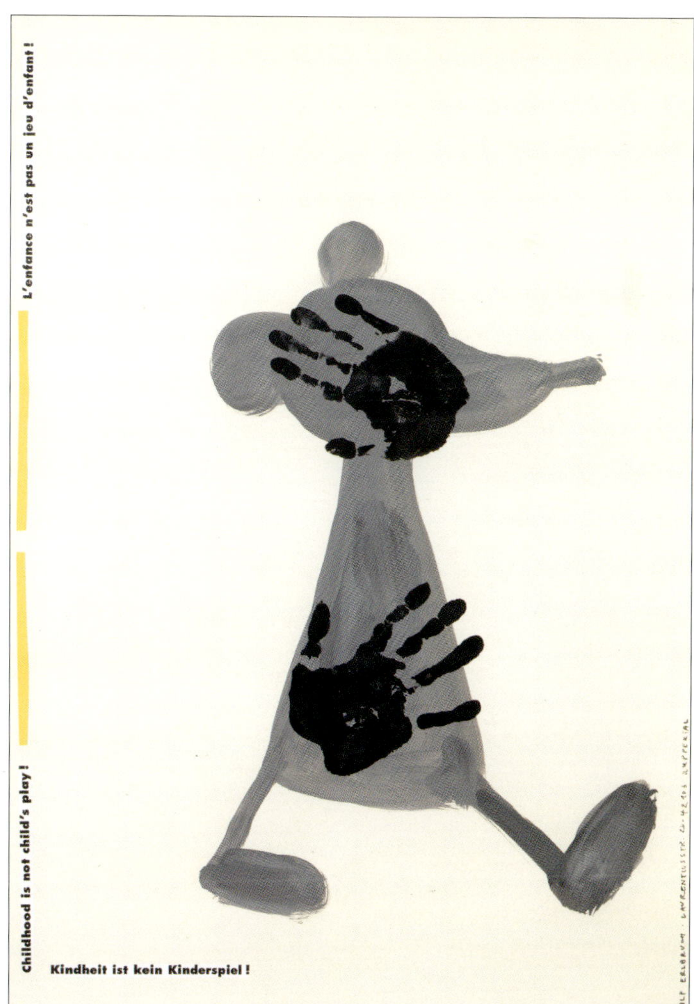

92

91. Childhood Is Not Child's Play, *by British artist David Hillman. Exhibited at UN Headquarters, New York in October 1999 under UNICEF sponsorship.*

92. Kindheit Ist Kein Kinderspiel *(Childhood Is Not Child's Play), by German artist Wolf Erlbruch. Won first prize in competition organized by Museum of Essen, Germany. Exhibited at UN Headquarters, New York in October 1999 under UNICEF sponsorship.*

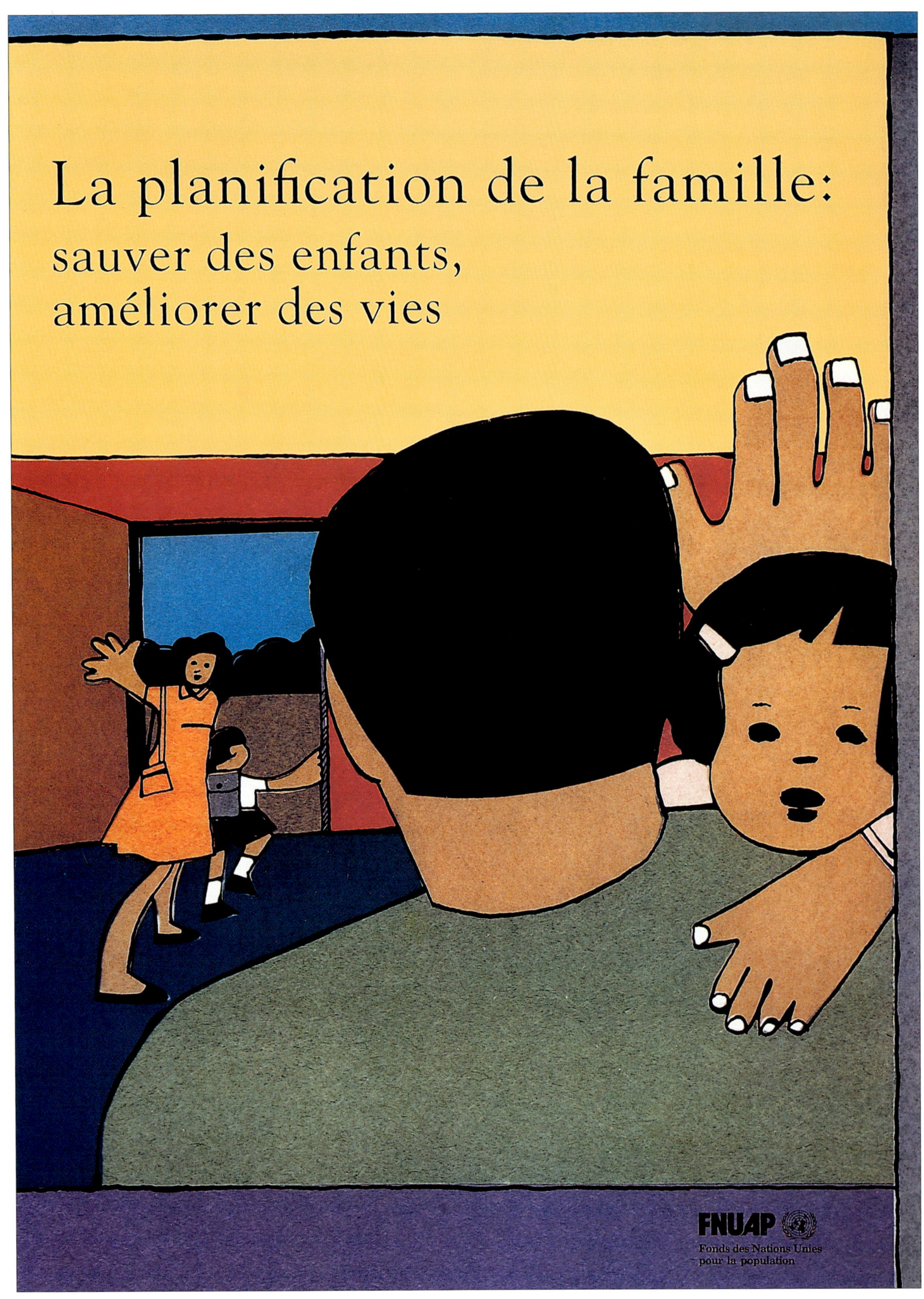

93. Save Children—Improve Life *(French version), art direction by Christian Delsol (UN Population Fund poster).*

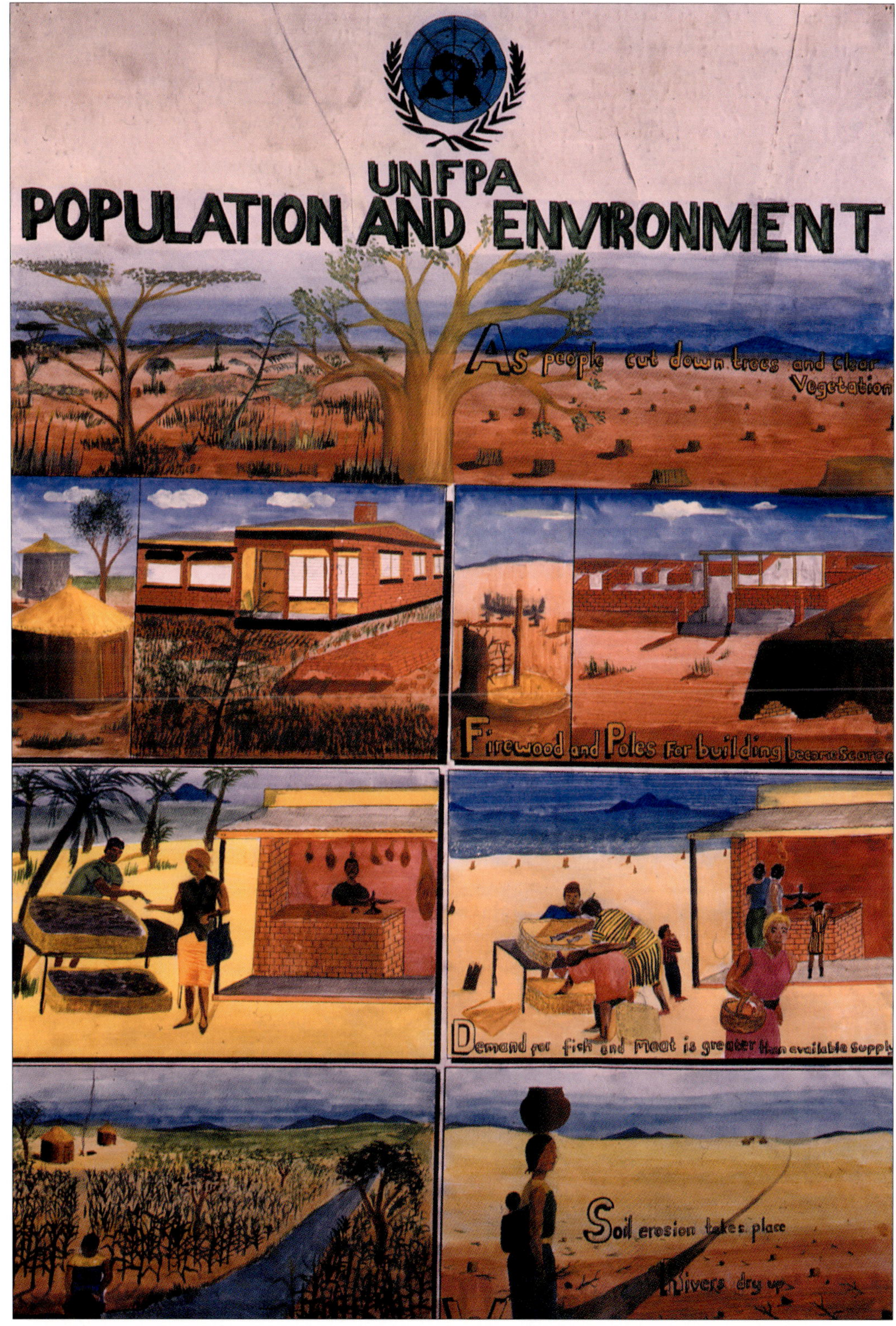

94. Population and Environment, *1992, by teenage Malawian artist Justin Malewezi, from the UN Population Fund poster contest.*

United Nations Population Fund (UNFPA), New York was established in 1969 at the initiative of the General Assembly, and it is the largest multilateral source of population assistance to developing countries. The fund's projects include family planning and improving the reproductive health of women, while promoting women's equality, sustainable development, and manageable population growth.

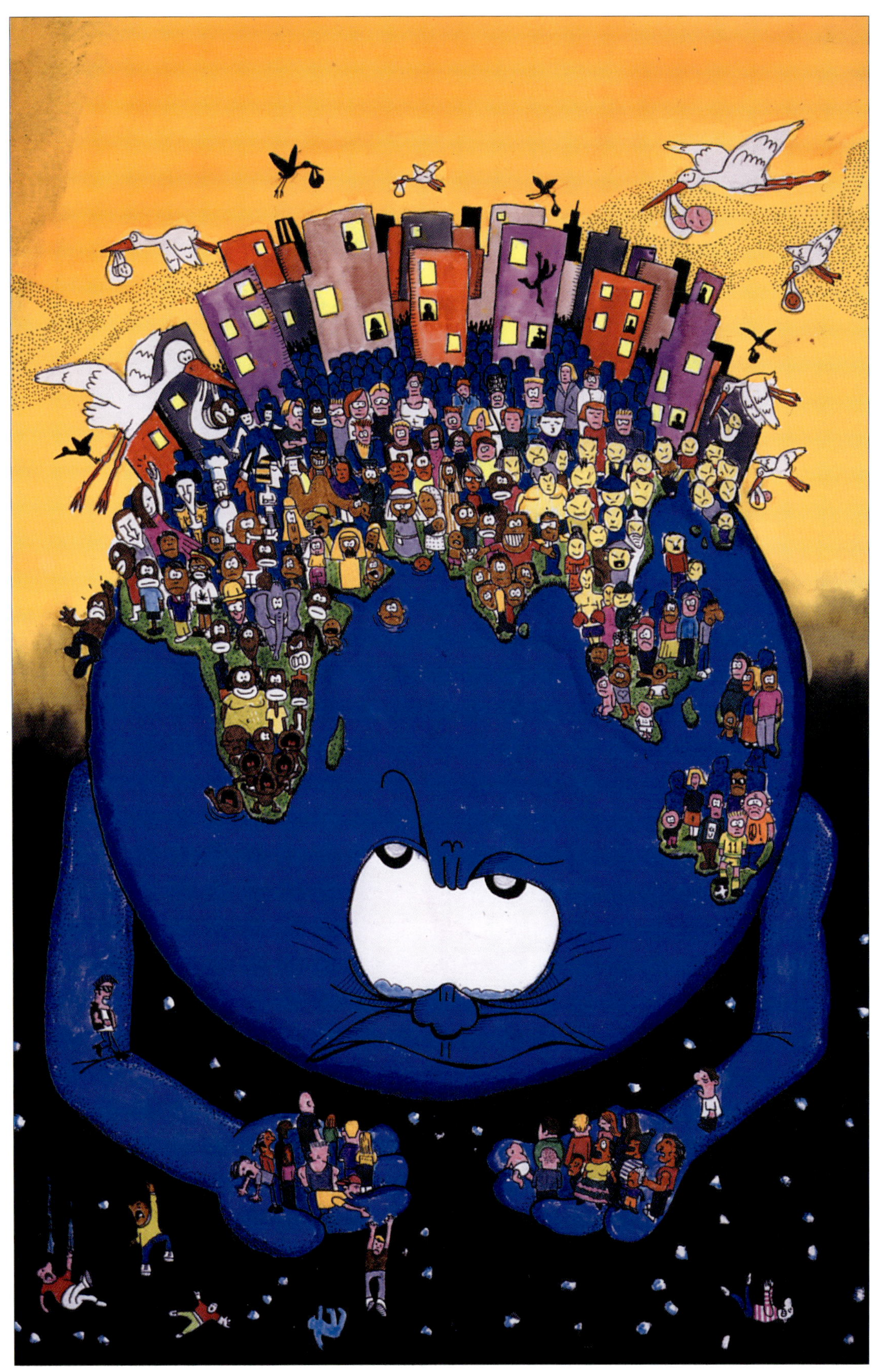

95. Population and Development—How Population Affects Our Quality of Life, *1994, by teenage Peruvian artist Fernando Carrasco Angulo, from the UN Population Fund poster contest.*

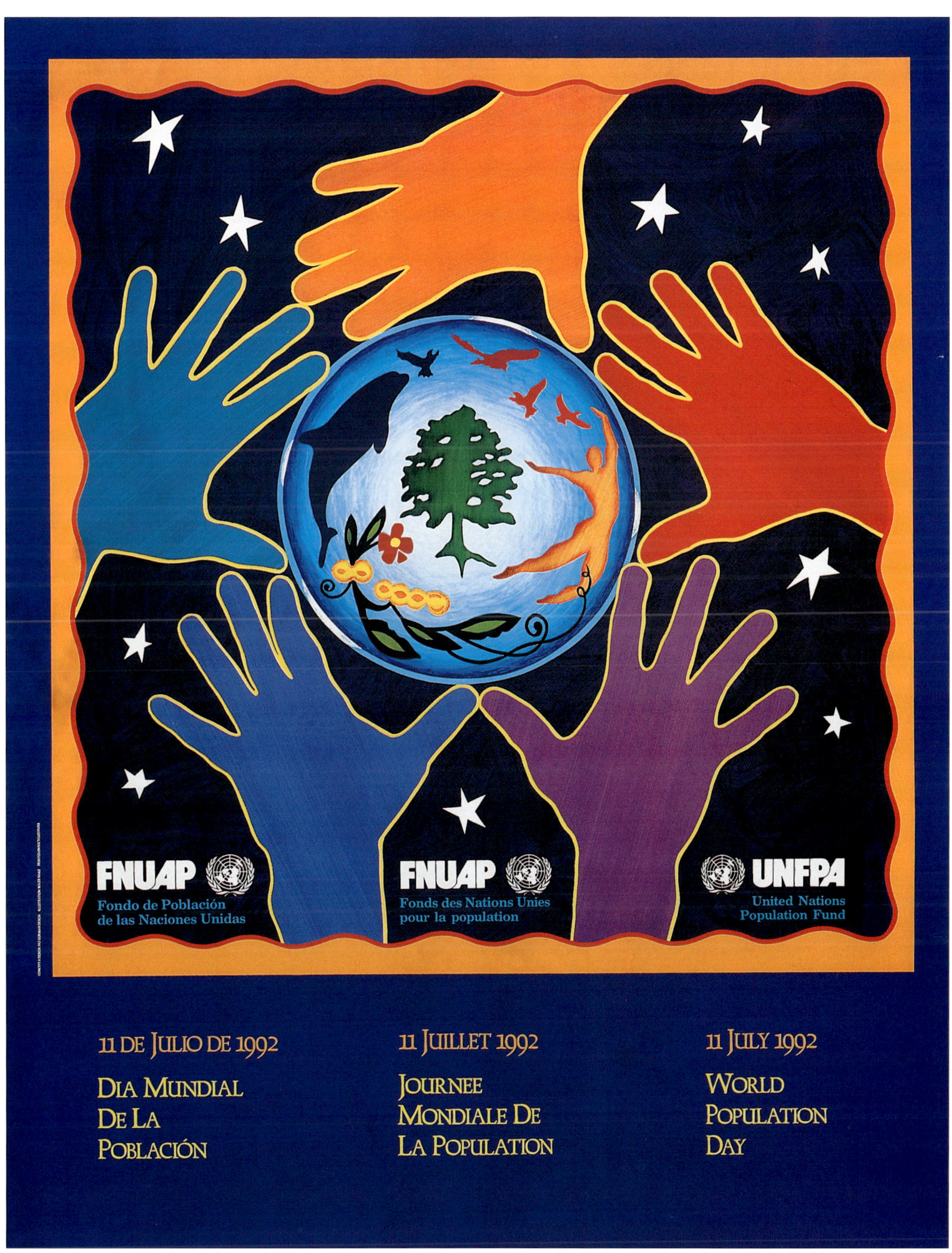

96. World Population Day, 1993, *concept and painting by Pat Gorman Design, art direction by Christian Delsol, UN Population Fund (UN Population Fund poster).*

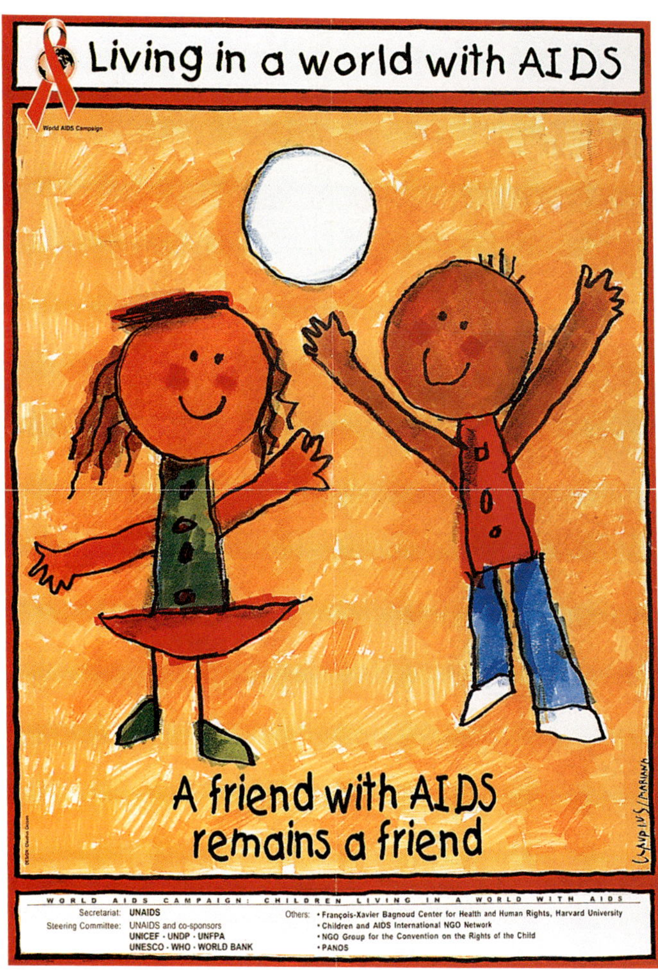

99. Living in a World with AIDS/A Friend with AIDS Remains a Friend, *from World AIDS campaign series, designed by Claudius Cercom (signed Claudius/Mariana) (World Health Organization poster in cooperation with other UN agencies).*

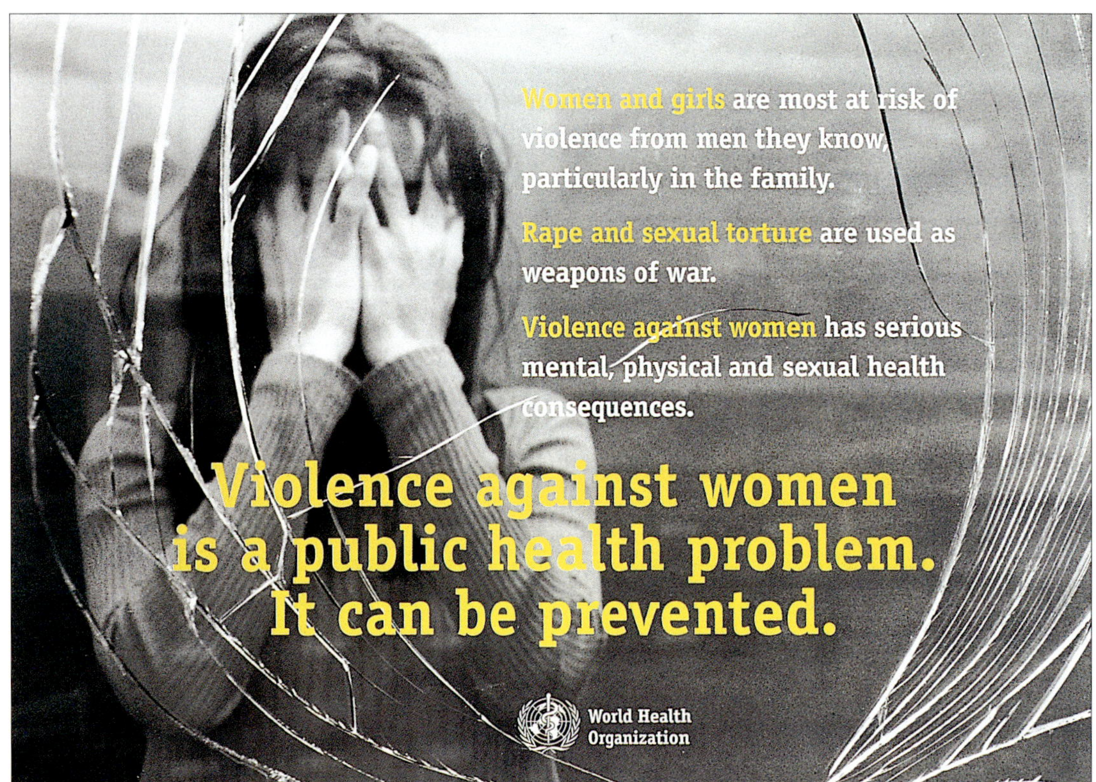

100. Violence Against Women is a Public Health Problem. It Can be Prevented *(World Health Organization poster).*

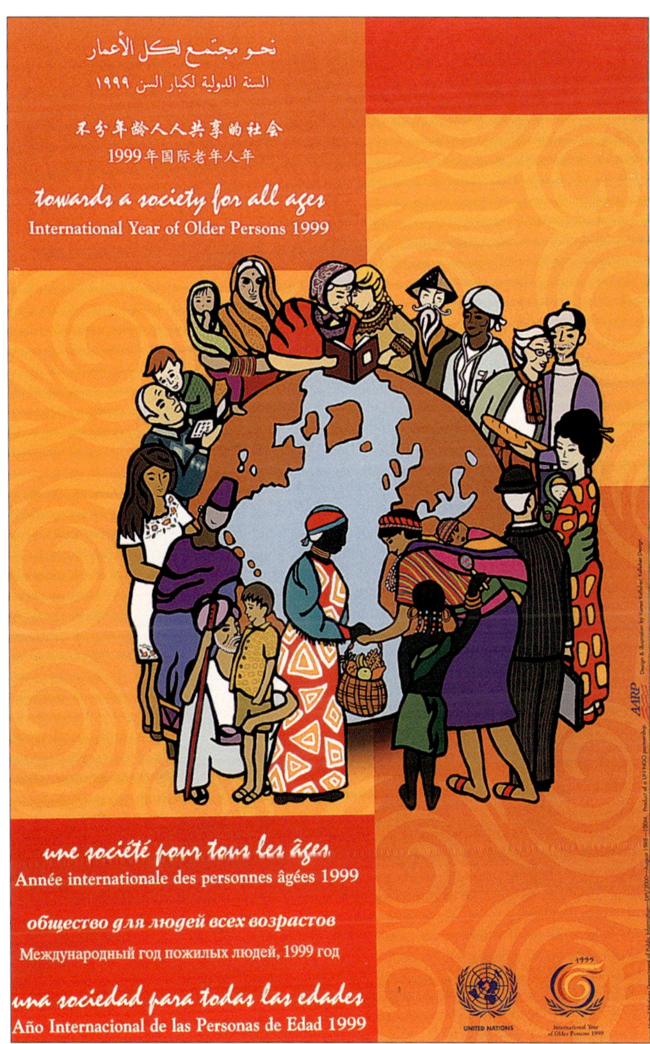

101. Towards a Society for all Ages, *1999, design and illustration by Karen Kelleher, Kelleher Design, in partnership with American Association of Retired Persons (AARP) and UN Department of Public Information (International Year of Older Persons poster).*

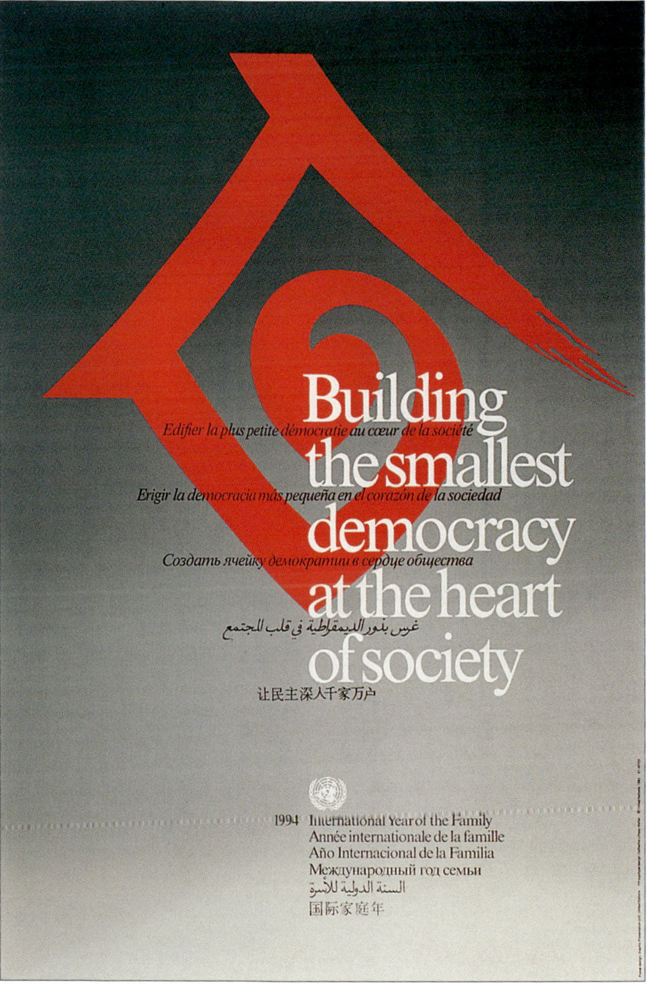

102. Building the Smallest Democracy at the Heart of Society, *1994, designed by José Castiñeira, emblem design by Catherine Littasy-Rollier, art direction by Maxim Żhukov, Graphic Design Section, UN Department of Public Information (International Year of the Family poster).*

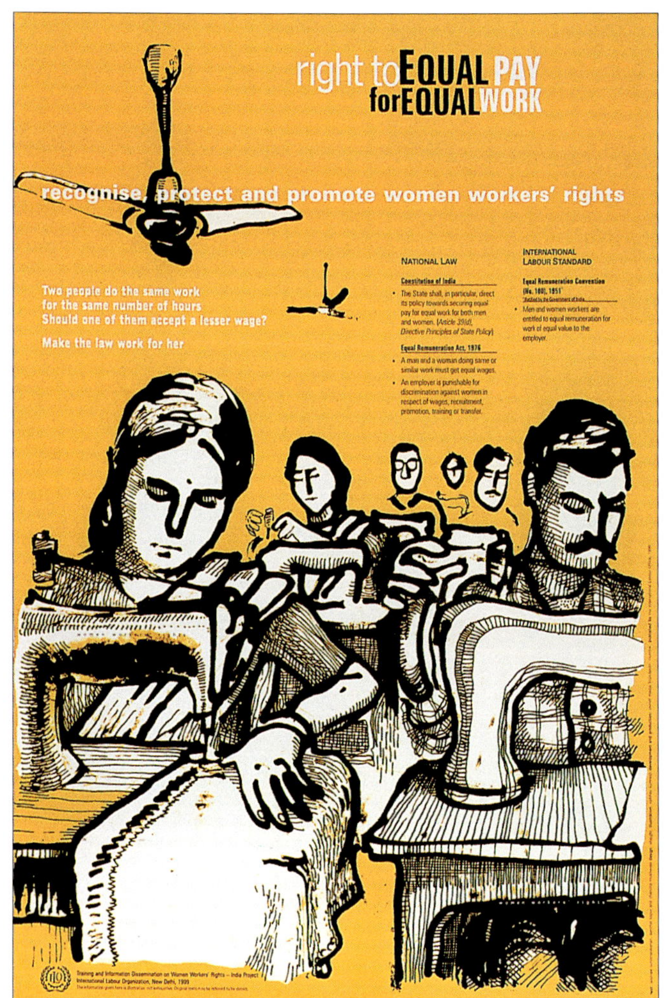

103

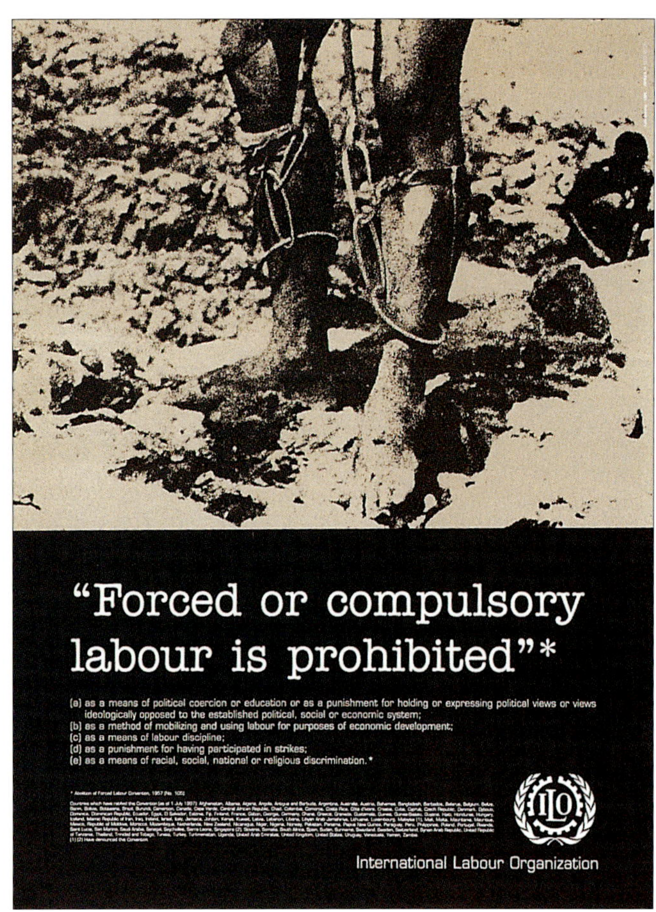

104

The **International Labour Organization (ILO), Geneva** has developed labor standards and guidelines that have served as the model for national legislation in numerous countries worldwide. Established in 1919, the organization is guided by the principle that social stability and integration can be sustained only if they are based on social justice—particularly the right to employment with fair compensation in a healthy workplace.

The ILO has long provided research, analysis, and advice to assist policy makers and its tripartite constituency (labor, management, and government) in making the right choices and formulating optimal strategies in the effort to create more and better jobs. ILO's technical cooperation supports democratization, poverty alleviation through employment creation, and the protection of workers. In particular, the ILO helps countries to develop their labor legislation and take practical steps toward implementing ILO standards.

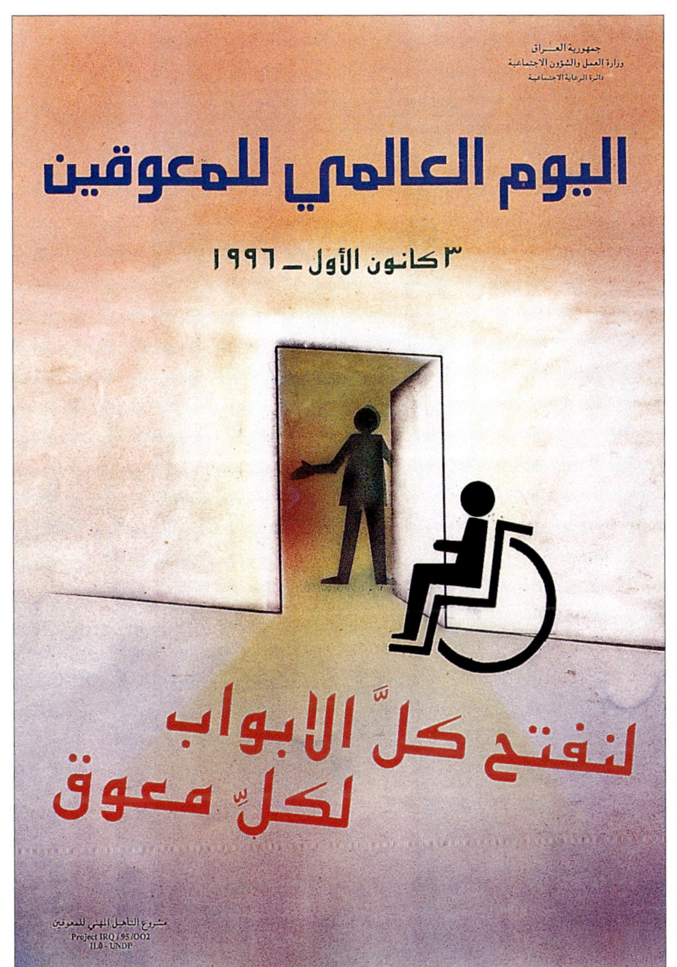

105

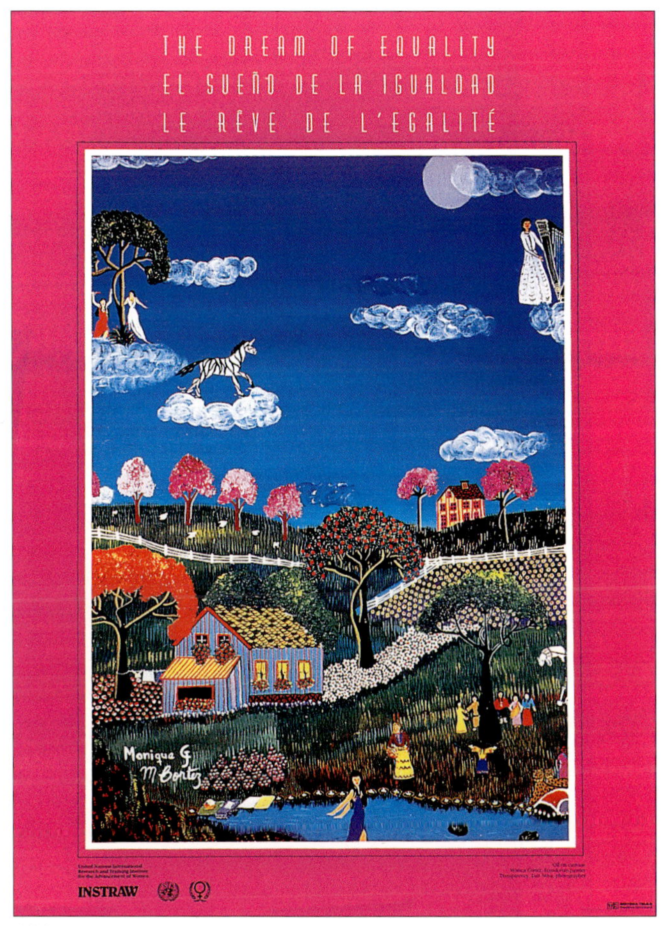

106

103. Right to Equal Pay for Equal Work, *1999 (International Labour Organization poster). Part of series to encourage rights of women workers.*

104. Forced or Compulsory Labour is Prohibited, *art by Faith Doherty, SAIN (International Labour Organization poster). Relates to 1957 ILO Convention (number 105). Shows legs of man bound in chains.*

105. Let's Open All Doors for All Handicapped *(Arabic version), produced by the Department of Social Affairs, Ministry of Work and Social Affairs, Republic of Iraq, for the International Day for the Handicapped, 3 December 1996 (International Labour Organization/UN Development Programme poster). IRQ-95/002*

106. The Dream of Equality, *by Ecuadorian artist Mónica Cortez, poster commemorating the UN International Training and Research Institute for Advancement of Women. Printed in Ecuador. Photo by Luis Nova.*

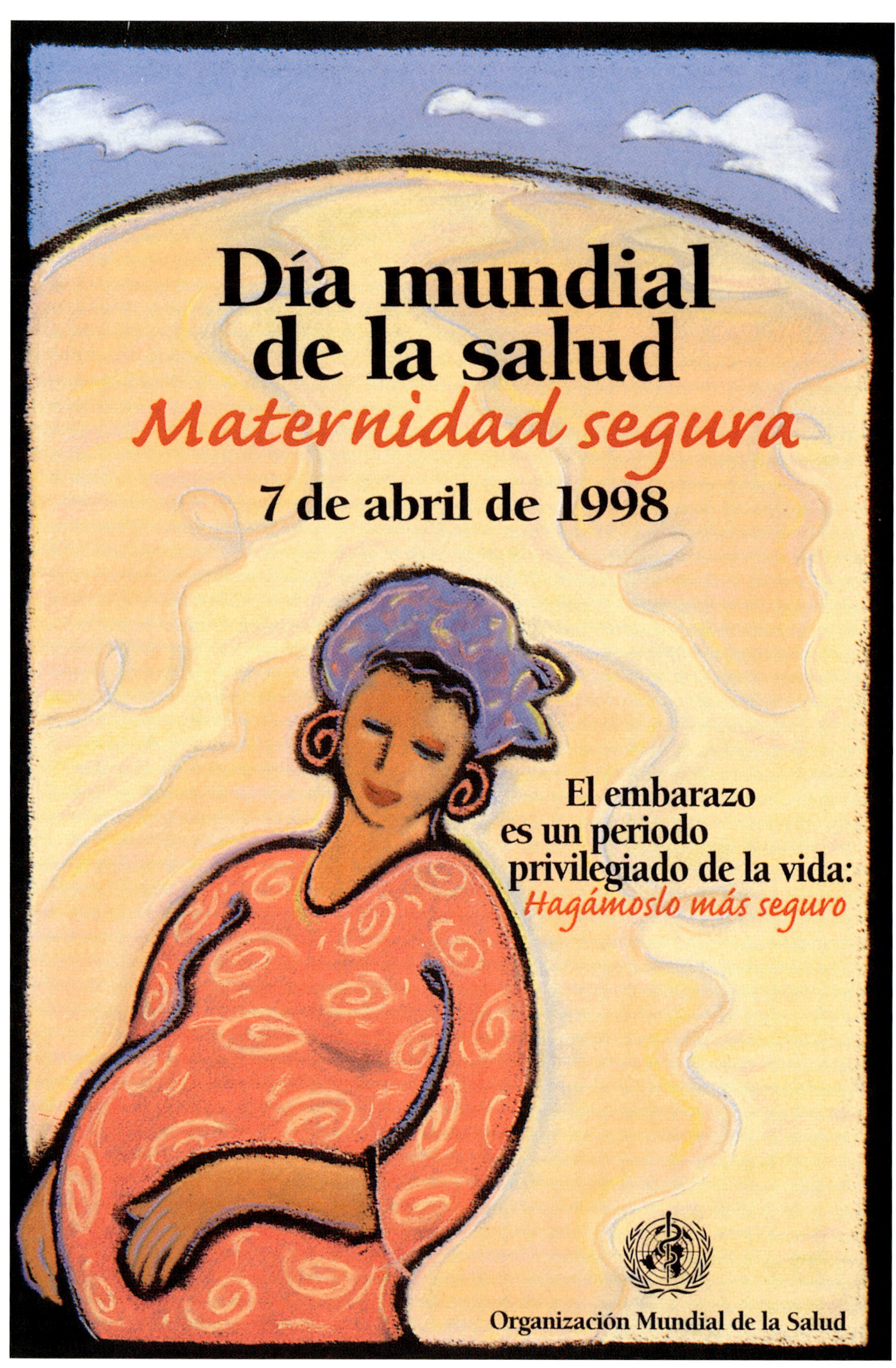

111. *Pregnancy is Special—Let's Make it Safe*, 1998 *(Spanish version), World Health Organization poster for Safe Motherhood for World Health Day, 7 April 1998.*

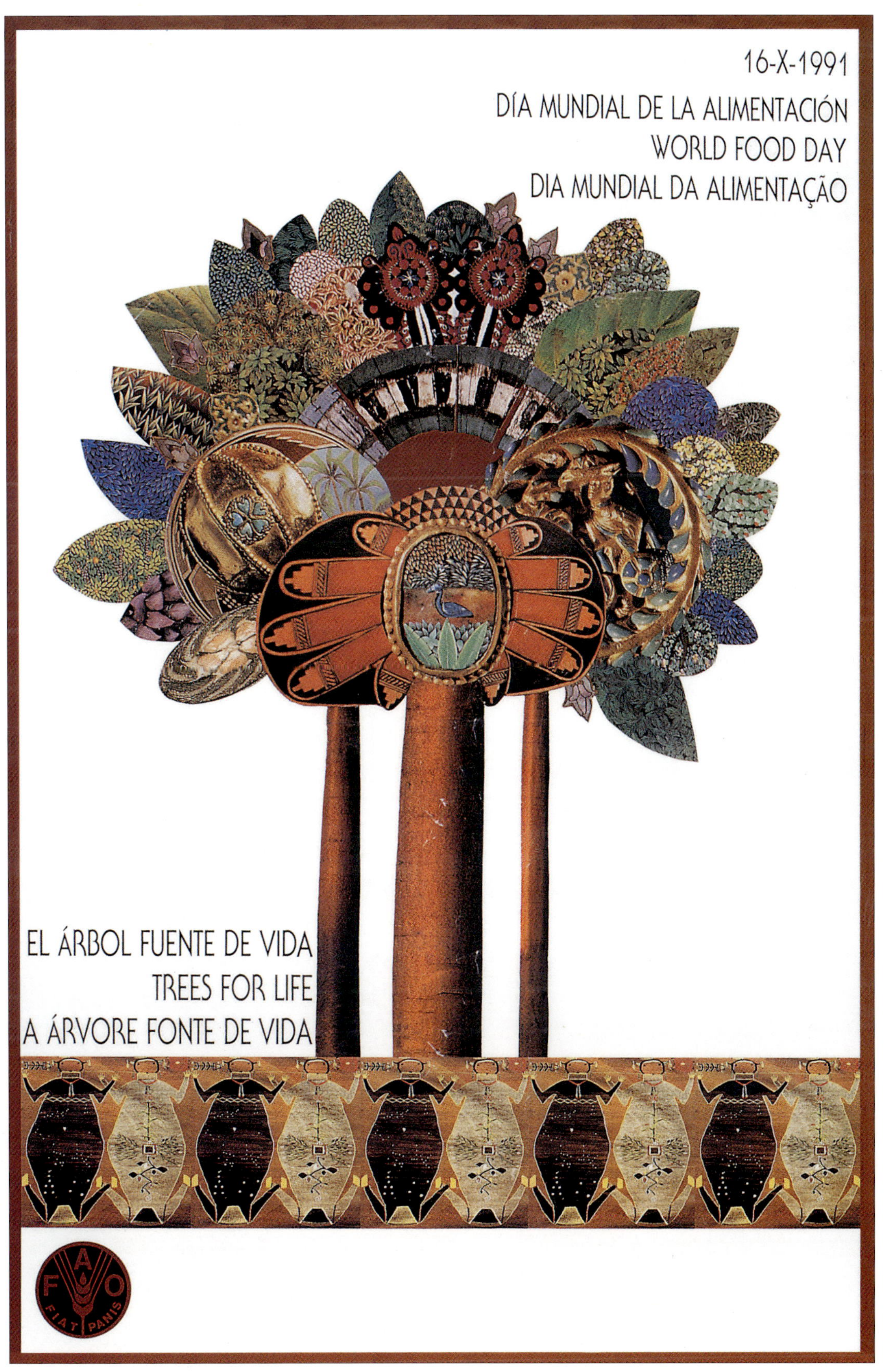

112. *World Food Day, 1991 (Spanish version), regional poster from Santiago, Chile, features local Indian artwork (Food and Agriculture Organization poster).*

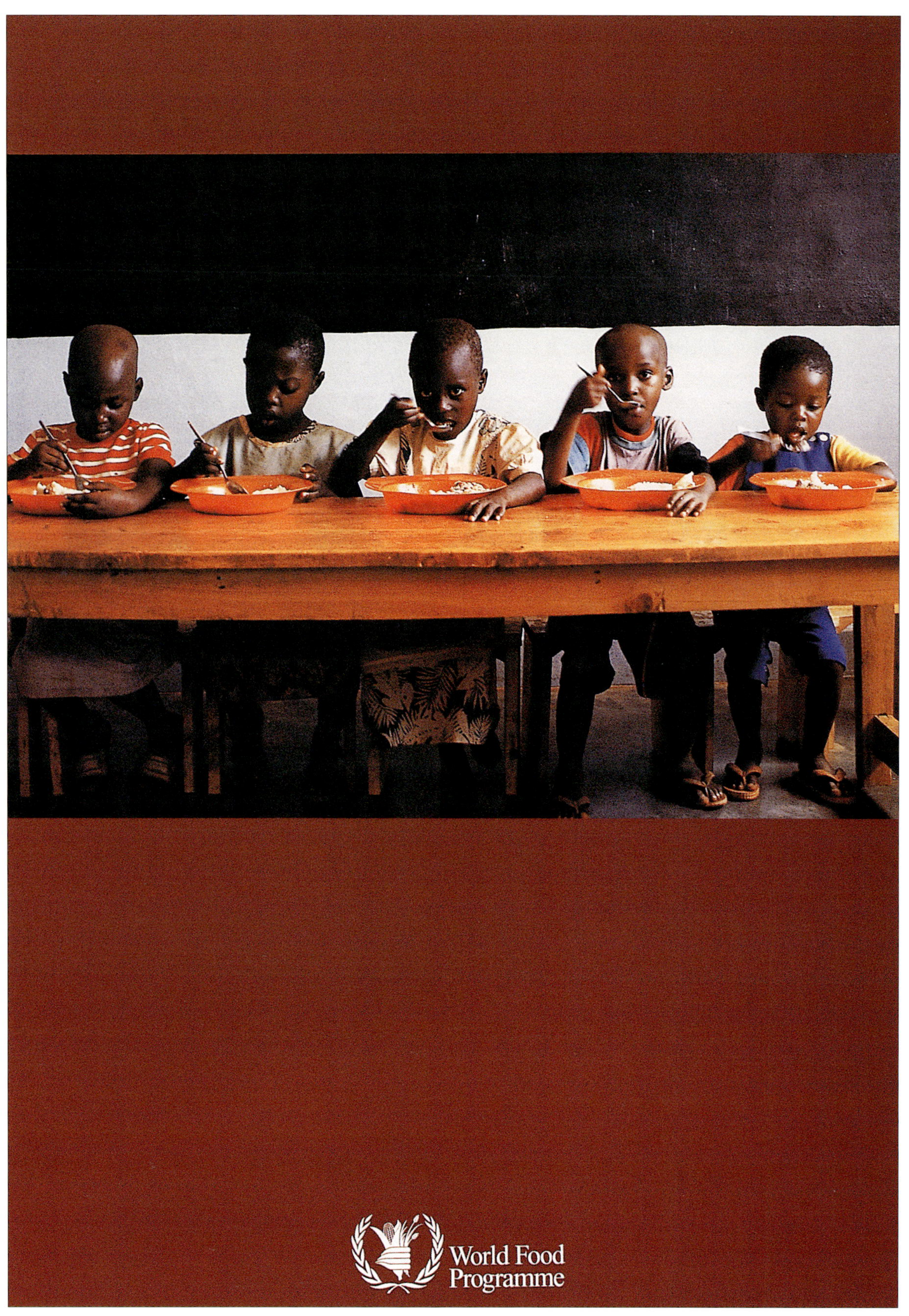

113. *World Food Programme, Africa. One of a series on global hunger.*

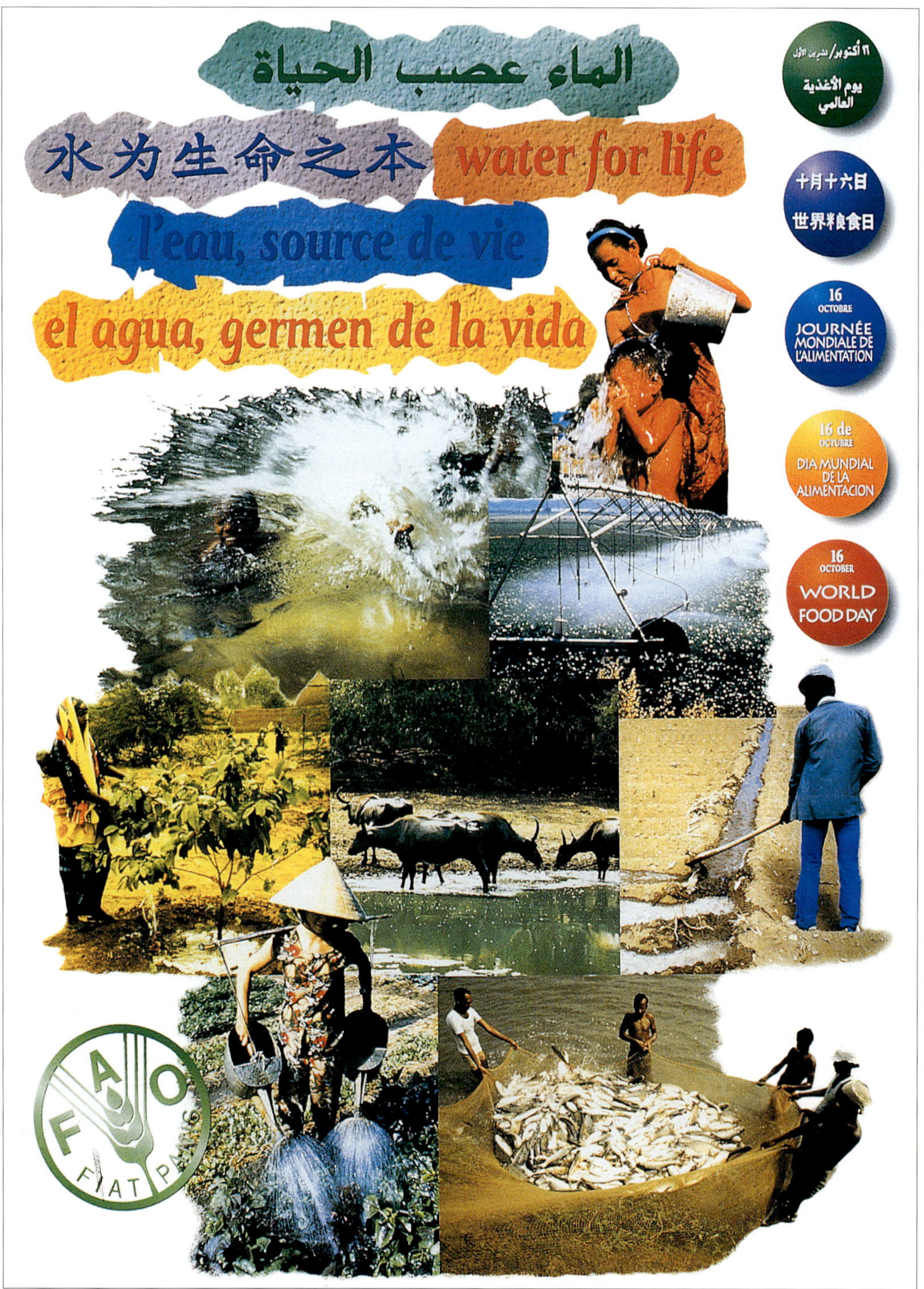

114. Water for Life, World Food Day (Food and Agriculture Organization poster). Depicts farm and daily life activities revolving around water.

The **Food and Agriculture Organization (FAO), Rome** was founded on October 16, 1945, at a conference in Quebec City—the date has, since 1981, been designated World Food Day. The FAO is the leading UN agency for rural development; it works to alleviate poverty and hunger by promoting agricultural development and improving nutrition and food security, ensuring access of all people at all times to the food they need for a healthy life. Some FAO programs help countries to prepare for food crises and provide relief when necessary.

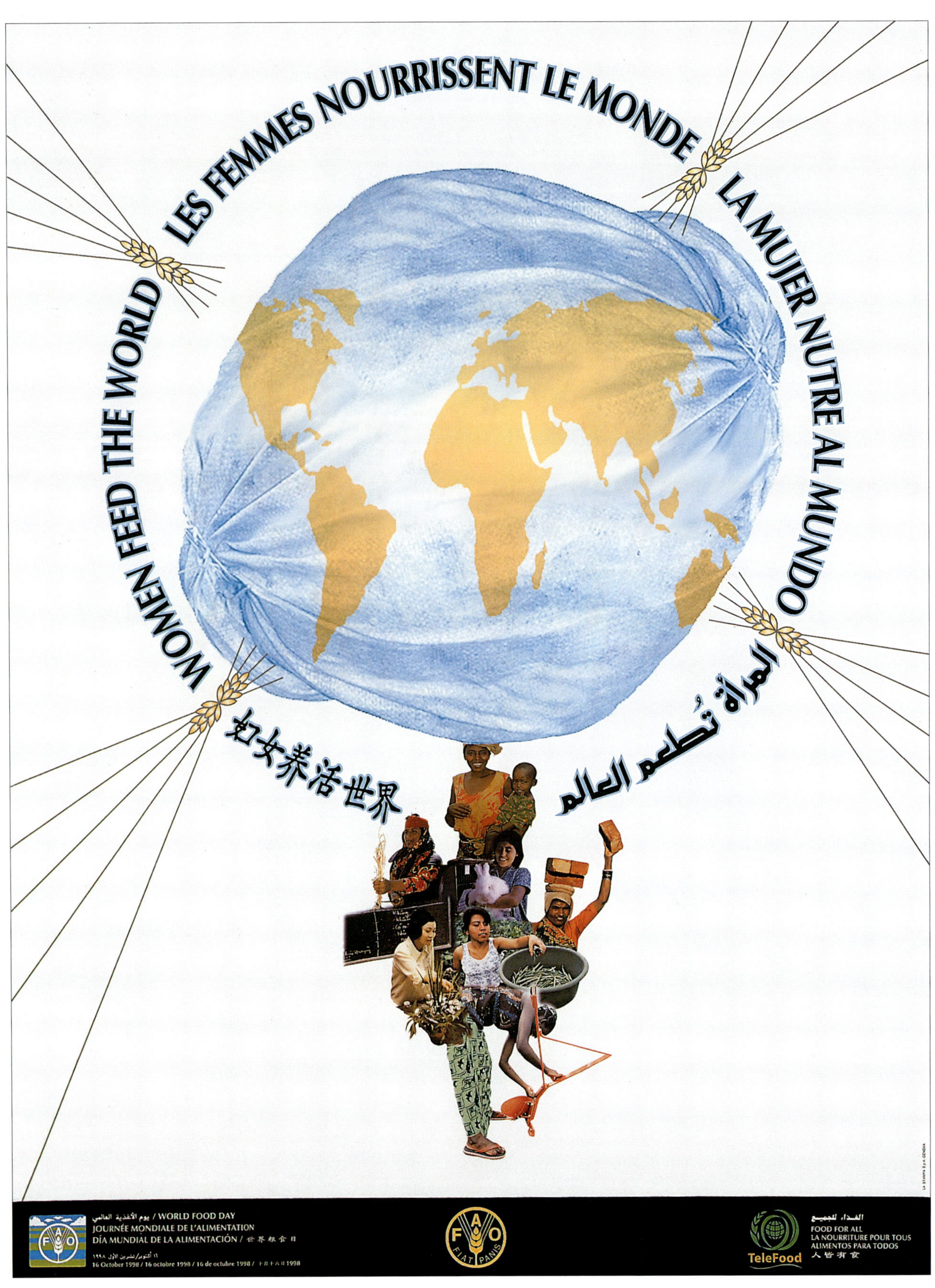

115. Women Feed the World, *World Food Day 1998, art by La Stampa SpA., Genoa, Italy, from* TeleFood *series (Food and Agriculture Organization poster).*

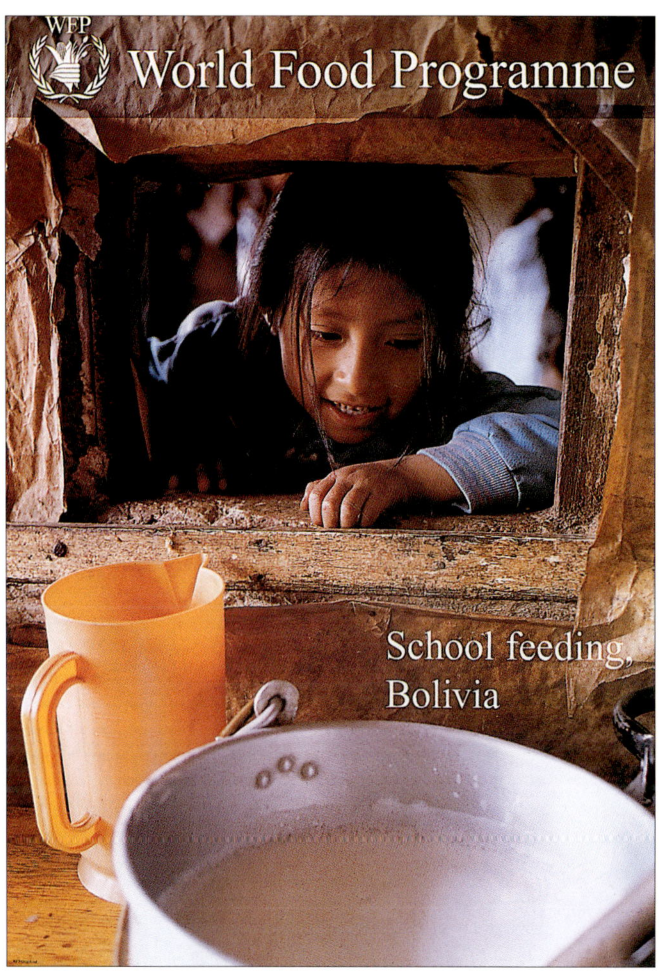

116. *World Food Programme, Bolivia. One of a series on global hunger. Photo by Greg Kind.*

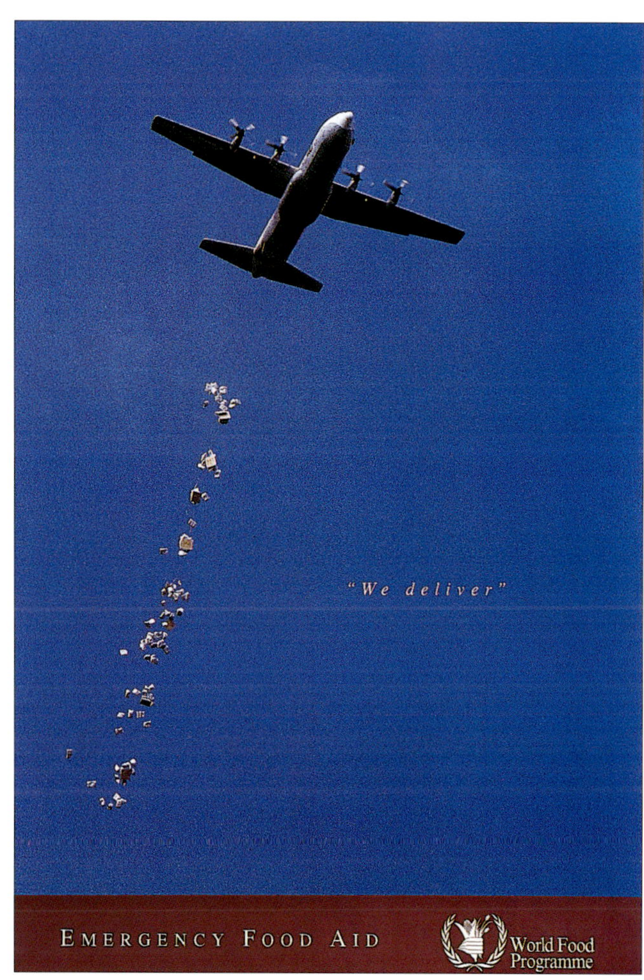

117. *We Deliver, World Food Programme. Shows air drop of relief food.*

The **World Food Programme (WFP), Rome** is the largest food aid organization in the world, buying more goods and services from developing countries—in an effort to reinforce their economies—than any other UN agency. The WFP has delivered two-thirds of the world's emergency food assistance, saving millions of lives. The program's "food-for-work" assistance helps recipients to become self-reliant, and other innovative social development projects help overcome the obstacles of hunger and poverty. The WFP provides food in ways that prepare people to help themselves and reduce reliance on international food assistance.

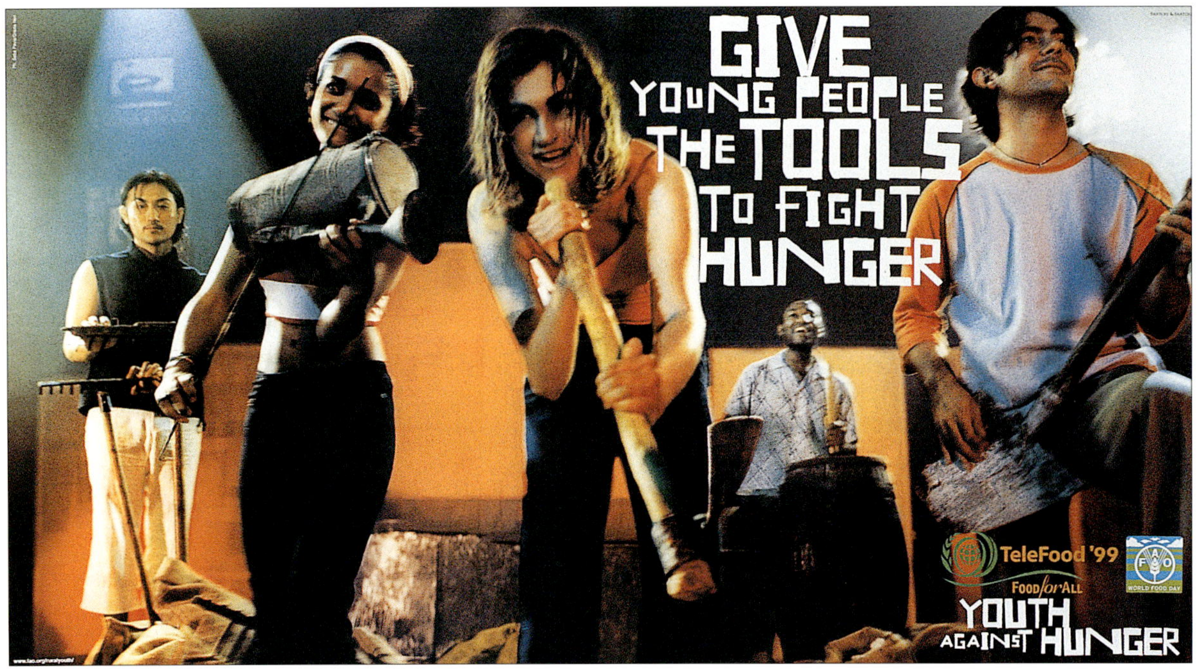

118. Give Young People the Tools to Fight Hunger, *art by Seba Pavia/Grazi Neri, from* TeleFood *series.*
Courtesy of Saatchi & Saatchi International Advertising Agency (Food and Agriculture Organization poster).

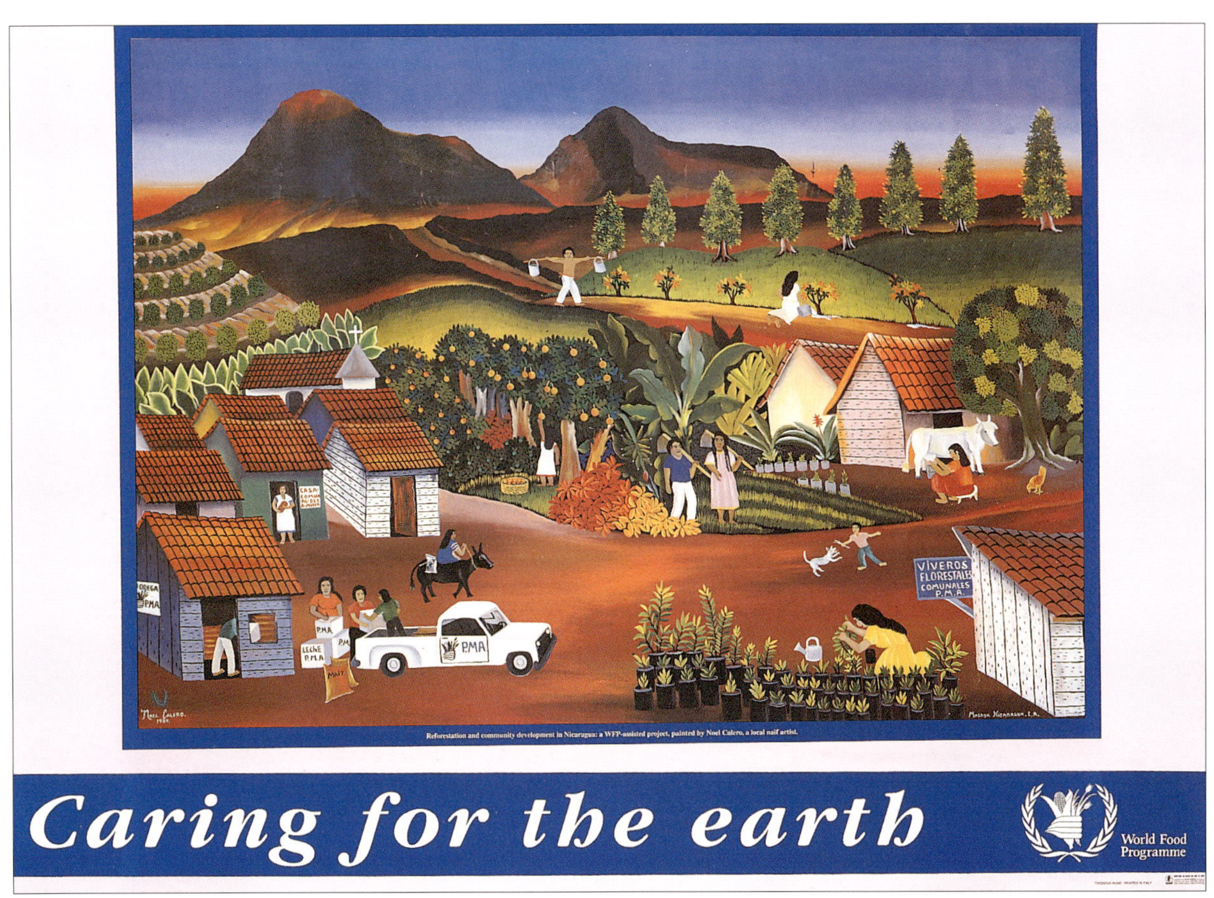

119. Caring for the Earth, *1989–90 by Nicaraguan artists Noel Calero and Otavio Fonseca, design by Masaya.*
Printed in Italy (World Food Programme poster).

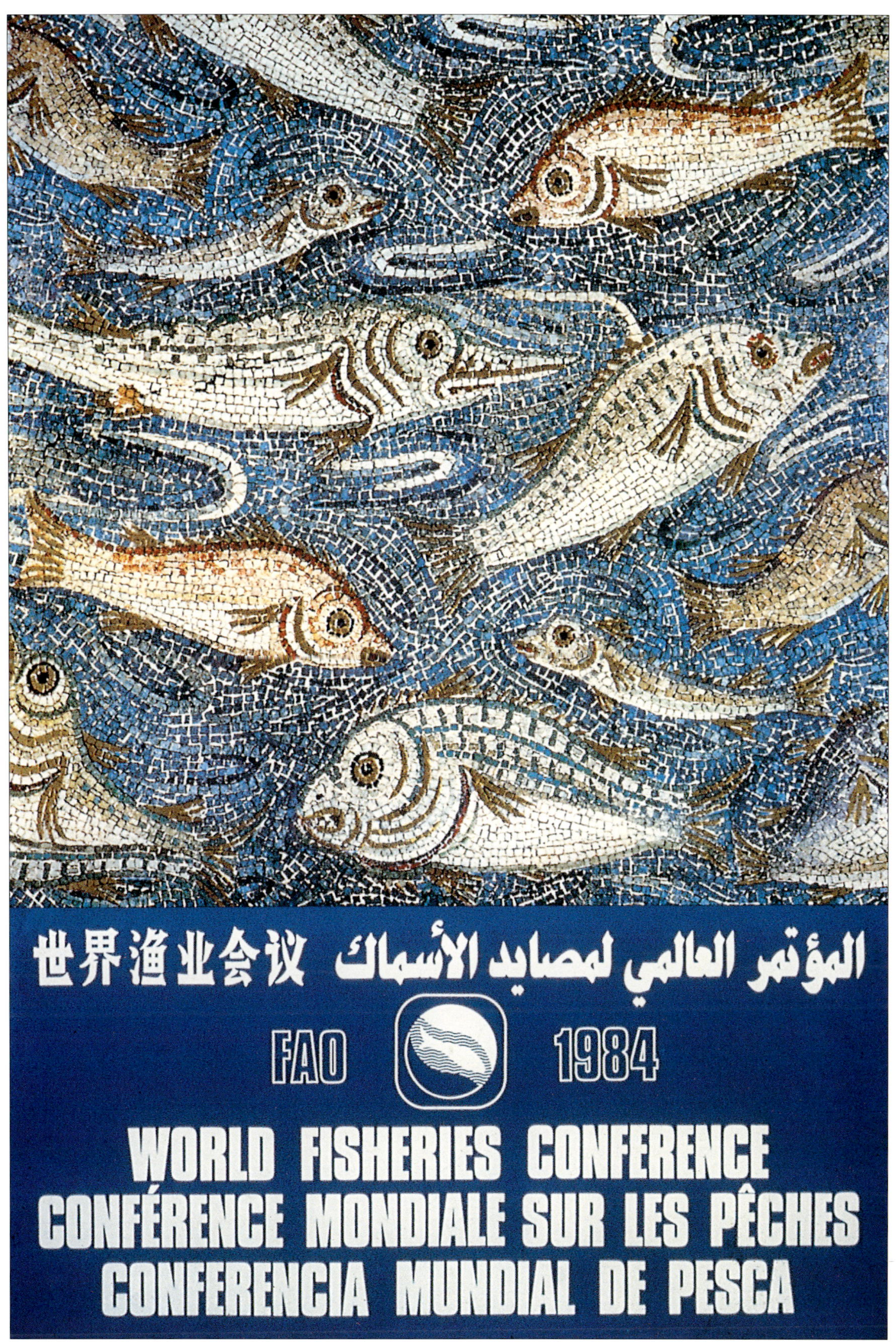

120. *World Fisheries Conference, 1984, printed in English, Spanish, French, Chinese and Arabic (Food and Agriculture Organization poster).*

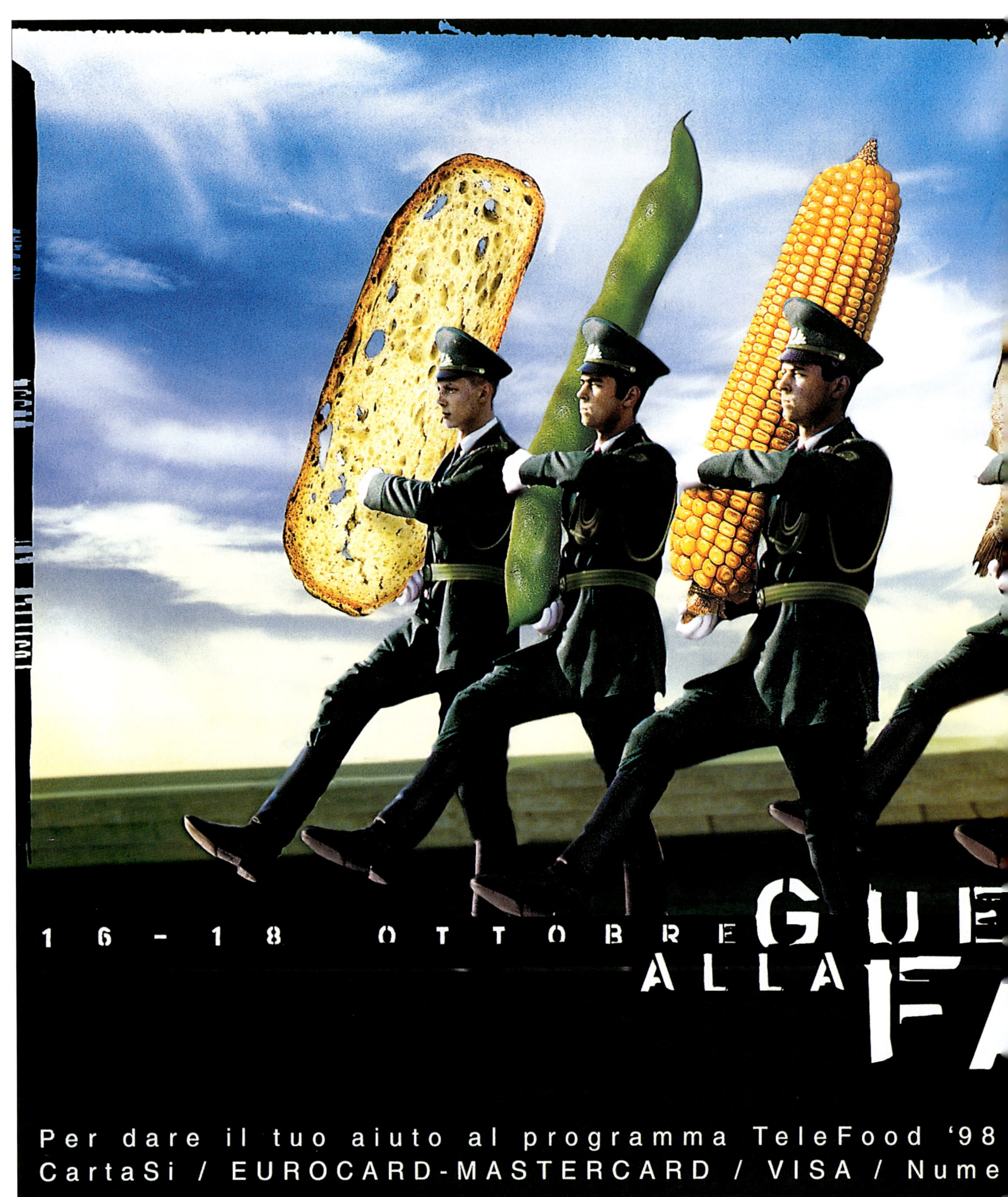

121. Food for All, 1998, *from* Telefood *series. Courtesy of Saatchi & Saatchi International Advertising Agency, printed in French and Italian (Food and Agriculture Organization poster).*

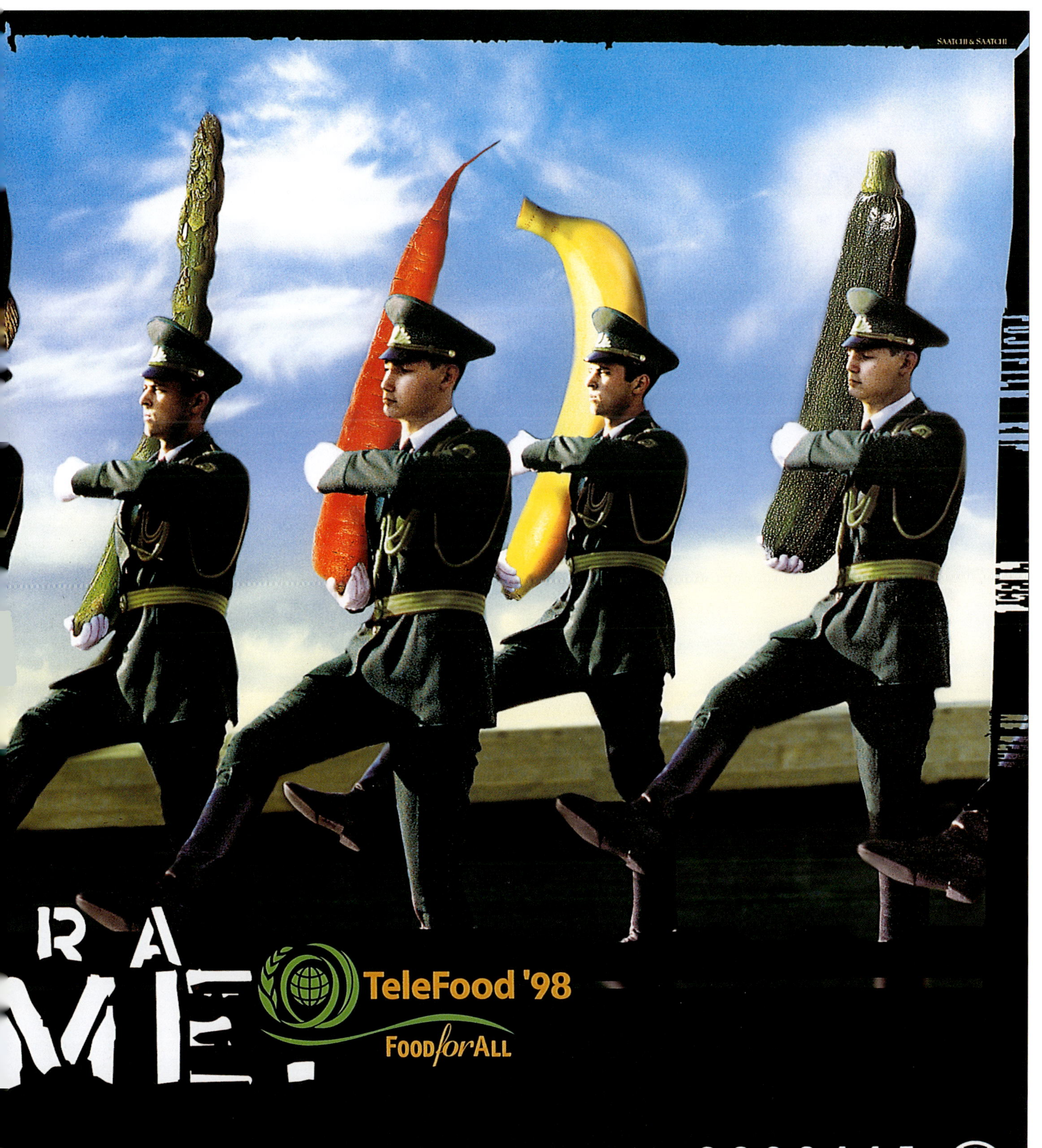

SAATCHI & SAATCHI
R A
ME!
TeleFood '98
Food for All
ICA COMMERCIALE ITALIANA C/C 2233445
rde 167.00.19.19 ■ C/C postale 997007
FAO

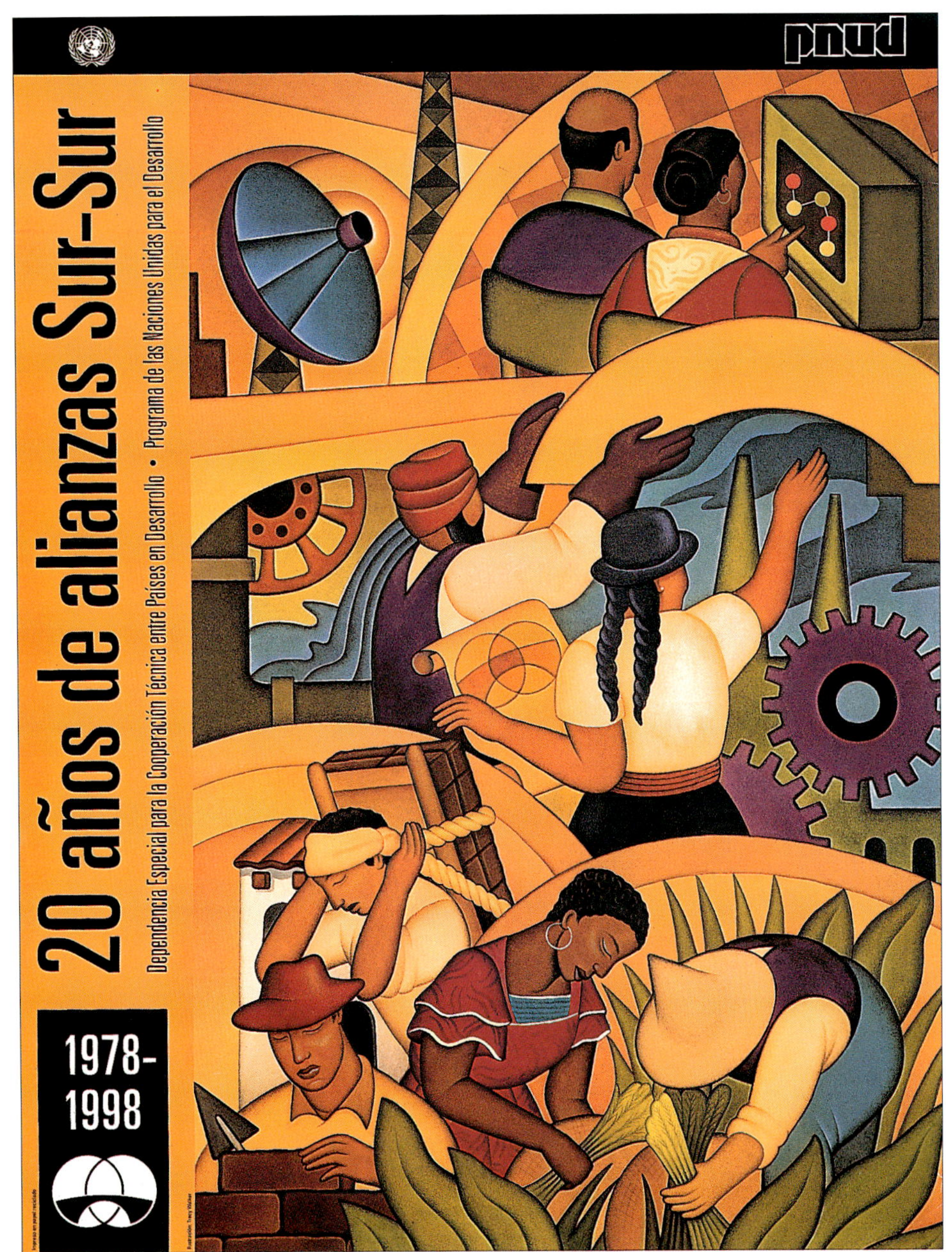

122. Twenty Years of South-South Technical Cooperation, 1978–1988 *(Spanish version), art by Tracy Walker (UN and UN Development Programme poster)*

The **United Nations Development Programme (UNDP), New York** is the world's largest multilateral source of grants for sustainable human development. Established in 1965, the UNDP was given three primary goals: help the UN become a powerful and cohesive force for sustainable human development, focus resources on objectives central to human development — poverty elimination, environmental regeneration, job creation and advancement of women — and strengthen international cooperation for sustainable human development while serving as a major substantive resource to facilitate this cooperation. The UNDP is governed by a thirty-six-member executive board with representatives from both developing and developed countries. Among UNDP's major publications is the annual *Human Development Report*.

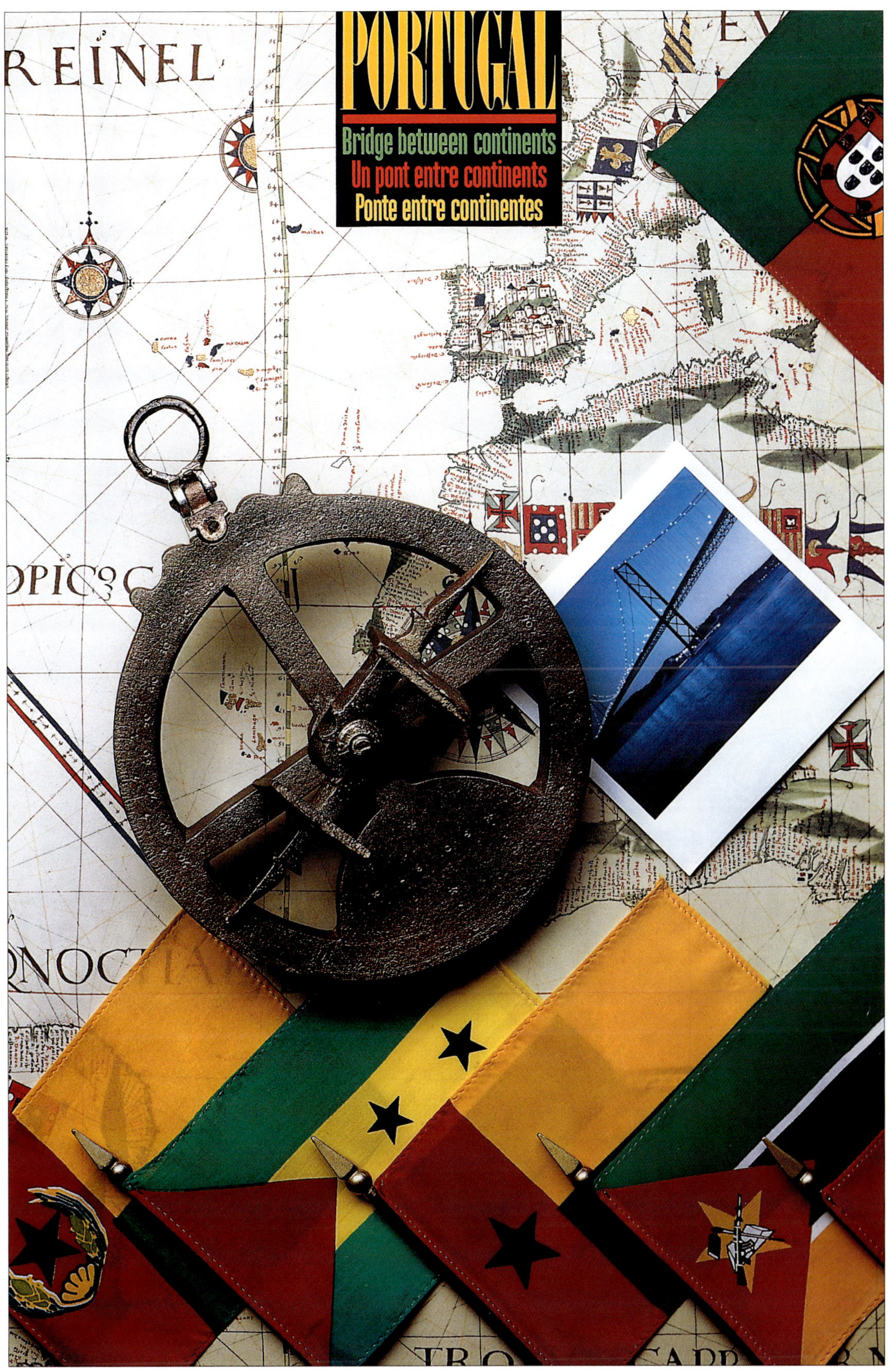

123. Portugal—A Bridge Between Continents, *designed by Emerson, Wajdowicz Studios, New York, art direction by Maureen Lynch. Photo by Terry Hefferman (UN Development Programme poster).*

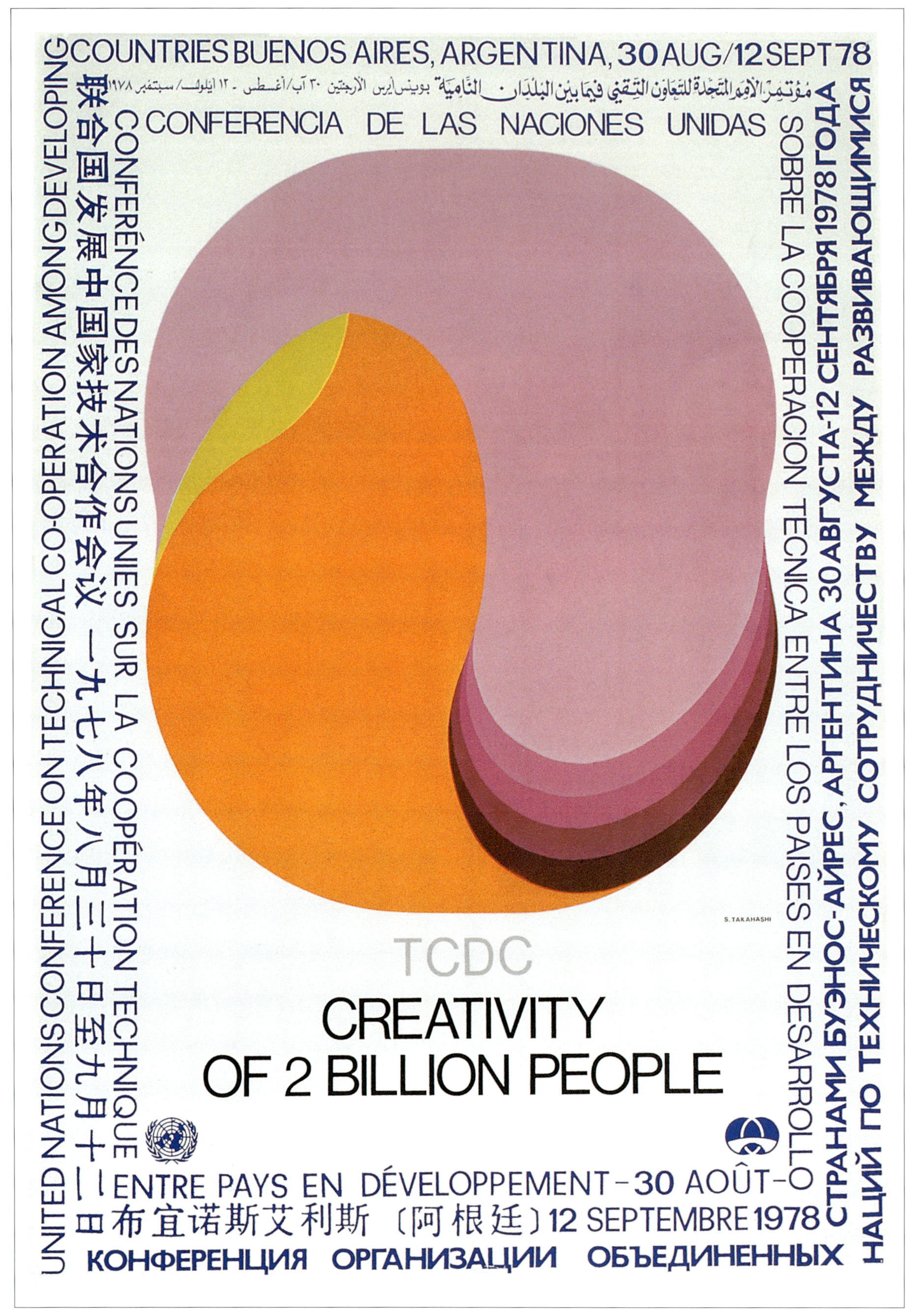

130. Creativity of Two Billion People, *art by Ikuo Hirayama (UN Development Programme/Technical Cooperation with Developing Countries poster).*

131. Shipping and the Oceans,
*poster commemorating
International Maritime
Organization's fiftieth
anniversary, produced by
Thai Harbour Department,
Ministry of Transport and
Communication, Apisara
Naree, Bangkok, Thailand.
Depicts a container ship with
dolphins and clown fish
among sea anemone.*

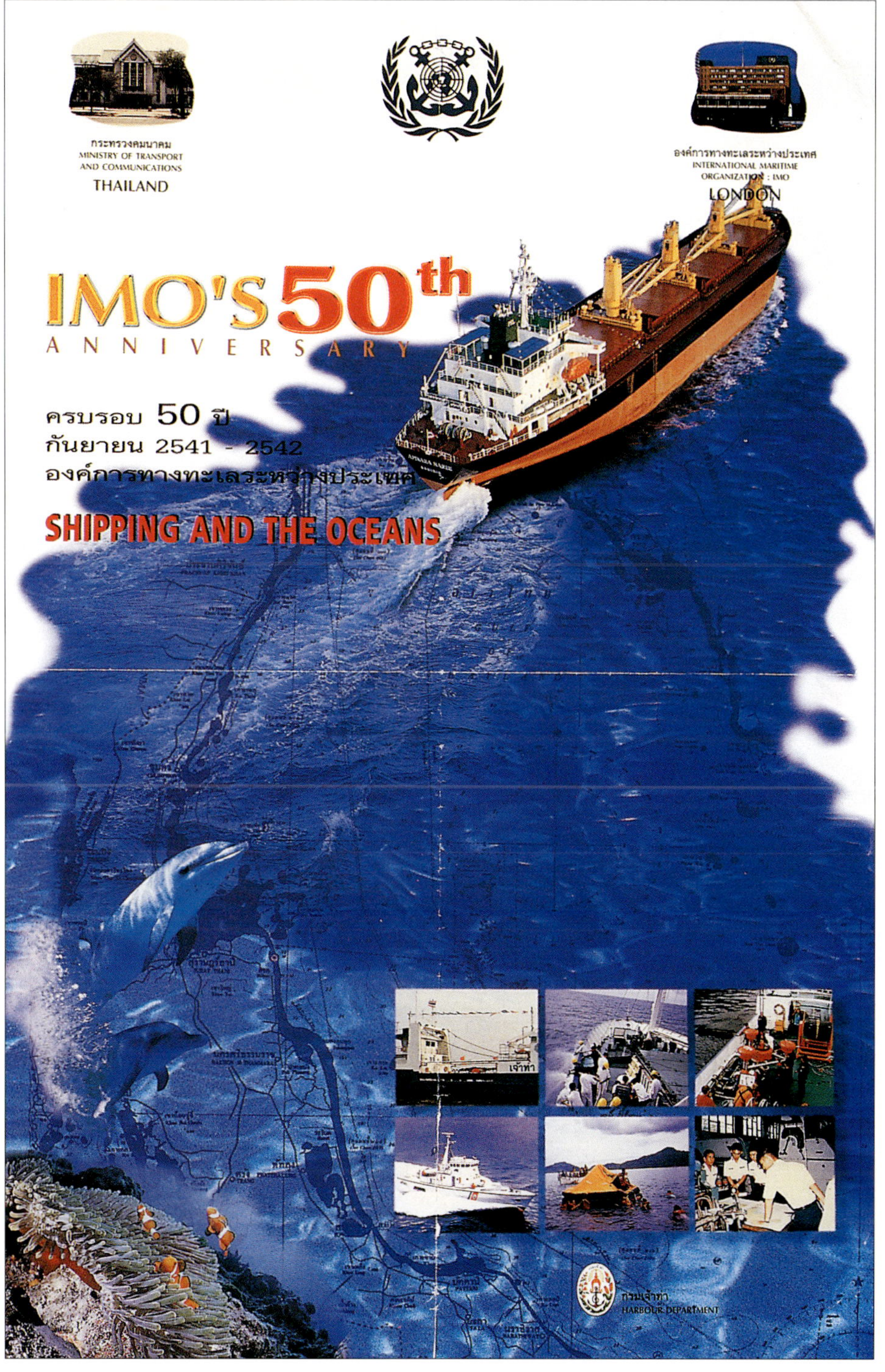

The **International Maritime Organization (IMO), London** is the UN agency exclusively concerned with safe shipping and clean oceans. The IMO's main objective is to facilitate cooperation among governments on technical matters affecting international shipping and thus achieve the highest standards of maritime safety and efficiency in navigation. Established in 1959, the IMO helps to protect the marine environment by preventing pollution caused by ships and other craft. It has drafted international conventions for the safety of life at sea, the prevention of marine pollution by ships, the training and certification of seafarers, the prevention of collisions at sea, and many others.

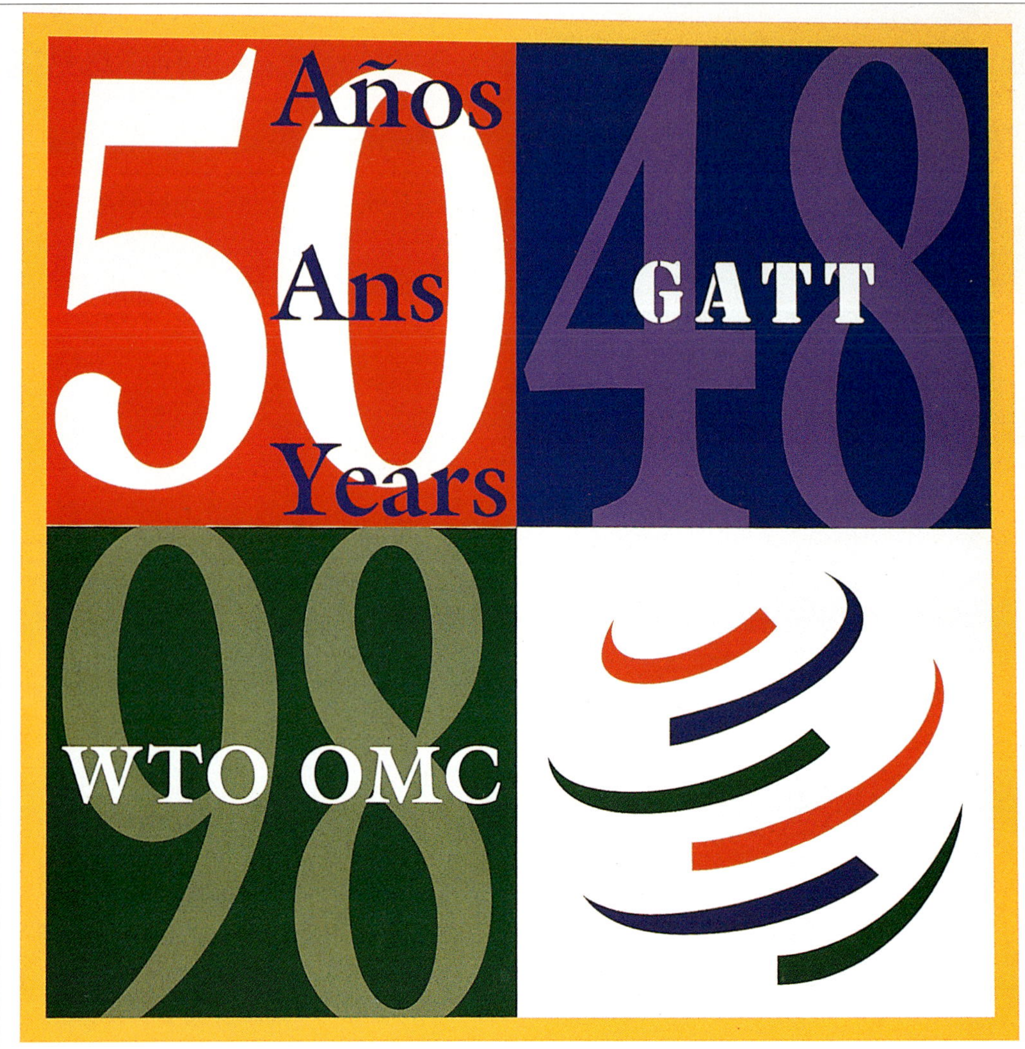

132. Poster commemorating fiftieth anniversary of the multilateral trading system, 1998. GATT (General Agreement of Tariffs and Trade) was a predecessor UN agency to the World Trade Organization (World Trade Organization poster).

The **World Trade Organization (WTO), Geneva** was established in 1995, following the dissolution of the General Agreement on Tariffs and Trade (GATT). The WTO focuses on technical cooperation in trade promotion.

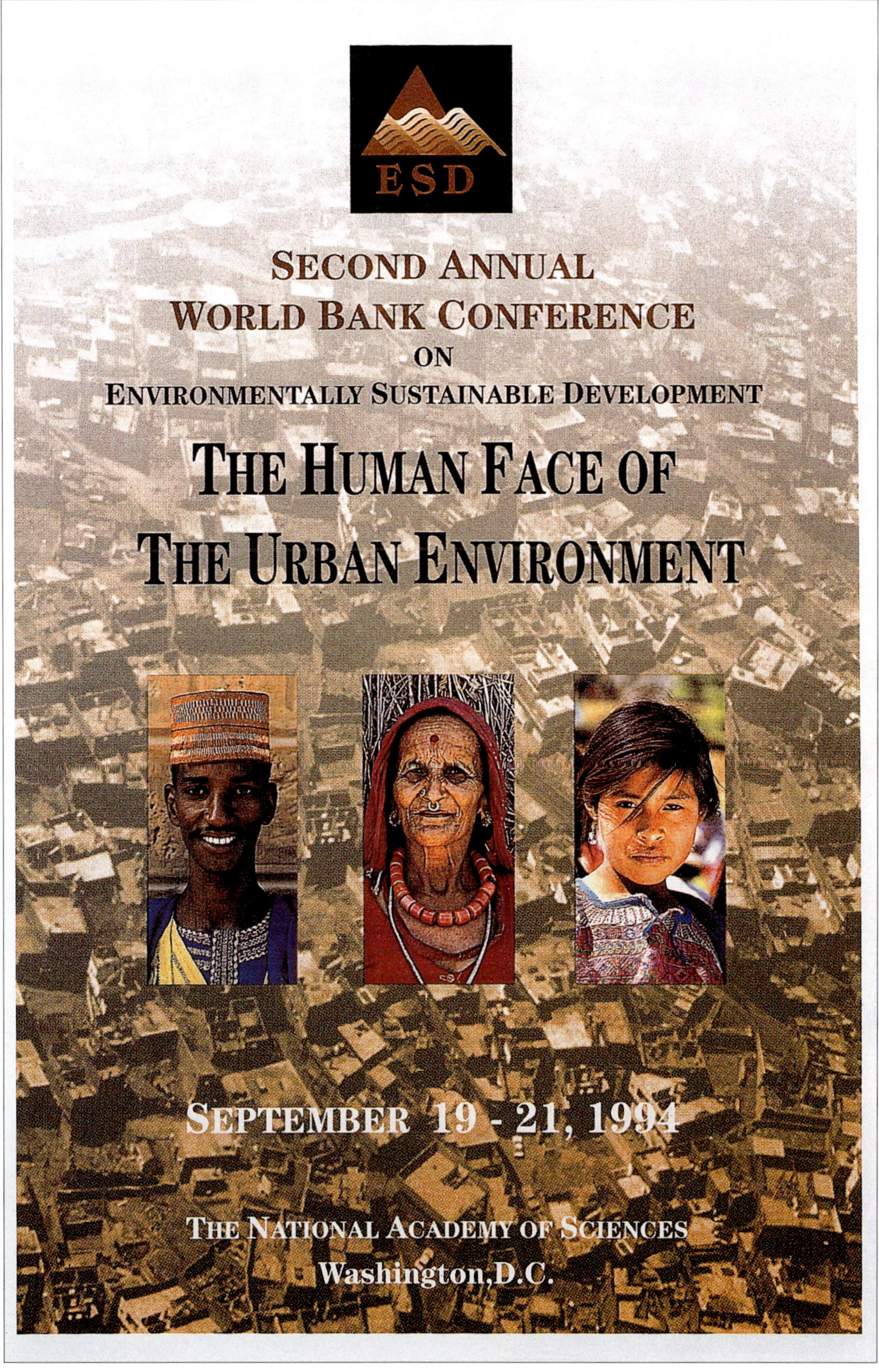

The **World Bank, Washington, D.C.,** was established in 1945. Its goal has been to reduce poverty around the world and strengthen the economies of developing nations by facilitating the international flow of capital for productive purposes and assisting in the reconstruction of nations devastated by war. International capital markets fund about 90 percent of the bank's lending, and $11 billion in capital has been paid in to the bank by its shareholders over the past fifty-four years. That amount has been leveraged into more than $280 billion in loans.

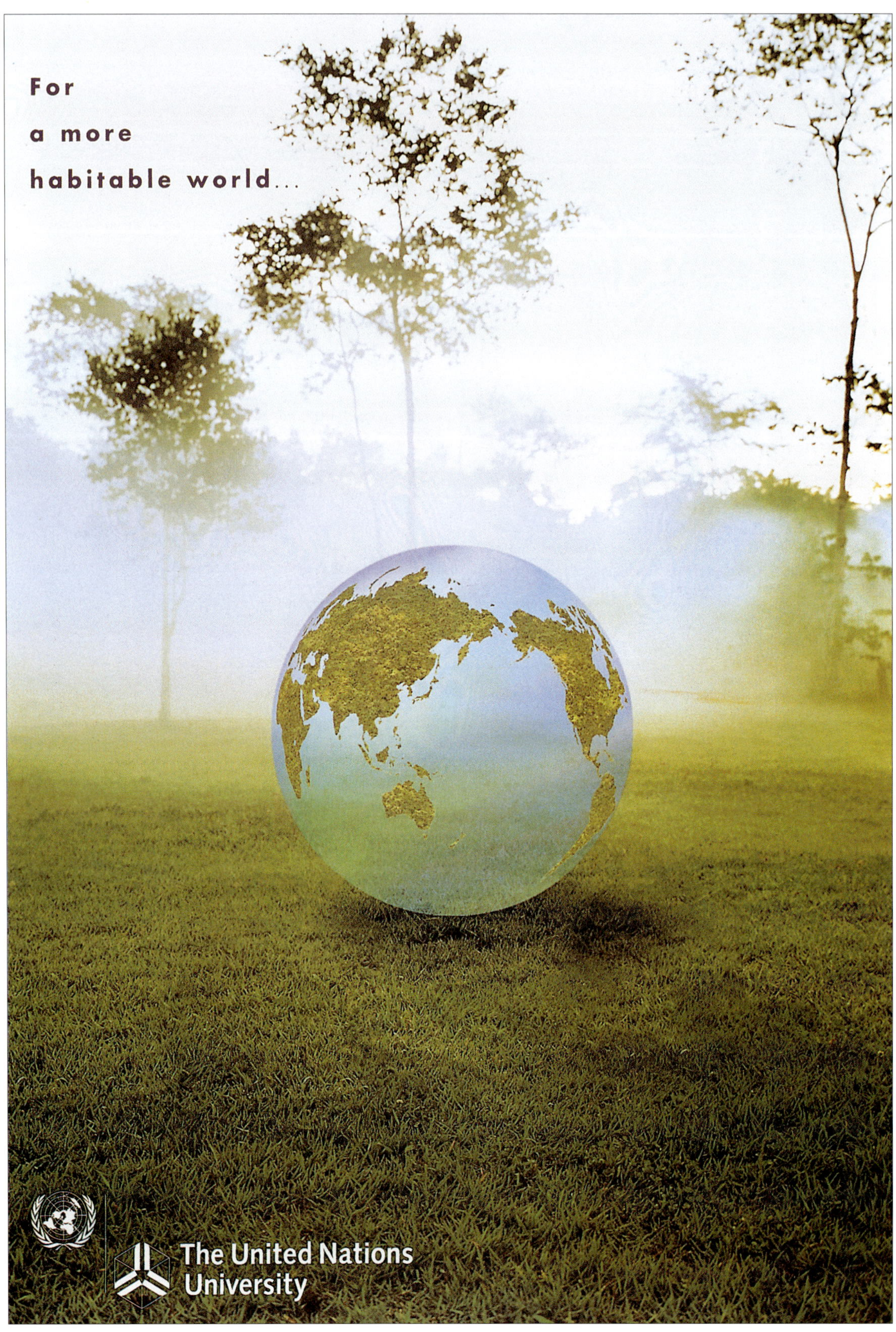

136. For a More Habitable World, *1997 (UN University poster).*

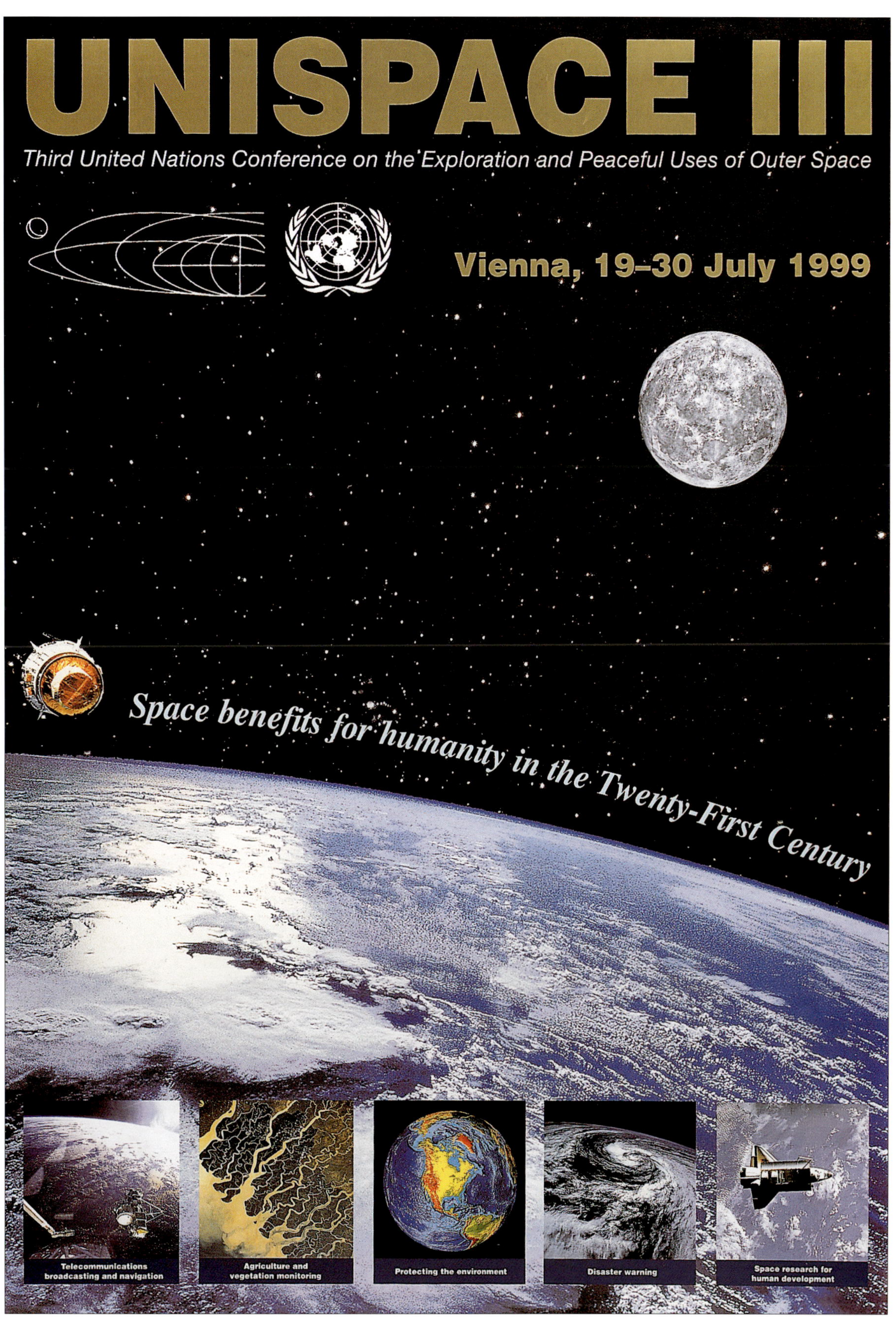

137. Space Benefits for Humanity in the Twenty-First Century, *poster for UNISPACE III, third UN conference on the exploration and peaceful uses of outer space, Vienna, 19–30 July 1999.*

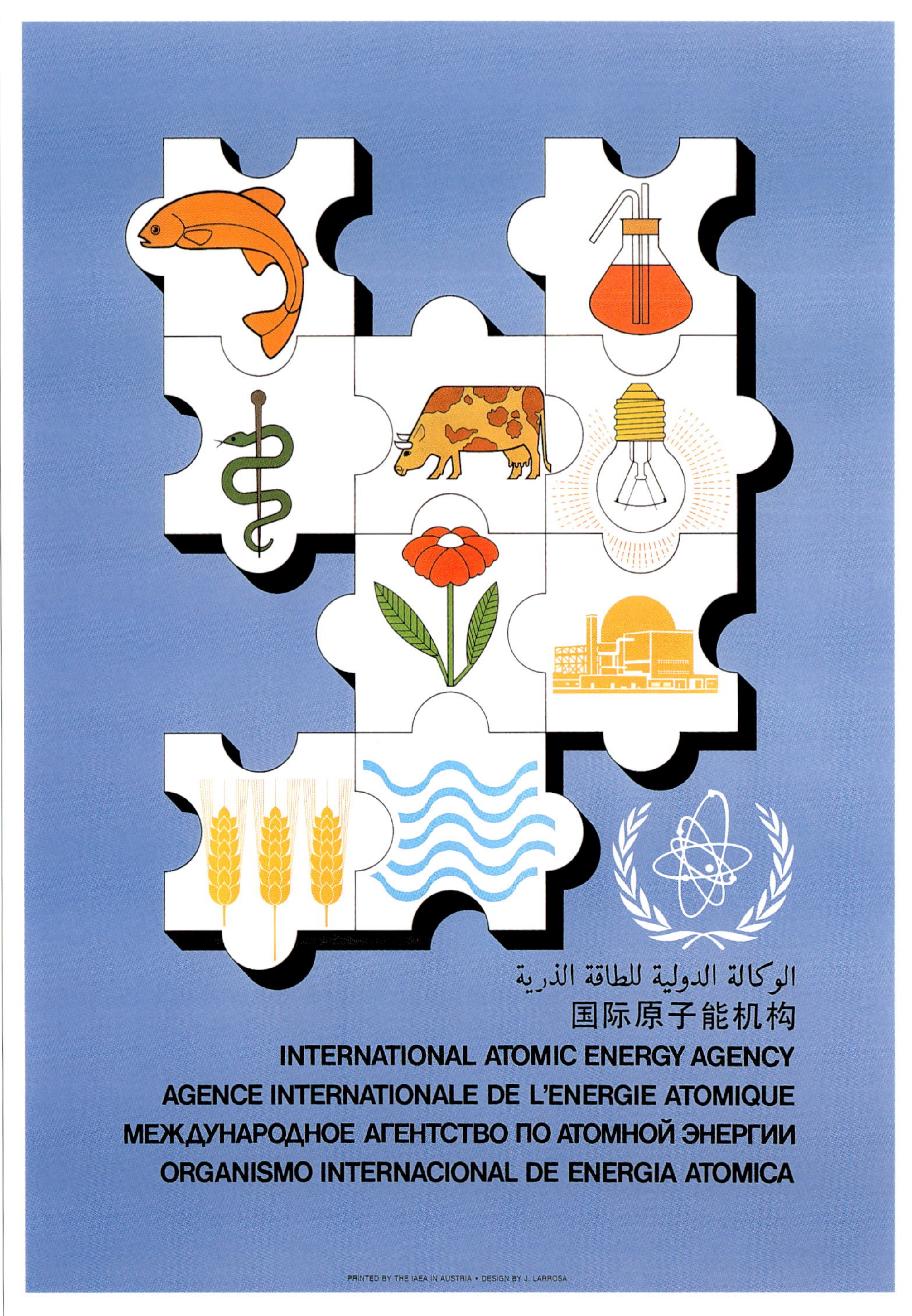

143. International Atomic Energy Agency poster, designed by J. Larrosa, printed in Austria. Puzzle pieces of various symbols: corn, wheat, fish, globe, flower, laboratory flasks.

The **International Atomic Energy Agency (IAEA), Vienna** plays a prominent role in international efforts aimed at preventing the proliferation of nuclear weapons. It serves as the world's international inspectorate for the application of nuclear safeguards and verification measures covering civilian nuclear programs. The IAEA's aim is to ensure that nuclear material held in a thousand nuclear installations in seventy countries is not diverted from legitimate peaceful uses to military purposes. It reinforces efforts to halt the spread of nuclear arms and aims to bring about a world free of nuclear weapons.

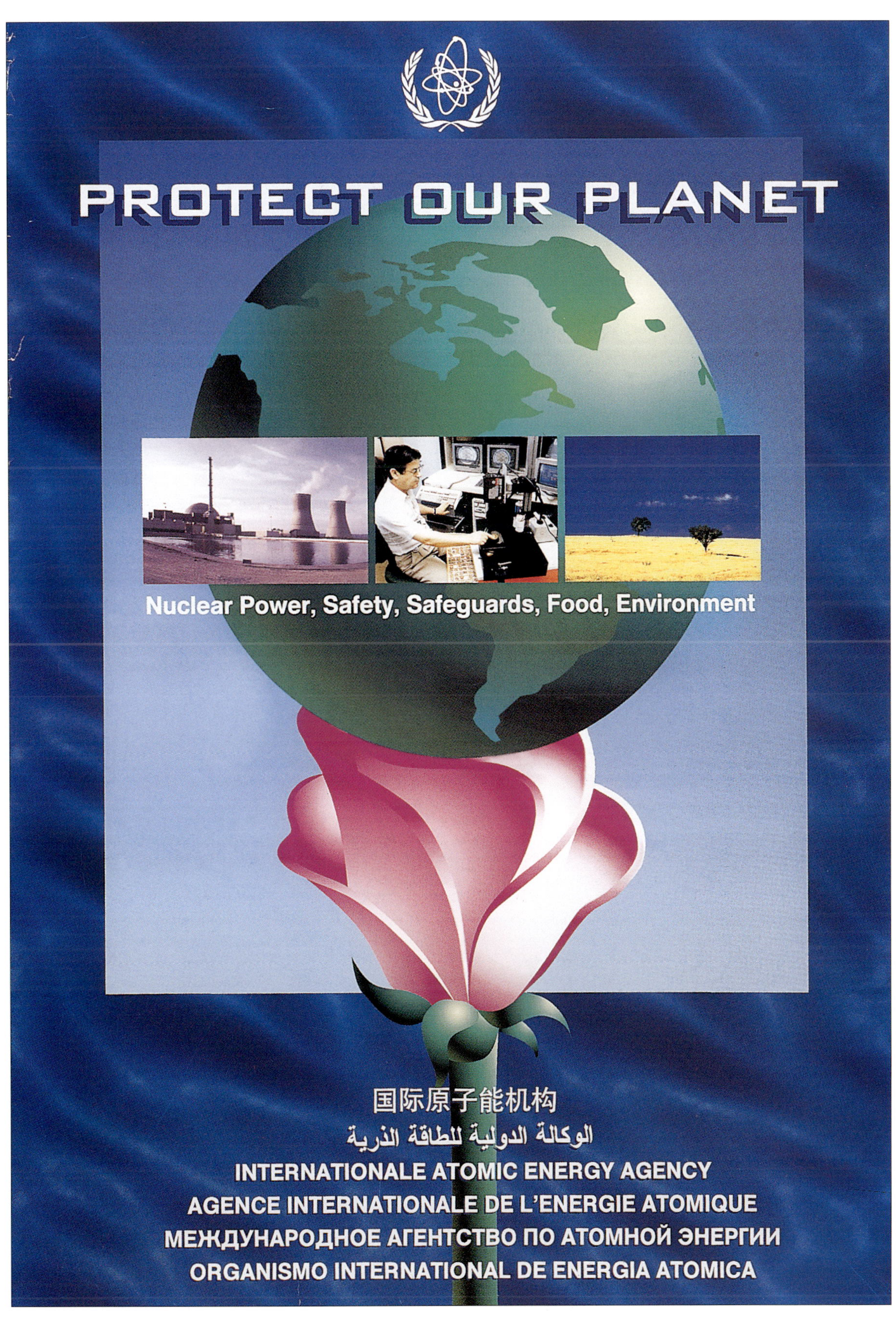

144. Protect our Planet, *International Atomic Energy Agency, Vienna.*
Globe and photos illustrate nuclear power safeguards.

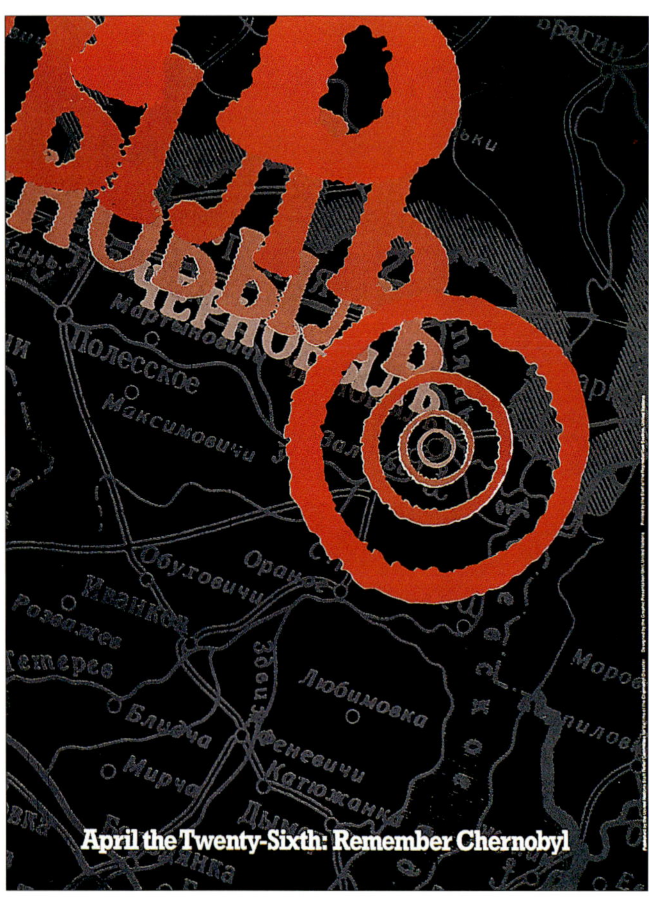

145. Remember Chernobyl, 1996, *designed by Maxim Żhukov, Graphic Design Section, UN Department of Public Information, for World Environment Day, April 26, (UN Staff Relief Committee for Victims of the Chernobyl Disaster poster).*

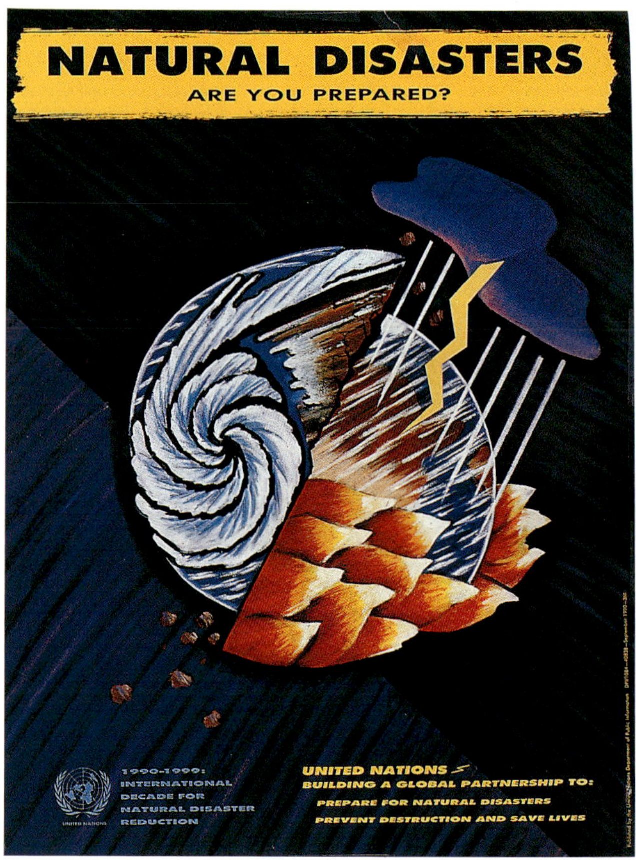

146. Are You Prepared? *illustration by Terrance Cummings, design and art direction by Jan Arnesen, UN Department of Public Information, for a conference on preparedness for natural disasters.*

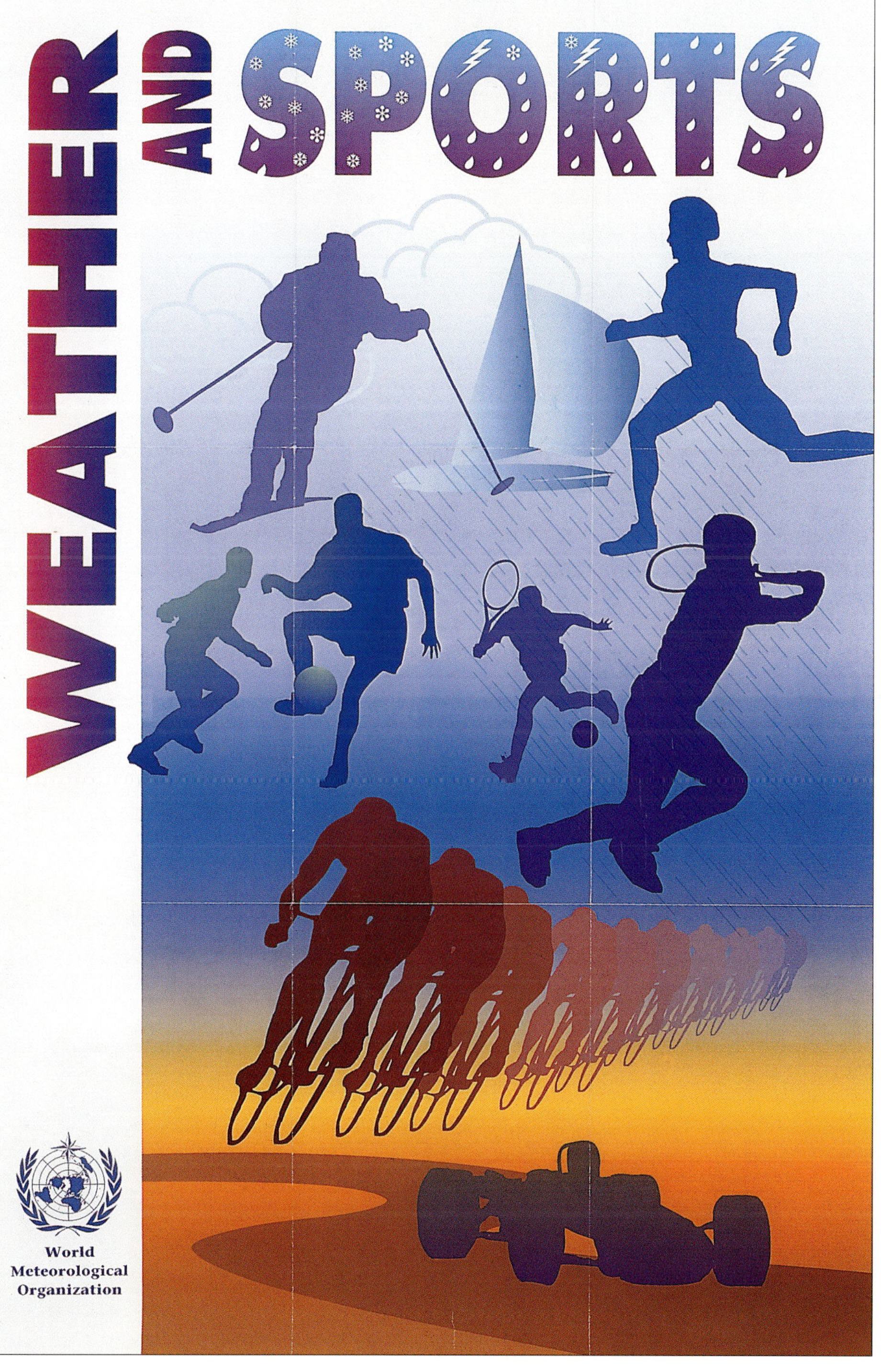

147. Weather and Sports,
*World Meteorological
Organization poster.*

The **World Meteorological Organization (WMO), Geneva** provides authoritative scientific information on the atmospheric environment, Earth's freshwater resources, and other climate issues. Established in 1951, the WMO offers weather-forecasting services, including seasonal forecasting. Through international collaboration, the WMO tracks global weather conditions, making the rapid exchange of weather information possible and facilitating better preparation and forewarning of severe weather. The organization's work has contributed significantly to our better understanding of the environment and the climate.

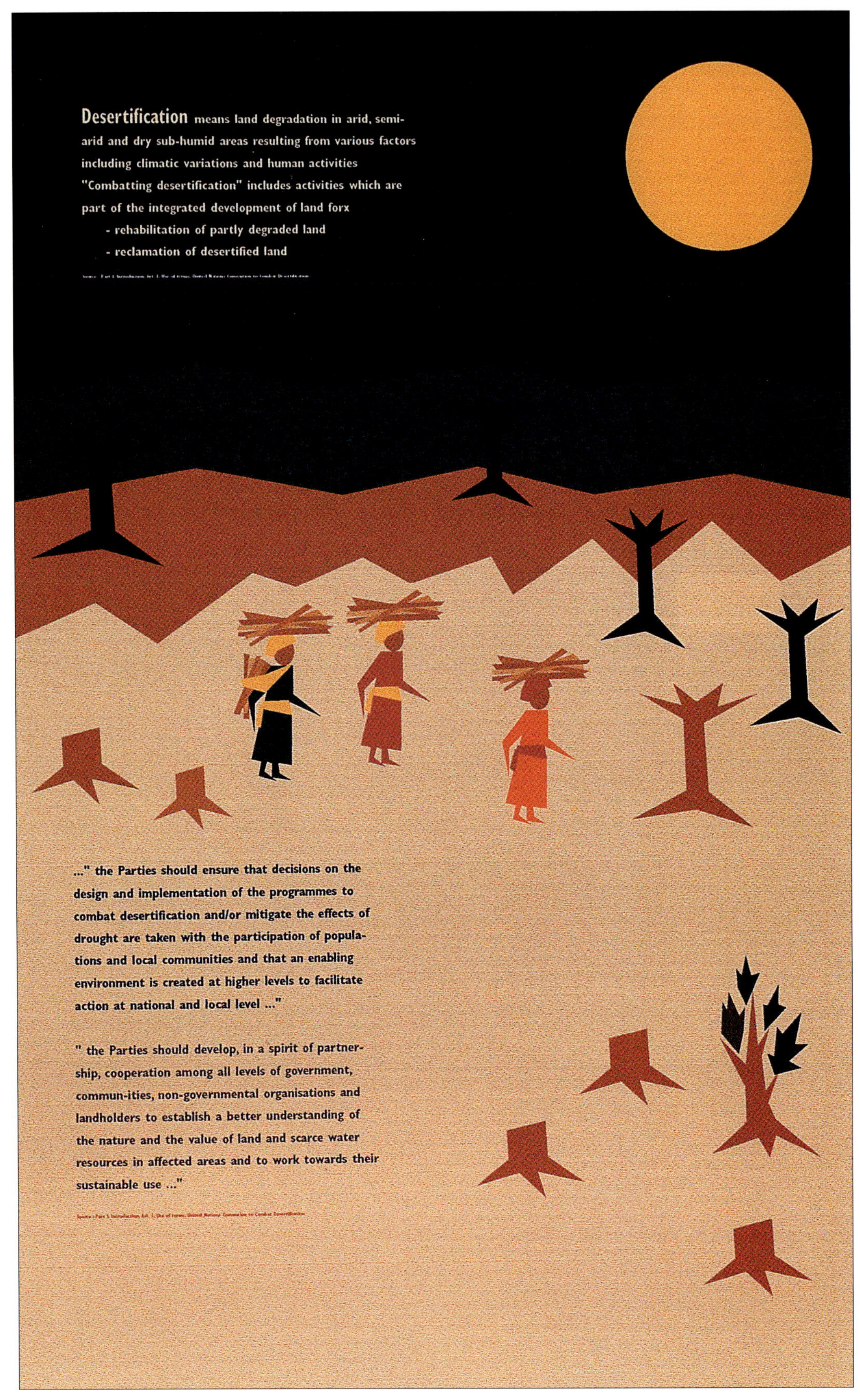

148. Desertification—South Sahel, Africa, *design and illustration by Jan Arnesen, UN Department of Public Information.*

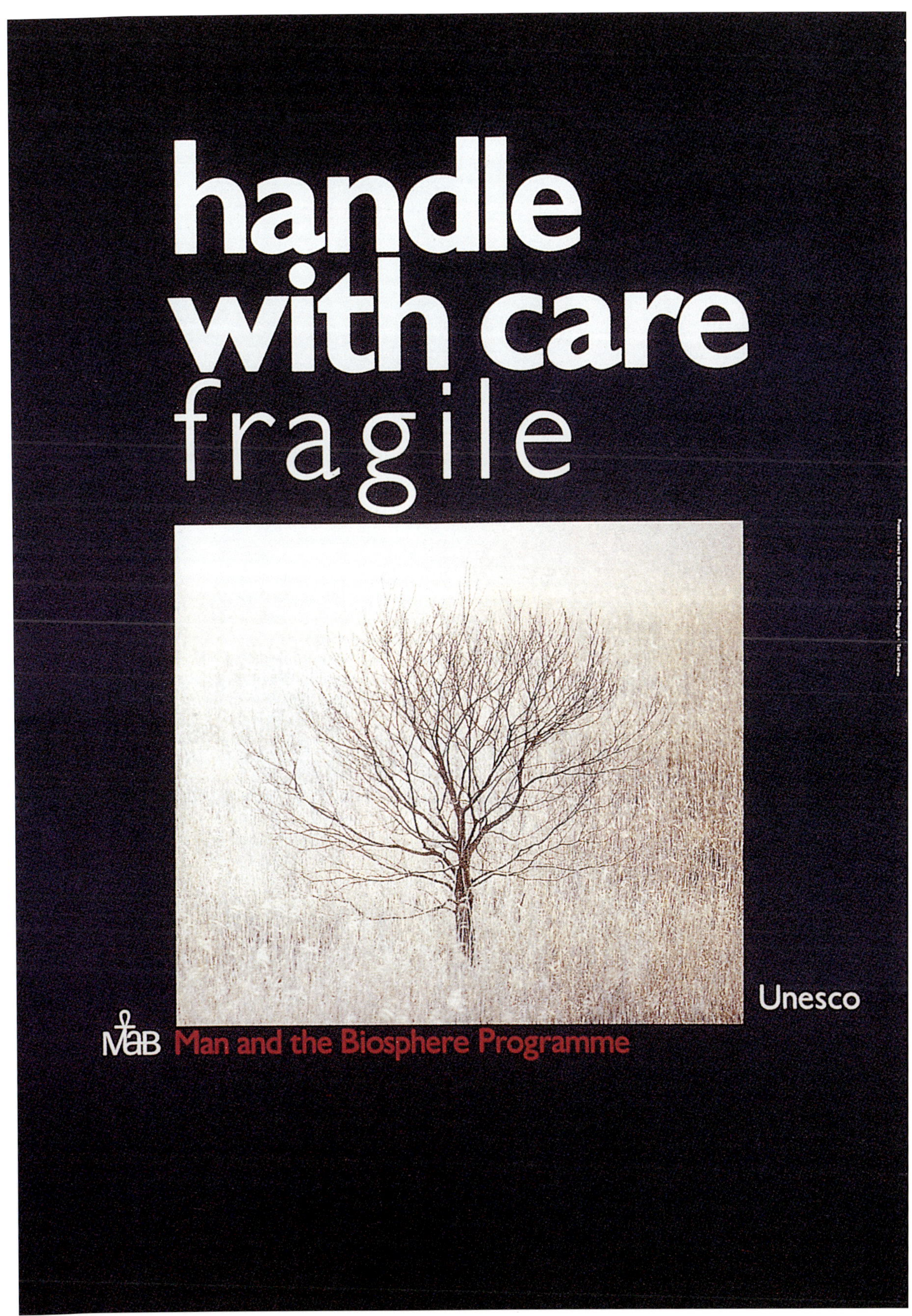

149. Handle with Care—Fragile: Man and the Biosphere Program, *1984, by Tad Wakamatau (UNESCO poster).*

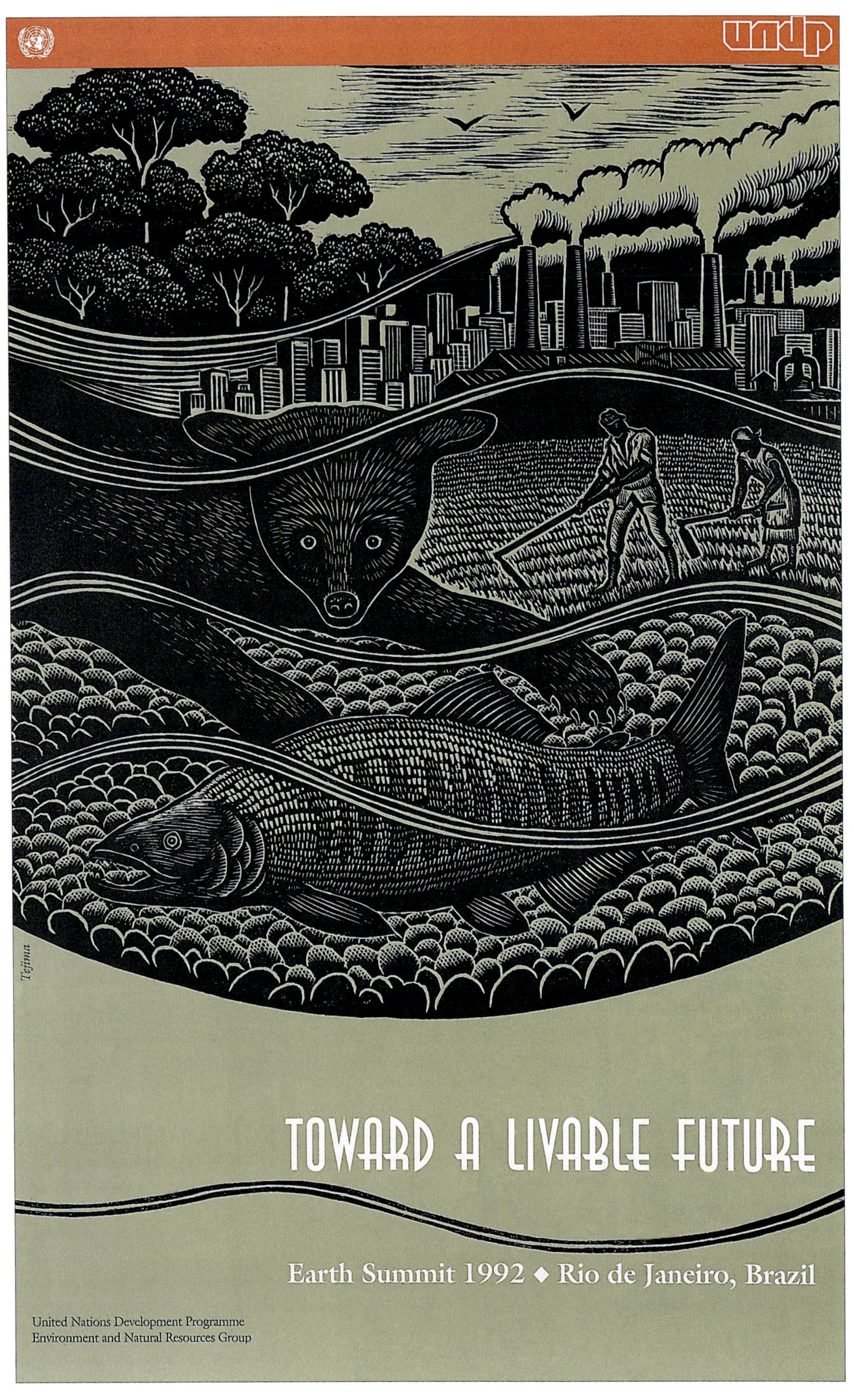

155. Toward a Livable Future, 1992, *for the Rio de Janeiro Summit Conference on the Environment. Design by Maureen Lynch, illustration by Tejima (UN Development Programme poster).*

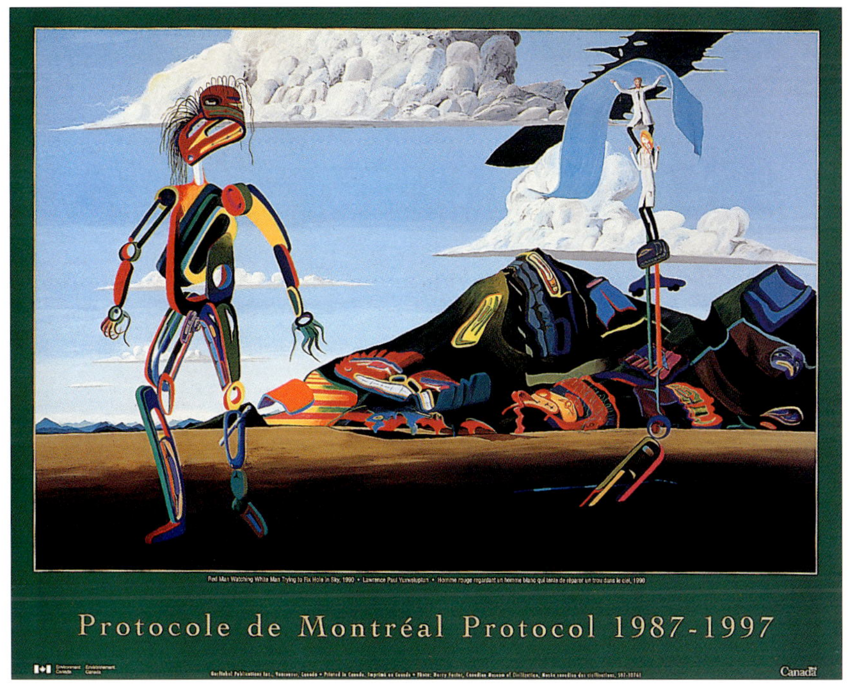

156. Montreal Protocol, 1987–1997 (French version), by Lawrence Paul Wuxweluptun, Garfinkel Publications Inc., Vancouver, British Columbia, produced in 1990 by Environment Canada. Photo by Harry Foster, Canadian Museum of Civilizations. Montreal Protocol is a program of the UNDP, UNEP, UNIDO, and the World Bank to assist developing countries protect the global ozone layer. Poster message: "Red man watching white man trying to fix hole in the sky."

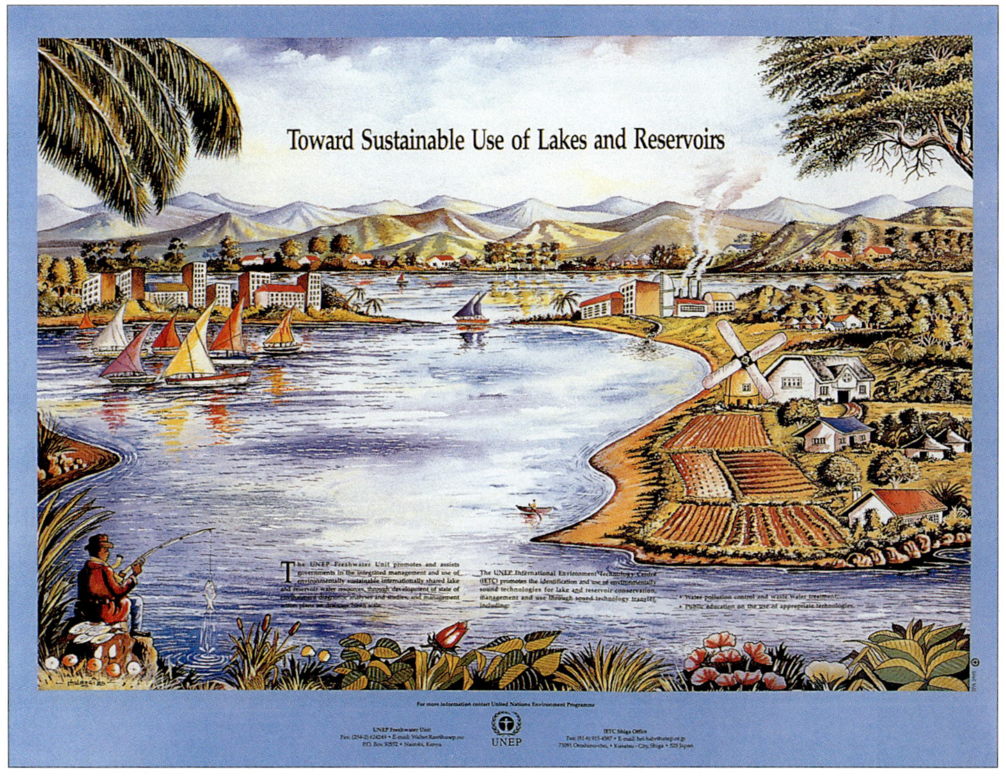

157. Lakes and Reservoirs, 1995, by Anthony Hiwangi, art direction by James Sneffen (UN Environment Programme poster).

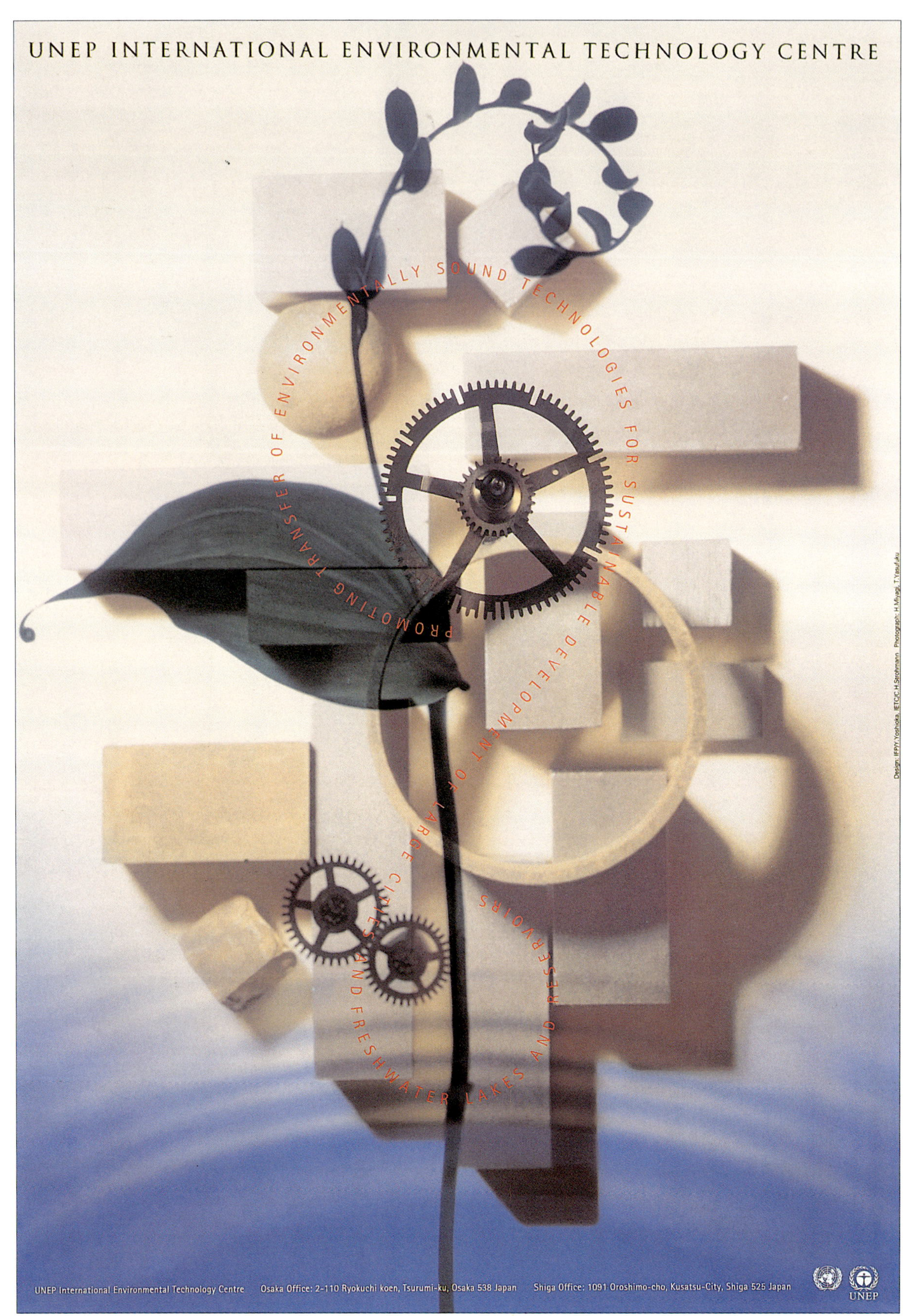

158. International Environmental Technology Center, *designed by IFP/Yoshioka and IETC/C. H. Strohmann, art direction by James Sneffen. Photo by H. Miyagi and T. Yasufuku (UN Environment Programme poster).*

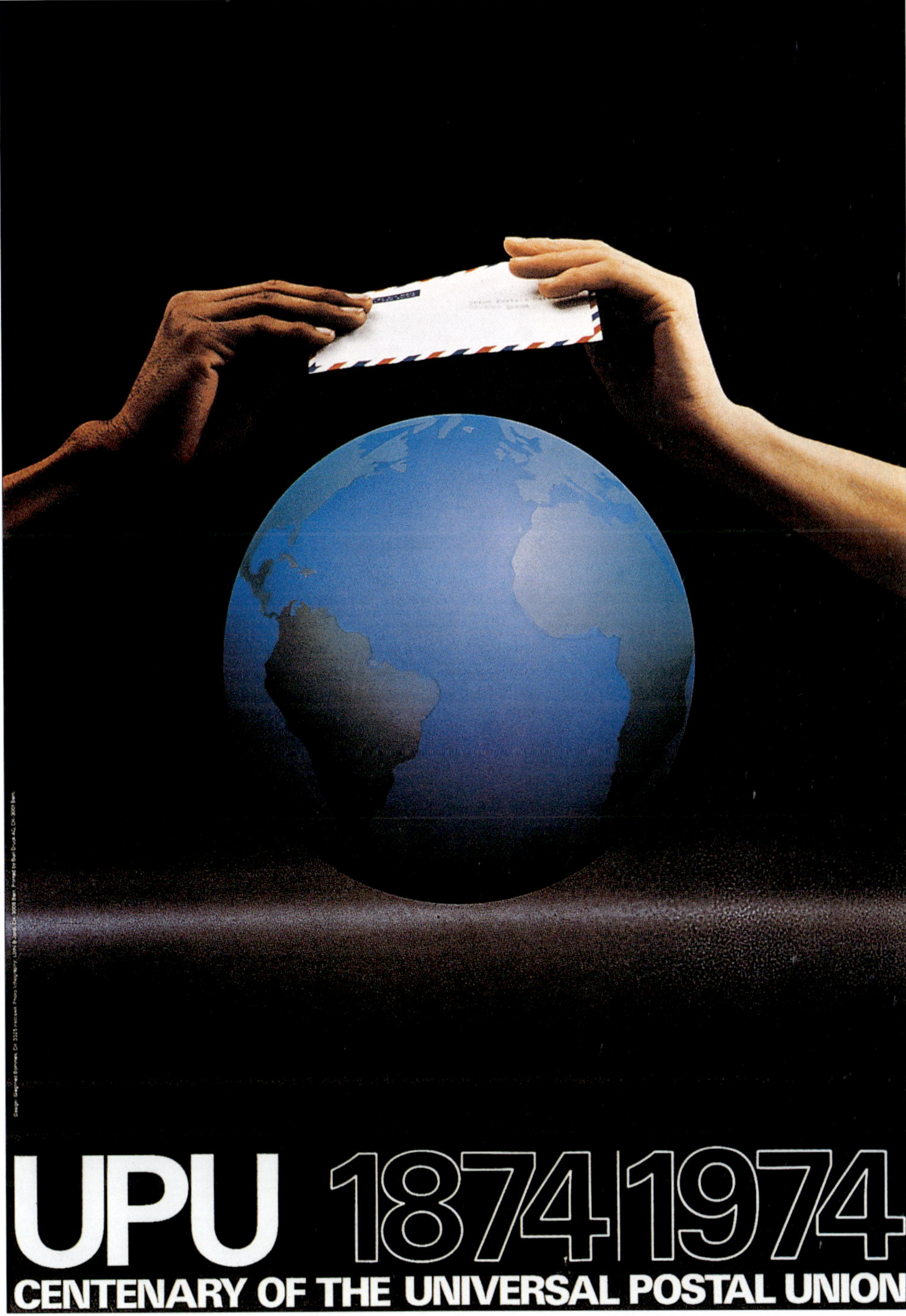

159. Poster celebrating centenary of Universal Postal Union 1874–1974, designed by Siegfried Bommeli, photo/lithography by Luthi & Jordi, printed by Buri Druck AG.

The **Universal Postal Union (UPU), Berne** was established by the Berne Treaty of 1874 and became a specialized agency of the UN in 1948. The UPU plays an important leadership role in promoting the postal services. With one hundred eighty-nine member countries, it is the primary vehicle for developing communication between all the people of the world and the cooperation between postal services. The UPU advises, mediates, and renders technical assistance. Its principal objectives include the promotion of universal postal services, growth in mail volume through the provision of up-to-date postal products and services, and improvement in the quality of postal service.

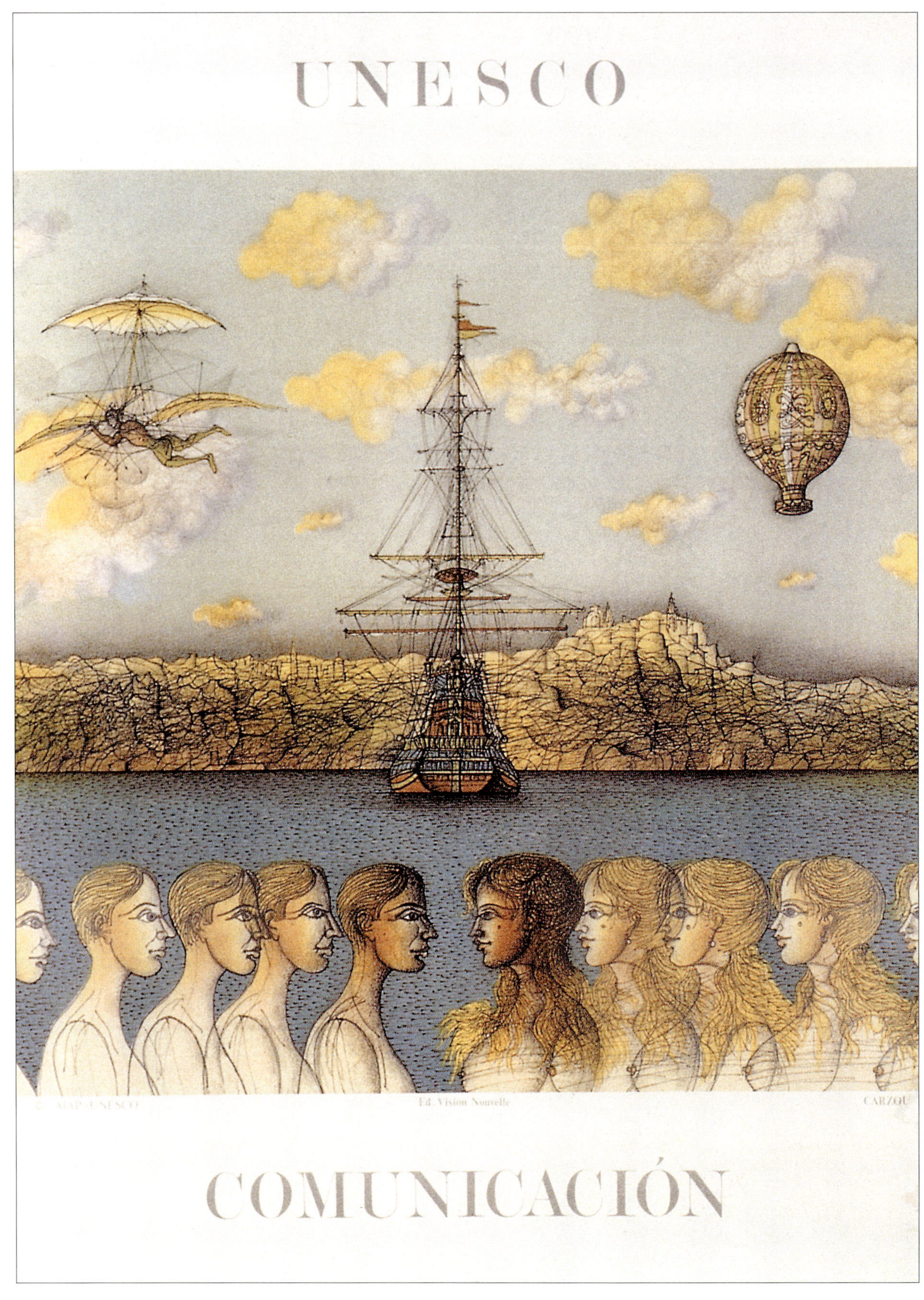

167. Communication *(Spanish version)*, 1986, by Carzou (UNESCO poster).

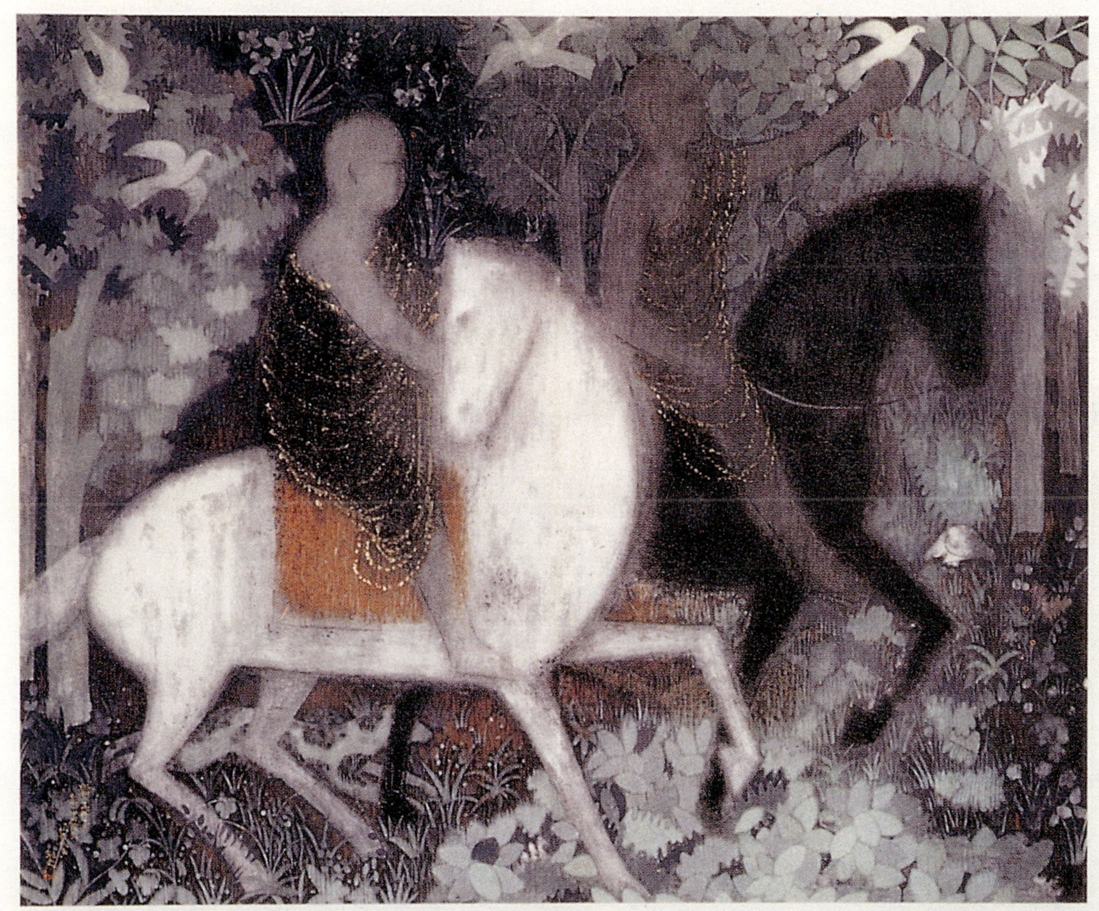

168. Silk Routes: Paths to Dialogue, 1988–1993 *(French version), by Ikuo Hirayama, 1988 (UNESCO poster).*

169. Solving Pressing Global Problems, *1997 (UN University poster).*

United Nations University (UNU), Tokyo is an international community of scholars engaged in research, postgraduate training, and the dissemination of knowledge to further the purposes and principles of the United Nations Charter. The UNU's two basic goals are to strengthen the capacities of institutions of higher learning in developing countries, carry out high-quality research and education, and make scholarly and policy-relevant contributions to the work of the UN. The UNU research and training centers collaborate with associated and cooperating institutions and individual scholars in many parts of the world. Currently, its activities are grouped within four program areas: development, environment, peace and governance, and science and technology.

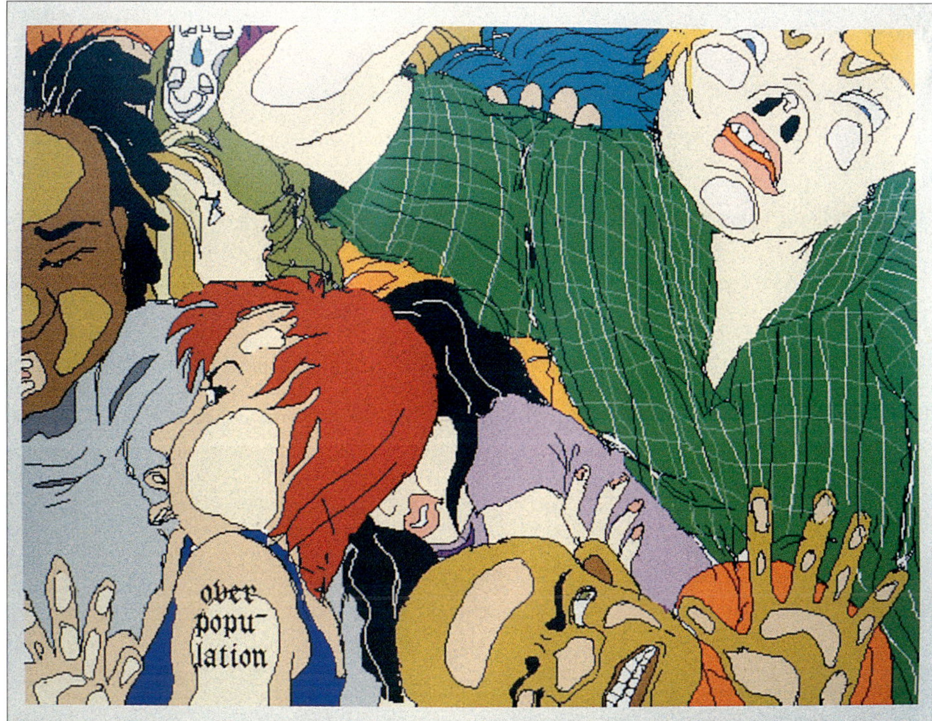

170

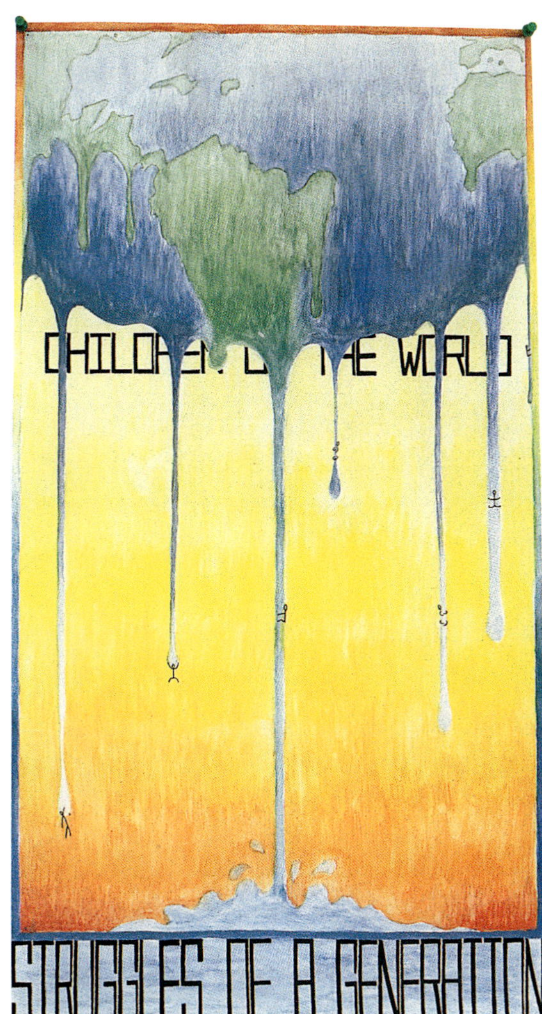

171

170. Towards the Millennium, a Search for Global Ethics, *1999, by Emi Noda (UN International School poster).*

171. Children of the World, Struggles of a Generation, *1997, by Sahe Kawahara (UN International School poster).*

The **United Nations International School (UNIS), New York** was founded in 1947 by a group of UN parents to provide their children with an education that fostered a global sensibility. What began modestly as a nursery school for twenty children is now a college preparatory school with two campuses, enrolling more than fifteen hundred children from more than one hundred countries. The academic program at UNIS is designed to offer every student a rigorous liberal arts program and to foster international understanding and effective living skills.

Jan Kristin Arnesen

Born in Cleveland and educated at the Chicago Art Institute, Hampshire College, and Harvard University, Jan Kristin Arnesen began her career as a graphic designer in Boston, and she later moved to Paris to work as an art director on projects for Peugeot and Canal Plus. In her career with the UN, Arnesen directed an information campaign on voting rights for elections in Namibia (1989–90). She has undertaken art direction for several UN conferences, including the World Conference on Human Rights and the Women's Conference in Beijing. She currently runs the exhibits service at UN Headquarters in New York.

Benn

Benn was born in 1905 in Bialystok, Poland (which at that time was a part of Russia) to an architect father and a mother whose family consisted of actors and musicians. While still an adolescent, he gave drawing lessons; in 1924 he founded an academy of painting in a garret. He constructed his first stage sets in 1926, gave his first exhibition in his native city in 1927, and was awarded a three-year scholarship in France in 1929, where he settled. Benn's best known work is a series entitled *Psalms*, which are paintings on biblical themes in memory of his parents, who were murdered during the war. He designed several posters for UNESCO, including *Peace and Justice* (page 38).

Graciela Rodo Boulanger

Born in La Paz, Bolivia, Graciela Rodo Boulanger was raised in an artistic environment. She studied piano with her mother, and it was at the age of twenty-five—after having studied music in Chile, Austria, and Argentina—that she decided to devote herself to painting. Since her first one-woman show in Vienna (1953), she has worked in many media: oil painting, etching, lithography, watercolor, pastel, sculpture, and tapestry. In 1979 she designed a poster for the International Year of the Child (see page 67); two of her tapestries were displayed in the public hall of the UN General Assembly during that year. In 1990 she designed a second poster for the UNICEF summit for children, attended by many heads of state.

Rocco Callari

Born in the United States, Rocco Callari is a graduate of Parsons School of Design and has studied at New York University. Callari joined the United Nations in 1971 after spending several years as a designer in advertising. He has spent most of his UN career as the head of the design studio of the UN Postal Administration. A designer of numerous UN stamps (see page 22), Callari has won several design awards, including the Gold Medal for Excellence from *Communication Arts* magazine, several awards from the Art Directors' Club, and the distinguished Gold Medal for Art Direction from the Society of Illustrators. For several years, Callari has been the chief of the UN's Graphic Design Section—the organization's premier design studio.

Carzou

Born in 1907 in Aleppo, Syria, Carzou created in his art a deserted, phantasmagorical world that has been described by Caillois as "a universe in a state of shock; as though abandoned, untouched by climate or event, made of silence and emptiness." Carzou's tangled-line style of drawing divests the world of its material substance, creating a realm of both enchantment and disenchantment, where amusement and sadness mingle. A member of the French Academy of Fine Arts, he designed *Communications* (see page 142) for UNESCO.

José Castiñeira

Born in Spain, José Castiñeira came to the United States at the age of fifteen. A graduate of New York's High School of Art and Design and the School of Visual Arts, he worked in the publishing industry before joining the UN's Graphic Design Section in 1980. During his twenty years with the organization, Castiñeira designed many posters; several are reproduced in this book, including *Day of Solidarity*, which won an award from the American Institute of Graphic Arts (see page 55).

Marc Chagall

Born in Vitebsk, Russia, Marc Chagall (1887–1985) is best known as a painter; he also produced etchings, mosaics, tapestries, sculptures, murals, and stained glass. A famous example of his work in stained glass—a memorial to Dag Hammarskjöld—is on display at UN headquarters in New York City.

In 1910 Chagall went to Paris where he met Picasso and Apollinaire. After the October Revolution in 1917, he returned to Russia with the hope of starting an art school, but as he found that his views clashed with the prevailing aesthetics of the new Soviet state, this dream was never realized. In 1922 he returned to France permanently. His best known works are those recalling childhood memories and Jewish legends. Two years after completing the ceiling at the Paris Opera in 1964,

---

*Many more artists and designers contributed to the creation of UN posters. This set of biographies was compiled based on available information.

Chagall completed two murals for the Metropolitan Opera in New York. Chagall created a universe of free-floating figures, animals, and scenes of Russian village life. The poster *America Celebrates Children* was based on Chagall's stained glass window at the United Nations (see page 71).

Laslo Cheffolway

Laslo Cheffolway was born in Hungary in 1943. Educated in Budapest in industrial and graphic design, he lived in Italy and Sweden and worked in jewelry and packaging design and as an art director in several advertising agencies. In 1985 he joined the United Nations, where he endeavors to find challenging solutions to international design projects (see page 56).

Paul Davis

An illustrator and graphic designer, Paul Davis was born and raised in Oklahoma and attended the School of Visual Arts in New York. His first illustrations were published in *Playboy* in 1959; since then, his work has appeared in *Life, Time, Look, Sports Illustrated, Evergreen Review, Harper's, Horizon, McCall's, The New Yorker, Mirabella, Fast Company, Worth, Money,* and many other publications. He was art director of Joseph Papp's New York Shakespeare Festival from 1984 to 1992. Recent clients have been UNITE!, Disney, Lincoln Center, McKinsey & Co., Scribner, Bernstein Real Estate, and Manhattan Plaza.

In 1997 Davis won the Rome Prize for design arts. He is a fellow of the American Academy in Rome and a member of the prestigious AppleMaster program, utilizing Macintosh technologies in new and creative ways. Currently on the faculty of the School of Visual Arts, Davis designed the *Blue Helmets* poster illustrated in this book (see page 38).

Ricardo Ernesto Jaime De Freitas

A native of Panama, Dr. Freitas is an architect, graphic artist, and a professor at the National University of Panama. He created the illustration for the poster that decorates the cover of this book (and also appears on page 20). It was chosen by a UN panel as the winner of a competition commemorating the fortieth anniversary of the world organization (1985).

Michel Delacroix

Born in 1933 in Paris, Michel Delacroix remembers that city during the war years as a sparkling place where the virtual absence of automobiles and carbon monoxide allowed Notre Dame and other ancient edifices to be washed clean. His cityscapes show not a city beset by war but a "magical theater." Delacroix was awarded the commission for the major print portfolio offered at the 1996 Olympics in Atlanta. He is also the chef-talent at Axelle Fine Arts, the Manhattan art publishing company and gallery. He presently resides in Lausanne, Switzerland. In 1998, Delacroix designed *The Spirit of Good Will* for the 1998 Good Will Games. It was later adapted and used by UNICEF (see page 70).

Sonia Delaunay

Sonia Delaunay was born in 1885 in the city of Odessa, Ukraine, which was then a part of Russia. In 1907, she came to France, settling at Meudon. Her first husband was the German critic and dealer Wilhelm Uhde, a great admirer of naive painting, and her second, the painter Robert Delaunay, whom she married in 1910. Delaunay devoted herself to the applied arts before painting the major works that were to make her known. In 1921 she founded her fashion studio, in the art deco style that was to make her famous. She was a joint organizer of the exhibition on "concrete art" and regularly exhibited in the Salon des Realites Nouvelles from 1946 on. For the rest of her life, Delaunay devoted herself to painting, which for her meant the pure exaltation of color. She died in Paris in 1979. Delaunay designed the 1976 UNESCO poster for the international women's year (see page 93).

Wolf Erlbruch

Born in 1948 in Wuppertal, Germany, Wolf Erlbruch was educated at the Folkwang Art School in Essen. A graphic designer and renowned illustrator, he worked for advertising agencies and trick-film studios in London before focusing his talents on creating illustrations for children's books. Erlbruch teaches illustration at the Arts and Design Department of Bergische Universitat in Wuppertal. His poster *Childhood Is Not Child's Play* won first prize in an international competition (see page 79).

Hans Erni

Born in Lucerne, Switzerland, in 1909, Hans Erni studied at the Lucerne School of Arts and Crafts and the Berlin School of Applied Arts. Influenced by the Cubists, he founded the Abstract-Creation group. Erni gave his first one-man show in Basle in 1935, subsequently exhibiting widely in Europe and the United States. His extensive body of work encompasses painting, lithography, illustration, stage sets, ceramics, and posters. Erni created a number of works for the UN art collection, including a portrait of Secretary-General Boutros Boutros-Ghali. Two of his posters are reproduced in this book (see pages 64 and 107).

James R. Eschinger

James R. Eschinger, a graphic designer, photographer, and illustrator, was born in 1944 in Washington, D.C. He has a master's degree in visual graphics and communication and is currently a senior designer with the UN Publishing Division. Prior to joining

Jacqui Morgan

Born in New York City in 1941, Jacqui Morgan studied with Richard Linder at Pratt Institute and received her master of arts degree from Hunter College. From 1961 to 1966 she designed textiles for different studios in New York. Since 1967 she has been a commercial illustrator for numerous firms, including Eastern Airlines, Irving Trust, Hilton Caribbean, Trevira, and IBM. Her color sensibility, a predilection for the use of 'love and peace' images—such as flowers and birds—and a shrewd understanding of the commercial marketplace contributed to her rapid emergence as a top illustrator.

Carlos Ochagavia

Born in Logrono, Spain, in 1913, Carlos Ochagavia moved with his parents to Argentina when he was two years old. He studied painting in Buenos Aires at the Academia National de Bellas Artes and at the Escuela Superior de Bellas Artes. In 1937 he was awarded a scholarship to study at the New York Art Students League. In Argentina he worked as both a painter and filmmaker—he had his own movie company dedicated to creating animation movies. In 1962 he won a first prize at the National Short Animated Film Festival for his film *La escoba de Lucinda,* and he participated at the de Tours and Annecy festival in France. In 1991 he painted three sets of stamps for the "Better Environment" Program for the UN Post Office (see page 120). His works also include several murals, illustrations for *Time, Newsweek,* and several other magazines, posters for the United Nations and private companies, and illustrations for limited edition books.

Pablo Picasso

Born in Malaga, Spain, Pablo Picasso (1881–1973) studied art in Barcelona and then in the Real Academia de Bellas Artes de San Fernado in Madrid. After several stays in Paris, he established himself there in 1904. His work *Les Demoiselles d'Avignon* (1906–1907) reflected the influences of Cézanne and African art. Until World War I, Picasso explored Cubism, and afterwards he began to work in another style, depicting figures in subtly detached classicism. During the mid-twenties he developed a powerful allegory in his work, describing the conflict between good and evil. The outbreak of the Spanish Civil War in 1936 inspired the famous and harrowing *Guernica* (1937), Picasso's first work about a political event. After World War II, his works centered on themes of war, peace, and human rights. The UNESCO poster based on his painting commemorates the centenary of Picasso's birth in 1881 (see page 14).

Jan Ralph

An Australian citizen who has served the UN for twenty-three years—primarily as the chief of the photographs and exhibit section and senior information officer of the communications and projects management division—Jan C. Ralph is currently a producer/writer for Ralph & Sarda Design Associates, with offices in New York and Guadalajara, Spain.

As UN technical director, Ralph was responsible for concept, design, production, installation, and operation of UN pavilions in major exhibitions, such as Expo-2000 in Hannover, Germany, and earlier pavilions in Genoa, Italy; Taejon, Republic of Korea; Osaka, Japan; Brisbane, Australia; and Vancouver, Canada. He was also editor/writer of *Visions,* the official UN fiftieth anniversary pictorial history, and he is on the board of directors of the International Photographic Council. Ralph studied photography and graphic arts at several New York institutions, received his B.A. from Hunter College, and earned a M.A. in film production from Columbia University.

Robert Rauschenberg

Born in 1925 in Port Arthur, Texas, Robert Rauschenberg studied at the Art Students League, in New York (1949–1950). He advanced toward paintings in which real objects such as photographs were affixed to, or combined with, the painted surface. Among the best known of these are *Charlene* (1954), *Rebus* (1955), and *Odalisk* (1955–1958). Since his first color silk-screen paintings of the early 1960s, Rauschenberg's work has been concerned with world events. He has designed seven posters for United Nations agencies (see pages 16–17).

Norman Rockwell

Born in New York City, Norman Rockwell (1894–1978) began studying art as a young child. At sixteen he entered the Art Students League of New York, and in the following year he received an assignment to illustrate magazines and children's books. Rockwell became known for the many covers he painted for *The Saturday Evening Post,* beginning with his first in 1916. These depicted ordinary, and often humorous, scenes from everyday life. Rockwell's work also included covers and illustrations for other well-known periodicals, pictures for editions of Mark Twain's *Adventures of Tom Sawyer* and *Adventures of Huckleberry Finn,* and illustrated calendars. His mosaic *The Golden Rule* is displayed at UN headquarters in New York City (see page 52).

Otavio Roth

Born in Sao Paulo, Brazil, Otavio Roth worked and lived in London, Oslo, New York, and San Francisco. His prints, drawings, and paper installations have been widely exhibited in numerous museums and galleries since 1972. Roth and Ruth Rocha illustrated several children's books about the United Nations, and one of Roth's illustrations became a UN poster (see page 121).

Théo Tobiasse

Théo Tobiasse was born to Lithuanian parents in 1927 in Jaffa, a backwater Mediterranean port in what was then Palestine. His father took the family to Paris in 1931. During the Nazi occupation, Tobiasse studied art privately at the École des Arts Décoratif. After the war, he worked for five years as an advertising artist. He settled in Nice where he worked as a commercial artist and concentrated on painting. In 1986, Tobiasse designed the UNESCO poster *Education for All* (see page 138).

Armando Paez Torres

Born in Córdoba, Argentina, in 1918, Armando Paez Torres was an autodidactic graphic artist who started out as an illustrator and layout person. He lived in Brazil from 1937–1947, and again from 1952–1955, working for advertising agencies and publishing houses. In 1948 he won a UN poster contest (see page 11).

Victor Vasarely

Victor Vasarely was renowned worldwide as one of the most original practitioners of geometric abstractionism. He is the undisputed leader of the Op Art movement and the major visual kinetic artist in France. Born in 1908 at Pecs (Hungary), he studied anatomy and the nude, then attended courses at the Hungarian equivalent of the German Bauhaus, the Mohely. In 1930, Vasarely took up residence in Paris, where he worked for ten years as a graphic designer for Havas, Draeger, and others. From 1944 on he devoted himself exclusively to painting. In the late forties, he became firmly committed to the constructivist-abstractionism school of painting, untiringly acting as its theoretician in his books and manifestos. He went on to discover the inexhaustible resources of the dialectic of the positive sign and the negative sign of black and white. In 1970 he established the "didactic museum" at Gordes in the south of France. In addition to his work as a painter, he created a large number of architectural compositions, in Europe and North America. Vasarely's kinetic line patterns and his famous stripes soon came to exercise a direct influence on fashion and advertising. He designed the symbol for the International Education Year (see page 15).

Maria Elena Vieira da Silva

Maria Elena Vieira da Silva was born in 1908 in Lisbon, where she studied drawing, anatomy, and sculpture. After moving to Paris, she followed courses given by the sculptors Bourdelle and Despiau, only to abandon sculpture for painting. Vieira da Silva paints in a limpid, abstract style; developed out of a mosaic pattern, it is the most distinctive feature of her art and is marvelously used to display her famous "library" and "subway" motifs. Renowned for her paintings, illustrations, and stained-glass windows, she is also interested in tapestry. In 1985 the Lisbon subway authority commissioned her to paint a gouache entitled *Metro,* using traditional Portuguese ceramic tiles to decorate one of its stations. She designed a poster for UNESCO on the International Year of Peace in 1986 (see page 53).

Maxim Żhukov

Born in Moscow in 1943, Maxim Żhukov worked for a number of major publishers in the USSR designing science and art books. He was also a presentation officer with the UN Graphic Presentation Unit (later Design Section) during 1977–1981, being promoted to unit chief during 1986–1993. His work has been featured in many domestic and international exhibitions, and he is a recipient of many design competition awards. Żhukov is presently a typographic coordinator for the United Nations. He has a broad background in graphic design (corporate identity, posters, exhibits) and publication design (books and periodicals). He is a member of the Russian Academy of Graphic Design and an honorary member of the Art Directors Club, New York. His poster designs appear on pages 56, 87, and 124.

Bibliography

Ades, Dawn. *The Twentieth Century Poster—Design of the Avant Garde* (New York: Abbeville Press, 1984).

Allner, W.H. *Posters* (New York: Reinhold, 1952).

Barnicoat, John. *Posters—A Concise History* (London: Thames & Hudson, Ltd., 1972; reprint 1998).

Basic Facts About the United Nations (New York: United Nations Department of Public Information, 1998).

Blue and Beautiful Planet Earth Our Home (New York: UN Department of Public Information and R.R. Bowker, 1990).

Denoon, Chris. *Posters of the WPA* (Seattle: University of Washington Press, 1987).

Exhibition Catalogue, Walker Art Center (Minneapolis and New York: Abbeville Press, 1984).

Funk & Wagnalls New Encyclopedia, 1983.

Granger, Michel. *La Surface Corrigée* (Paris: Le Cherche Midi Éditeur, 1993).

Heyman, Therese Thau. *Posters American Style* (New York: National Museum of American Art, Smithsonian Institution, in association with Harry N. Abrams, Inc., 1998).

Kindheit ist kein Kinderspiel (Childhood is not Child's Play). Illustrated catalogue of International Poster Competition organized by the German Poster Museum, 1999.

Marks, Edward B. *A World of Art—The United Nations Collection* (Rome, Italy: Il Cigno Galileo Galilei, 1995).

Steiner, Henry A. with Ken Haas. *Cross-Cultural Design—Communicating in the Global Marketplace* (London: Thames & Hudson, Ltd., 1995).

UNESCO Through Its Posters (Paris: United Nations Educational, Scientific, and Cultural Organization, 1989).